The Rise of the Public Authority

The Rise of the Public Authority

Statebuilding and Economic Development in Twentieth-Century America

GAIL RADFORD

The University of Chicago Press
Chicago and London

Gail Radford is associate professor of history at the University at Buffalo. She is the author of *Modern Housing for America: Policy Struggles in the New Deal Era*.

The University of Chicago Press, Chicago 60637
The University of Chicago Press, Ltd., London

Printed in the United States of America

22 21 20 19 18 17 16 15 14 13   1 2 3 4 5

ISBN-13: 978-0-226-03769-1 (cloth)
ISBN-13: 978-0-226-03772-1 (paper)
ISBN-13: 978-0-226-03786-8 (e-book)

Library of Congress Cataloging-in-Publication Data

Radford, Gail.

The rise of the public authority : statebuilding and economic development in Twentieth-Century America / Gail Radford.
pages ; cm
Includes bibliographical references and index.
ISBN 978-0-226-03769-1 (cloth : alkaline paper)—ISBN 978-0-226-03772-1 (paperback : alkaline paper)—ISBN 978-0-226-03786-8 (e-book)
1. Corporations, Government—United States—History—20th century.
2. Federal land banks—United States—History—20th century. I. Title.
HD3885.R33 2013
338.6′209730904—dc23

2012047522

Portions of chapter 1 appeared in an earlier version as "William Gibbs McAdoo, the Emergency Fleet Corporation, and the Origins of the Public-Authority Model of Government Action," *Journal of Policy History* 11, no. 1 (1999): 59–88.

Portions of chapters 3 and 5 appeared in an earlier version as "From Municipal Socialism to Public Authorities: Institutional Factors in the Shaping of American Public Enterprise," *Journal of American History* 90, no. 3 (2003): 863–90.

♾ This paper meets the requirements of ANSI/NISO Z39.48–1992 (Permanence of Paper).

CONTENTS

ACKNOWLEDGMENTS

One of the pleasures of finishing this book is reflecting back on all the people and organizations that helped make it possible. At the outset of my career, Richard M. Abrams played a crucial role. After many years, I still think back to his stimulating lectures on the Progressive Era, which gave rise to my long-term interest in this period. At Columbia, Kenneth T. Jackson was a model advisor, both encouraging and challenging in his trademark good-natured way. I am deeply grateful for the support he has always shown to me and my work.

I gratefully acknowledge the help I received from a number of organizations while researching and writing this book. The project was supported by fellowships from the American Council of Learned Societies, the National Endowment for the Humanities, and the Woodrow Wilson International Center for Scholars. I was lucky to be able to present a first draft of the project to the Chicago Urban History Seminar, a vibrant forum led for many years by Michael H. Ebner. During a semester living in Princeton, through the good offices of Jameson W. Doig, I was a visiting fellow at the Woodrow Wilson School. I benefited from stimulating discussions when I presented my work to the Urban History Group in Leeds, England; the Baldy Center for Law and Social Policy at SUNY–Buffalo; the American Bar Foundation; the High Road conference in Buffalo; and a seminar in my home department organized by Erik Seeman. The library and librarians at SUNY–Buffalo have been invaluable resources. For special thanks I would like to single out Edward Herman, whose vast knowledge of government materials is only surpassed by his willingness to help. An informal, but very productive, organization was my writing group. Many thanks to Patricia Mazón, Claire Schen, and Gwynn Thomas.

Many individuals provided a variety of kinds of aid during the time spent researching and writing this book. I would like to acknowledge my colleague Tamara Plakins Thornton, who on two different occasions, at significant inconvenience to herself, made it possible for me to take leaves from teaching. For his interest and help since the very beginning of the project, thanks to A. Scott Henderson. Thanks also to Nelson Lichtenstein, whose belief in the project from an early stage has been very important. Judy Kramer and Paula Schwartz, two close friends from graduate school, provided encouragement over many years. One of my only disappointments regarding this book is that Judy's untimely death means I won't be able to send her a warmly inscribed copy. I would also like to acknowledge: Richard Briffault, Peter H. Brown, Cecelia Bucki, Mary Ann Clawson, Kevin Connor, Philip Ethington, David M. P. Freund, Stephen Halpern, Clifton Hood, Robert D. Leighninger, Jr., Ajay K. Mehrotra, Joanne Meyerowitz, Stephen Mihm, Daniel Nolan, James Stuart Olson, Terrianne Schulte, Erin Sobkowski, Daniel Stone, Joel Tarr, Christopher Tomlins, Alexander von Hoffman, Michael Vorenberg, Mark R. Wilson, and James A. Wooten.

For permission to use the cartoon of Hoover in chapter 4, I thank the Jay N. "Ding" Darling Wildlife Society. The Department of Special Collections of the library of the University of Iowa, which hosts a comprehensive website of Ding Darling editorial cartoons, was exceedingly helpful. Adam Zyglis, whose pointed and entertaining cartoons appear in the *Buffalo News*, graciously gave permission to use the one found in the epilogue. At various points in the book I draw on "From Municipal Socialism to Public Authorities: Institutional Factors in the Shaping of American Public Enterprise," which appeared in the *Journal of American History* 90, no.1 (December 2003). I thank the journal for permission for its use. I also thank the Pennsylvania State University Press for permission to use parts of "William Gibbs McAdoo, the Emergency Fleet Corporation, and the Origins of the Public-Authority Model of Government Action," which appeared in the *Journal of Policy History* 11, no. 1 (1999). Last but not least, the Library of Congress shows the virtues of general-purpose government by providing access without charge to an enormous collection of historical graphics, including the fleet corporation poster reproduced in chapter 1.

I am privileged to again have the experience of working with the University of Chicago Press. Thanks are due to the anonymous readers of the manuscript for their insightful comments. Robert Devens, my astute and encouraging editor, helped me put many of their suggestions to use, to the benefit of the final product. On the production end, I appreciate the help of the organized and agreeable Russell Damian. I am indebted to my copyeditor, Jennifer Rappaport, whose keen eye and good judgment have greatly improved the book.

My greatest debt is to Stephen Hart, whose ideas, computer skills, and great charts have done so much to improve the book—and whose companionship has done so much to improve the life of its author.

INTRODUCTION

Starting in the late nineteenth century, public officials in the United States began to experiment with new tools by which government could engage directly in the economy. Over time, these efforts would culminate in the emergence of a powerful institutional sector of quasi-public agencies, best known as "public authorities." Although created by general-purpose governments to pursue goals defined as being in the public interest, these agencies are largely independent—administratively, financially, and legally—of the governments that create them. Operating with little publicity and less citizen input, they have been called America's "shadow government."[1]

Quasi-public agencies are varied, but they have many features in common. This is not by accident or through simple imitation. Rather, the public authority as an institution represents a model or template (more precisely, a family of templates) that is supported by federal and state laws, the practices of financial institutions and markets, and perceptions of what is normal and acceptable held by politicians, citizens, and judges. These supports make it easy to build new agencies that fit the mold.

This book is different from previous work on public authorities in several ways. Most existing accounts, by scholars and journalists, concentrate on the period since the Second World War. The great bulk of this literature deals with state and local agencies. By contrast, this account examines the early history of these agencies, in order to understand the goals of the people who first proposed them, as well as the political struggles and legal pressures that shaped them in their formation and subsequent evolution. A major part of this early history concerns federal corporations. Furthermore, interactions between events at the federal and subfederal levels require attention, since in this earlier period local initiatives often influenced federal officials, while federal policies and actions had a great impact on the development of public authorities at the state and local level.

Another difference has to do with point of view. Many, perhaps most, writings on public authorities are first and foremost critiques of these agencies, expounding with vigor their unfortunate qualities. The critiques are often based on copious and rigorous research, but a major part of their agenda is to describe in detail the failings of public authorities. Other writings defend them, based on similarly careful research.

I am sympathetic to the critics. Like them, I believe that growing reliance on public authorities over the last century has had unfortunate consequences. These mechanisms generally lack democratic accountability, have a tendency to fragment and commercialize the public sector, and are poor tools for social justice or regional planning. This is not to say that any particular authority is useless or harmful, or to deny the accomplishments of this institutional sphere. Nevertheless, I believe that as a nation we could benefit by finding other ways to achieve the purposes that the statebuilders had in mind when they first started developing this organizational form.

Yet the basic purpose of this book is quite different from that of either the critics or defenders. It is *an attempt to understand how and why this institution came into being and took its present form*. I believe that for engaging today's policy debates such an understanding is a better starting point than a list of the pros and cons of quasi-public agencies. Any attempt to shift away from our reliance on public authorities must address what it was that led public officials to create these mechanisms in the first place. The early architects of public authorities were trying to meet modern needs. In the end they chose to do so by detouring around, rather than confronting, obstacles they found in the administrative, legal, and institutional framework that constitutes democratically accountable government in the United States. Why they did this and what consequences flowed from this choice are important questions to answer if we are to seek new ways forward in the future. Hope for doing better depends upon surmounting the obstacles faced by earlier generations, and that in turn requires a deep understanding of those obstacles, many of which are still with us.

What Are Public Authorities and Why Is So Little Known about Them?

Institutions built on the public authority model operate throughout the country, at all levels of government. They come in a variety of sizes. Many are huge. The Tennessee Valley Authority (TVA), created by the federal government during the New Deal to generate electricity, among other responsibilities, posted revenues of close to $12 billion in FY 2011.[2] At the state level, the New Jersey Sports and Exposition Authority (NJSEA), owns and operates over $1 billion worth of facilities. Among these are the Meadowlands Sports Complex (including Giants Stadium, Meadowlands Racetrack, and a twenty-thousand-seat indoor arena known as the Izod Center), Monmouth Park Racetrack, the Atlantic City Convention Center, the Wildwoods Convention Center, and the NJSEA Insurance Company.[3] Another giant set up by a state is the Tampa Port Authority, which took over the city's deteriorated commercial waterfront and transformed it into a profitable cargo port, a major cruise center (attracting over three-quarters of a million passengers in 2008), and a popular entertainment destination. It has served as a development engine for Tampa's downtown.[4]

In contrast to these behemoths, most public authorities are small to medium-sized affairs, in charge of a single operation. For example, the Springfield Parking Authority (SPA), in Springfield, Massachusetts, operates five garages and eight lots, generating, in 2004, $1.4 million in income. The SPA identifies itself on its website as "a public enterprise which is financially independent of the city of Springfield."[5] While a common rationale for establishing independent agencies is that they can provide more effective management than typical government departments, the SPA offers evidence that such an outcome is not assured. A scathing independent review in 2005 castigated the authority for the poor physical condition of its properties, a computer system so inadequate that cashiers in garages were reduced to writing receipts by hand, and payment machines in its lots so decrepit they were completely nonfunctional. According to the report, four of its parking lots were actually losing money.[6]

Despite the size of entities such as the TVA, NJSEA, and the Tampa Port Authority, and the ubiquity of their smaller cousins such as the SPA scattered across the landscape, even close observers of American government have been apt to overlook the existence of this sector. Robert A. Caro, whose widely read biography of the "power broker" Robert Moses did so much to publicize the significance of self-supporting, administratively independent agencies, confessed that before starting the book he wondered "what a public authority was, anyway." And Caro was a journalist who specialized in politics![7]

At the national level, the so-called government corporations, which are structured on the same lines as public authorities, are if anything less understood. In addition to the TVA, some of the better known entities that were set up to function outside the standard departmental structure of the executive branch are the Reconstruction Finance Corporation, Fannie Mae, the Federal Deposit Insurance Corporation (FDIC), the Federal Savings and Loan Insurance Corporation (FSLIC), the Resolution Trust Corporation (RTC), Sallie Mae, and Amtrak.[8] While these entities were created to perform a variety of tasks, the most important function of this sector as a whole has been to channel credit to parts of the economy such as housing and agriculture identified as inadequately served by private capital markets. To give a sense of the magnitude of these kinds of operations, in 2008, federal corporate agencies held $6.3 trillion in outstanding loans.[9] Historian Jordan A. Schwarz highlighted the importance of such programs during the 1930s, contending that the principal achievement of the New Deal was "a revolution in expanded credit supported by public capital."[10] The massive public investment to which Schwarz called attention flowed largely through government corporations. Today, despite the scale of activities carried out by these institutional structures, most citizens are only vaguely aware of them. Few perceive their positive achievements as the result of *government* activity; indeed, unless they run into trouble they are hardly noticed.

One reason for the obscurity of these agencies at all levels of government is that basic information about them is hard to get. Experts in public administration cannot even say how many there are. Using different definitions and hindered by lack of data, scholars estimate their total number at anywhere from five thousand to over eighteen thousand. The difficulty in identifying and counting these agencies stems from the fact that the federal government and states create them in a bewildering variety of legal formats and do not keep track of them in any systematic way. Indeed, most states would be hard-pressed even to list their authorities. In 2004, the New York State Comptroller's office conducted an investigation that initially determined that the state had 643 authorities, but after several more months of digging discovered almost 90 more. Nor do labels provide a useful guide, since revenue-producing, administratively independent units have been given an array of titles. They have been called boards, commissions, agencies, trusts, districts, administrations, public corporations, public benefit corporations, and government corporations—in addition to the name by which they are best known: public authorities.[11] Just to add to the confusion, some of these labels can also be used to designate units within general-purpose government.

Although we cannot reliably count public authority–type agencies, we can get a rough sense of the scale of their activities by looking at patterns in public borrowing. Most authorities fund their capital facilities by borrowing against future earnings, issuing what are called "revenue bonds" (as op-

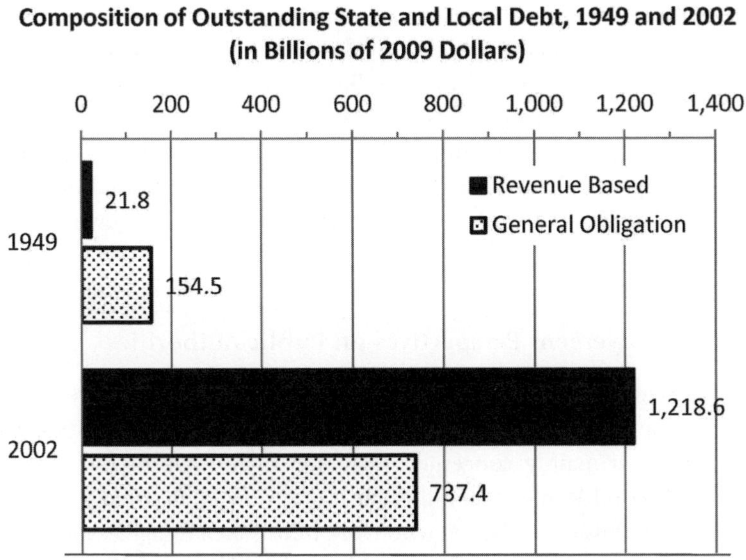

Figure I.1. Patterns in public borrowing illustrate the rise of public authority–type agencies since the mid-twentieth century. Such agencies borrow through revenue bonds, while standard governments issue bonds backed by the "full faith and credit" of the government—that is, its taxing power. This chart shows that revenue-based debt, which represented only one-eighth of subfederal public debt in 1949, grew far more rapidly than full-faith and credit debt and by 2002 constituted five-eighths of total borrowing at the state and local level.

posed to the "general obligation bonds," backed by taxing power, used by general-purpose governments). Figure I.1 indicates trends in the two kinds of debt. From 1949 to 2002, revenue-based debt increased fifty-six-fold (in constant dollars). General-obligation debt also increased, but only five-fold. As a result, revenue bonds, which made up only one-eighth of total subfederal public indebtedness fifty years earlier, constituted five-eighths of such debt by the end of the century.[12] This represents a sea change in the institutional character of public economic activity.

Just as striking as the extent of publicly initiated economic activity happening through public authorities is the fact that this activity generates so little opposition. Standard accounts of American ideology ascribe to the United States a deep, principled hostility to government involvement in the economy. Yet, when public authorities are set up to run business operations, the only kind of resistance that is actually expressed (and this only occasionally) concerns the usefulness or cost-effectiveness of particular activities. Challenges to the basic concept of publicly sponsored business ventures are almost never heard. For example, in the 1990s, when the Cleveland Teachers Union protested the building of city-owned sports complexes for the Cleveland Indians, Browns, and Cavaliers sports teams, they denounced the projects as "a metaphor for a society's [misplaced] priorities." The teachers maintained that public money would be better spent dealing with the city's high adult illiteracy rate and crumbling school buildings—not that it was wrong for local government to own money-making facilities.[13]

Divergent Perspectives on Public Authorities

Political scientists, students of public administration, and investigative reporters have produced most of the research on public authorities. This work has been mainly concerned with the functioning of these bodies since the Second World War, although it often contains cursory accounts of their earlier history. Scholars who work in this area disagree, sometimes vehemently, about how to evaluate public authorities.

Supporters laud authorities for their ability "to get things done." They point to how these institutions are able to avoid the rigid budgeting, personnel, and procurement rules to which standard government agencies must conform. Most significantly, supporters highlight the ability of these agencies to generate and utilize their own sources of revenue, which liberates them from the contentious politics of taxation and public borrowing that often stymie efforts to use standard government to accomplish the task at hand. In addition, by being able to borrow against their future revenue streams for capital investments, authorities are able to make long-range plans. Political scientist Jameson W. Doig, a leading expert in the field, regards the organizational structure of the public authority as highly successful. Many, he says, "behave in ways not unlike the well-run private corporation." This perspective on the virtues of independence is probably most strongly held by pro-development business groups (for which, it must be noted, these structures tend to be more permeable than they are for other parts of civil society). In a 1986 op-ed in the *Boston Globe*, Harold Hestnes, a longtime leader of the Greater Boston Chamber of Commerce, praised public authorities for having built "many of the most significant public works in this nation," an achievement he attributed to the fact that these agencies are "removed from the vicissitudes of political interference."[14] The basic point is that quasi-public agencies are able to accomplish tasks that their proponents take to be otherwise impossible given what they see as the American political system's tendencies toward stasis.

Critics of public authorities reject these positive evaluations. They charge that the businesslike efficiency of these devices is overrated, and that whatever gains in effectiveness they do achieve come at the expense of democratic accountability. In the words of noted public administration scholar Annmarie Hauck Walsh, the public authority "involves public ownership without public policy."[15] Another major criticism is that reliance on public authorities fragments the power of government and commercializes the public sector. Political scientist Alberta M. Sbragia argues that public authorities have "diluted the power of general purpose governments, have insulated themselves from the electorate, and have transformed taxpayers into ratepayers subject to user fees."[16] Some commentators even allege that the public authority sector is in effect an "underground" government that poses systemic risk to the economy because of its size and the fact that it is constrained neither by the electorate nor the market.[17] All the critics acknowledge that standard government agencies are often slow moving and ineffectual at certain kinds of tasks, but they maintain that a far better solution would be "to attack the weakness in government rather than search for new forms of independence."[18]

Assumptions about the Origins of Public Authorities

Surprisingly, given these divergent positions with regard to the merits of public authorities, there is widespread agreement about how and why these mechanisms emerged. Most scholars seem to have absorbed the revisionist interpretation of the Progressive Era first popularized in 1955 with the publication of Richard Hofstadter's *Age of Reform*. Breaking with long-standing assumptions in American historiography, Hofstadter raised questions about the character and potential of social movements such as Populism, and the personal motives of middle-class Progressive reformers, in particular their much-vaunted aspiration to institute greater democracy. Hofstadter's intent was to infuse American political history with a greater sensitivity to the nonrational springs of human action and—with both fascism and McCarthyism in mind—to caution against taking at face value the self-proclaimed goals of individuals, organizations, and governments.[19]

While rejecting Hofstadter's suspicion of social movements, New Left historians of the 1960s adopted his skepticism with regard to the democratic aims of Progressive reformers. Fueled by disillusionment with the character of American liberalism at the peak of its power in the 1960s, given the role of liberals in directing the war in Vietnam and the ways Progressive Era reforms seemed in retrospect to have primarily advantaged big business, New Left historiography emphasized the elitism of early twentieth-century reformers, their comfort with an economy dominated by large corporations, and their admiration for the organizational techniques of large-scale business. As these authors recounted American political history, the Progressives were no longer heroic initiators of a social democratic trajectory toward greater democratic participation and economic equality, but rather architects of what Martin J. Sklar, coining a term that came to be widely used, referred to as "corporate-liberalism."[20] Cast in less pejorative terms, this perspective assumes that early twentieth-century reformers believed that "it was possible to create a nonpolitical, essentially technical, government organization and management."[21]

While this interpretive framework no longer dominates American political history, it continues to hold sway in other disciplines and is particularly influential among those who study public authorities, supporters and detractors alike. For example, Annmarie Hauck Walsh, a leading critic of public authorities, charges that "Progressive dogma supplies the rationale for the autonomy of public authorities and for the business dominance of their boards of directors." Jameson W. Doig, a more sympathetic observer, also believes that the motives of Progressive reformers provide the best guide to understanding how public authorities took the form they did. According to Doig, a key goal of the Progressives was to "insulate complex public programs from politics and ineffective management," and he sees this aspiration most fully embodied in the public authority tradition.[22]

A final element of the usual story line, this one not based on revisionist views of Progressivism, is that Americans have always had a deep-seated hostility to anything that deviates from pure private enterprise, such as government provision of goods and services beyond policing and national defense. The assumption here is that only public enterprise done outside of standard government, by semiprivate corporations that act in almost all respects like for-profit businesses, is culturally acceptable or politically possible in America.

Thus the story line provided by critics and supporters of public authorities is basically the same. It is also basically wrong. First, it is wrong in that most of the statebuilders who crafted the early versions of quasi-public agencies did *not* desire the organizations they proposed to be insulated from the electorate or to be predominantly market-driven and profit-oriented. (They did, to be sure, desire relief from some of the sources of inefficiency plaguing normal government agencies, such as reliance on annual legislative appropriations for capital expenses or multiple layers of control over even small expenditures.) Second, whatever their intentions, statebuilders had little ability to put them into practice. Their goals were weak forces compared with the legal, financial, and political constraints they faced. And third, the shared story line is wrong in assuming an unbending ideological commitment to pure capitalism. Proponents of municipal enterprises, as we will see in chapter 3, have often been able to win elections, not just for themselves but for their proposals. And grassroots criticism of public authorities is seldom against the basic idea of public involvement in the local economy, but almost always focused on what is taken to be wrong with the particular activity being proposed. Americans seem more pragmatic than ideological on the issue of government economic activity.

Thus the widely shared presumption that the contemporary character of public authorities originated from conscious efforts by early twentieth-century public officials is not supported by the evidence. Nor is the commonly held belief that these entities emerged in response to a transhistorical hatred of government. Instead, the authority evolved as a result of preexisting institutional arrangements, ad hoc choices, and political conflicts.

The political conflicts were affected by the varying interests and structural positions of many powerful actors, internal and external to the state. Business interests—including developers, the real estate industry, and companies that benefited from new quasi-public infrastructure or services—tried to influence the operations of public authorities, even though these groups did not take the lead in setting up the agencies. Meanwhile, courts and legislatures wanted to shape the form taken by public involvement in the economy. Statebuilders operated in this political matrix, which added constraints beyond the ones they encountered from preexisting legal and institutional frameworks. Furthermore, those who desired to build a more activist government in the United States lacked a coherent vision for how to reshape the relationship between government and the economy, and were therefore not well positioned to foresee or forestall the institutional trends to which they were contributing.

The public authority emerged by trial and error in an intense period of institutional experimentation when Americans were seeking to build state capacity for economic intervention. In the early twentieth century, many public officials and policy intellectuals wanted to develop administrative tools that would allow them to transcend the limitations of a fragmented polity imprisoned in an archaic legal structure that severely restricted its ability to engage in economic activity. A variety of motives were in play. For some, it was simply an effort to find ways to finance infrastructure. Others aimed at creating public agencies that could break free of the annual funding cycle controlled by legislative bodies, in order to respond dynamically to changing market conditions and to allow for long-range economic planning. Still others envisioned institutions able to address issues having to do with social justice and economic equality in ways that unconstrained markets cannot. For many it was some mixture of all these purposes. In another context general-purpose governments, perhaps using nonstandard but still accountable agencies, might well have been capable of meeting those goals, but the structure of government as it had developed historically in the United States made this path difficult.

One might question why it matters to pin down the origins of this obscure, if powerful, class of institutional structures. The answer is that the conviction that either elites or the larger public actually desired the kinds of institutions that exist today is not only inaccurate factually, but deleterious politically. It conveys a false sense of inevitability and thereby inhibits clear thinking about how to overcome the obstacles that public authorities merely circumvented.

The Story of Public Authorities Told in This Book

Public authorities in the United States in the early twenty-first century are predominantly state and local, but the federal government played a major role in how they emerged, took their present form, and became so dominant. So the story presented here moves back and forth between federal and subfederal levels of government. It also pays attention to how the different levels affected each other, and in particular how the federal government shaped the institutional character of public-sector economic activity in state and local government.

The story begins in chapter 1 with the creation of the U.S. Emergency Fleet Corporation. In 1914 President Woodrow Wilson and his secretary of the treasury, William Gibbs McAdoo, came up with the idea of a federally owned merchant marine. They envisioned a mechanism through which the administration could guide national trade policy. Despite widespread upset over the decrepit state of the U.S. commercial shipping industry and the shortfall in foreign carriers once the war in Europe began, the plan was a tough sell. Business groups recoiled at the idea of public ownership and lawmakers resisted ceding control over economic policy, which had historically resided in Congress, to the executive branch. After two years of effort by the administration and increasing anxiety about war preparedness, Congress authorized a federal shipping company on a temporary basis. However, the plan was much altered. McAdoo and Wilson had proposed a separately incorporated entity, but one whose governing board would consist of cabinet members; thus, basic policy would be integrated with other executive branch plans and the electorate could hold the administration accountable for the corporation's behavior. The enacted version had an independent board on the model of a regulatory agency, insulating the fleet corporation from democratic accountability. The change resulted from political compromises, and went against the vision of the fleet corporation's sponsors.

Chapter 2 describes the origins of the Federal Land Banks, established by Congress in 1916 to provide a national agricultural credit system. While the formation of the fleet corporation illustrates how incorporated federal agencies gained administrative freedom, the land banks pioneered, at the federal level, an organizational model for fiscal freedom. Here again, the aspirations of the program's designers do not correspond with the imperious motives generally ascribed to the Progressive Era statebuilders who pioneered the public authority template. Actually, the intentions of the sponsors were quite the opposite. The land banks as proposed, and even as originally established by Congress, had large elements of local self-governance, akin to co-ops, but this democratic component evaporated in the course of implementation and revision.

Although largely forgotten today, the land banks constitute a significant chapter in the history of the authority device. For one thing, they survived a legal challenge to their constitutionality, in a 1921 decision by the Supreme Court. As a result, their design became a template for federal lending agencies established in later years. Thus, the land banks represent the earliest exemplar of what has become the most important single way that incorporated national agencies operate in the economy: shaping capital markets. Fannie Mae is only the largest of the host of agencies based on this model. Also, the banks are significant for initiating an experiment—unfortunately aborted—in integrating grassroots activism with government involvement.

The story shifts to the local level in chapter 3, which traces the search by municipal officials, starting in the 1890s, for ways to fund the expansion of infrastructure. Some of this infrastructure produced services that could easily be charged to users, raising the possibility that these investments could pay at least part of their way. Despite widespread public support for municipal ownership of revenue-generating operations, most state courts initially blocked this option on the basis that direct involvement in the economy was an unconstitutional expansion of the power of government.

Courts became more lenient on such matters by the 1920s, but cities still faced the barrier of public finance laws left over from the nineteenth century. These laws imposed debt caps that made it impossible to borrow the sums necessary to build infrastructure needed for an increasingly urbanized environment. By trial and error, public officials came up with two basic strategies for circumventing the rules. One was the special taxing district, a legally separate governmental institution not subject to the debt caps that constrained general-purpose government. The second strategy was the "revenue bond," a financial instrument based on the concept that a city should be able to borrow beyond its legal limit if no burden was incurred by taxpayers. Revenue bonds would be used for projects that could ultimately pay for themselves through charging user fees. The revenues from the facilities, but not the city's taxing power, would be pledged as collateral. Both special taxing districts and revenue bonds proved useful for funding public-sector activities. The drawback was that municipal officials had to seek permission from their state legislatures each time they wanted to employ one of these maneuvers, a process that was always laborious and often unsuccessful.

In chapter 4 the narrative returns to the national level, where it follows the history of federal corporate agencies. Modeled after the Emergency Fleet Corporation and the Federal Land Banks, government-owned corporations became a familiar part of the federal government's administrative repertoire during the First World War, and these mechanisms were again called into service during the Great Depression by both the Hoover and Roosevelt administrations. While President Hoover initiated this practice when he asked Congress to establish the Reconstruction Finance Corporation (RFC) and the Federal Home Loan Banks, it was FDR and his officials who extensively used these devices as they struggled to expand government capacity under emergency conditions. For those involved in running New Deal programs, the corporate agency presented an appealing way to sidestep the required procedures and legal rules that constrained standard units of the federal bureaucracy, as well as to achieve a measure of financial autonomy.

In a hurry to tackle pressing problems and finding little in the way of preexisting bureaucratic apparatus, the New Dealers made almost indiscriminate use of this organizational device. In Great Britain, during this same period, left-of-center politicians were openly discussing whether and how government corporations could be developed into useful administrative machinery for managing socialized sectors of the economy. In contrast, American liberals did not try to connect these structures to a larger strategic vision of activist government, or articulate any overall rationale for when and how these mechanisms should be used. The result was a helter-skelter array of semiautonomous agencies that began to worry even those who had enthusiastically employed them to deal with particular needs. A backlash built, and in 1945 Congress restricted use of these instruments with the Government Corporation Control Act. After this, the wartime corporations were largely abolished; some of the others were absorbed into standard departments; and few new ones were created. Still, this institutional format has remained part of the federal administrative toolbox and has continued to be used sporadically.

Chapter 5 explains how the two lines of institutional development, federal and local, came together in the 1930s to forge a template for the public authority agencies that would become integral to subfederal government in the postwar years. The precipitating factor was the difficulty both the Hoover and Roosevelt administrations encountered trying to loan money to municipalities for construction projects that would produce needed jobs. Congress had authorized such loans, but all over the country local governments were legally blocked from borrowing because they were already up against their debt ceilings. After RFC loans for public works became available in the last part of the Hoover administration, states scrambled to find ways of taking advantage of the money, but progress was minimal. Dealing with debt limits written into state constitutions was especially challenging.

The Public Works Administration (PWA), which had some of the characteristics of the government corporation, took over from the RFC once the New Deal began. To overcome the problems that confounded Hoover's program, PWA director Harold Ickes threw his formidable legal department at the task of systematizing and disseminating the work-around strategies that had been developed on an ad hoc basis over the previous several decades. PWA lawyers went so far as to draft model statutes that state legislatures could adopt, based on the specific constitution and laws of each state. Even the president got into the act. In 1934 Roosevelt sent a letter to all forty-eight governors urging them to draw on the expertise of the PWA's Legal Division to revise their municipal finance laws so they would be able to "legally take full advantage" of the public works programs of his administration. He specifically recommended the creation of legally independent instrumentalities that could finance themselves by borrowing against future revenue.[23] In essence, Roosevelt and the PWA revised, standardized, and popularized the model for what has come to be known as the public authority, an institutional template that combined the funding strategy of revenue bonds with the organizational device of special districts.

Chapter 6 provides an overview of the ways that public authority agencies have been employed since the Second World War. At the federal level, new corporations were rare and some of what had been done by federal corporations was outsourced to independent organizations such as Los

Alamos National Laboratory that were run by private contractors but entirely or mostly funded by the U.S. government. At the same time publicly launched corporations at the state and local level mushroomed, and also evolved into new forms. Whereas traditional public authorities were the direct builders and operators of income-producing infrastructure such as ports, bridges, parking lots, or stadiums, as time went by authorities came to be increasingly used simply as vehicles to obtain low-cost capital from the tax-exempt capital market. The so-called financing authority, pioneered by Governor Nelson Rockefeller in New York State, has become a staple of public finance throughout the country. Thus the nature as well as the number of public authorities has expanded. By now, as shown in figure I.1, these institutions account for the majority of subfederal public borrowing.

Conclusion

What are the implications of the proliferation of public authority–type structures? Given their robust financing capabilities, authorities now exert enormous influence on development patterns throughout the country. Yet because they are not accountable to the electorate this influence is hardly discussed in public debate and almost totally beyond the control of public policy. Rather than pursuing goals determined by democratically elected legislatures and executives, they are guided by the logic of the market, an inevitability given that attending to their revenue flow is their only assured path to continued existence. Meanwhile, these self-contained units fracture the capacity of the public sector. How is it possible for coherent regional planning to take place when metropolitan regions all over the country are divided, not only into states, counties, and municipalities, but also into freestanding sewer authorities, water boards, redevelopment agencies, industrial development commissions, and the like, each pursuing its own vision for the future—a future with its own institutional well-being at the head of the priority list? Another way these agencies undermine the capacity of government is through their inability to cross-subsidize those public activities that cannot or should not become self-supporting. A post office that is fully a part of the national government can be expected to provide service at a loss to people who are unprofitable to serve, or to deliver periodicals at a low rate as a contribution to lively public discourse, but a post office spun off and considered to be essentially a business, even with some subsidies, is not nearly as likely to make such choices.

When one thinks back to the kinds of people who staffed the New Deal—people who believed in collective solutions, who wanted government in the United States to be more robust, more effective, more prestigious vis-à-vis the business world, and more able to aid the less fortunate—it seems curious that they would have built up government structures with attributes so at odds with their values. How can we explain their actions? Put simply, they took the path of least resistance. They did this by largely accepting the institutional environment they inherited, and by expanding and routinizing preexisting institutional innovations, such as special districts and revenue-bond financing, that were essentially methods of evading roadblocks built into the status quo.

Of course, one might argue in their defense that the New Dealers were faced with a crisis, and that the obstacles to pursuing any other path were insurmountable in the near term. The weak link in this argument is that serious problems with local public finance did not originate with the Great Depression. For many years municipalities had not been able to borrow and build in straightforward ways because they were, in the words of the PWA's chief legal officer, "enmeshed in a labyrinth of limitations."[24] This inability to borrow was layered on top of an even deeper problem: that the fiscal basis of local government was the property tax. This method of funding government has always been hated by voters, works regressively, and provides less revenue in hard times, exactly when responsibilities expand.

New Deal officials wanted to respond to a crisis that was generating enormous human suffering, but by attempting to work around the existing dysfunctional institutional structure, rather than trying to overhaul it—by failing even to argue for changes, while at the same time popularizing new institutional forms that in some ways deepened the dysfunctions—they made matters worse. They weakened, ideologically and institutionally, government as a means for citizens to take common ownership of and responsibility for the character of the economy as a whole, and for the well-being of individuals.

As we look at the stories that make up this account, we will pay attention to other voices: the people who advocated alternatives to the organizational template we ended up with. In the epilogue, we will return to these voices, and to contemporary ideas for better forms of government activism, better ways in which we might collectively respond to the kind of needs that sparked the creation and growth of public authorities.

ONE

The Campaign for a Federal Fleet Corporation

Critics of America's vast, uncoordinated sphere of government-created but democratically remote agencies, commonly known as public authorities, often assume that these mechanisms mirror the intentions of the political leaders who initially proposed them. However, the history of the Emergency Fleet Corporation, one of the first public authority–type agencies in the United States, illustrates how these mechanisms only partially reflected, and in some ways contradicted, the aims of those who first advocated their use.

William Gibbs McAdoo

It was William Gibbs McAdoo, secretary of the treasury under Woodrow Wilson, who in 1914 came up with the idea for a merchant marine that would be run by a corporation owned and controlled by the government. His aim was to give the federal government a tool by which to shape international trade. It may seem surprising that a nationally acclaimed business hero who had never held public office before taking over the Treasury Department would champion governmental activism. Yet even during his days in the private sector, McAdoo never embraced the prevailing economic attitudes of his time. He was, in the words of Walter Lippmann, "an outsider who knows the inside wires."[1] This was the case in part because McAdoo, like Wilson himself and others in the president's inner circle, was a transplanted Southerner who had made his mark in the North. His grueling climb from obscurity before achieving financial security in his forties seems to have checked any temptation to idealize the benevolence of unrestrained market forces. Indeed, during one particularly low point in his personal fortunes, he began writing a book on poverty, which he described as "the most serious indictment of our vaunted civilization."[2]

Trained as a lawyer, McAdoo essentially functioned as an entrepreneur before entering public life. Throughout his career, he was continually drawn to technologically innovative and financially complicated, even risky, projects to expand and rationalize transportation networks. After his attempt to electrify the Knoxville, Tennessee, street railway system ended in failure, leaving him nearly bankrupt and "very much mortified," McAdoo moved his family to New York City. He arrived without any real connections and just in time for the severe depression of the 1890s. Nevertheless, by the turn of the century, he had built up a solid practice based on selling corporate securities and reorganizing financially shaky railroads.[3] Shortly thereafter, he established a company that tunneled under the Hudson River, providing the first rail links (now PATH tunnels) between Manhattan Island and New Jersey. Impressive as this achievement was, McAdoo saw it as only the first step toward the comprehensive, integrated transportation network for the entire metropolitan region that he dreamed of creating. He was ultimately frustrated in his hopes to achieve this larger vision, but the opening of the Hudson Tubes in 1908 and the accolades he received for his management of the Hudson and Manhattan Railroad Company transformed him into a respected public figure and propelled him onto the national political stage.[4] The press hailed him as "probably the most popular citizen of New York," and groups around the country invited him to address them on his vision of business-government relations.[5]

According to one biographer, the humanitarian strain in McAdoo's thinking placed him "outside the broad spectrum of business thought." Whether or not this is entirely accurate, given the popularity of "welfare capitalist" ideas in the early twentieth century, the future cabinet secretary did have quite liberal ideas.[6] Despite being on a first name basis with many of the biggest names in American business—men such as Elbert "Judge" Gary, who headed U.S. Steel, and J. P. Morgan, the financier, put hundreds of thousands of dollars of venture capital into McAdoo's projects—the future treasury secretary was openly critical of standard corporate practices of the day. He ran his own firm as something of a counterexample. The company's slogan, "the public be pleased" (an obvious reference to William Henry Vanderbilt's notorious "the public be damned" comment), turned out to be more than a clever public relations gambit (see figure 1.1). At a time of widespread hostility toward urban rail companies for poor service, the Hudson and Manhattan acquired a reputation for clean, modern cars, convenient schedules, and courteous staff. Few riders bothered to use

Figure 1.1. As this 1909 cartoon in the *Jersey City Evening Journal* suggests, McAdoo gained widespread recognition as a visionary and progressive corporate executive during his years as head of the Hudson and Manhattan Railroad. Under his leadership, the company successfully completed commuter rail tunnels under the Hudson River linking New Jersey to Manhattan and garnered widespread praise for its customer service. The company's motto—a play on railroad entrepreneur William Henry Vanderbilt's notorious saying, "the public be damned"—expressed McAdoo's belief that businesses could make good, if not spectacular, profits and simultaneously serve the public interest.

the complaint forms that the company distributed as one of its customer-friendly policies.

Cordial labor relations were also the rule at the Hudson and Manhattan. The way the company introduced women ticket sellers in 1909 suggests some of the reasons. McAdoo explained later that the idea came from one of his managers who suggested women would increase customer satisfaction, since they were "quick and courteous."[7] The manager also recommended female workers on the basis of economy, but McAdoo refused to pay his new female employees at a lower rate than men doing the same job. As predicted, riders responded positively to the innovation. In addition, his decision to pay women comparable wages boosted McAdoo's reputation after it was publicized by female teachers in New York City as part of their campaign to equalize their salaries with those of their male counterparts.[8]

McAdoo also embraced change when it came to government intervention into the economy. Invited in 1910 to address the Harvard Business School, he told his audience: "I believe in the Commission idea." Regulatory commissions were necessary and beneficial, he said, always assuming that everyone understood that business was "essential to the public welfare" and had to show a profit to survive. Moreover, McAdoo believed the government had a role in labor relations. He told the same Harvard audience that he applauded the movement then under way in which some corporations were voluntarily beginning to offer employee pensions, and he looked forward to the time when what he called "wise legislation" would compel all business concerns to provide disability and accident benefits.[9]

One could summarize McAdoo's views on political economy by saying that despite his success as an entrepreneur, he was never in thrall to the mystique of business. While certainly no socialist, his strongest commitment was to a stable and expanding economy that met ordinary people's needs, rather than the sanctity of private property. During his years in Wilson's cabinet, he continually inveighed against the idea that business alone could manage the economy, and he even challenged the assumption that the profit motive guaranteed that businessmen would run their own companies in the most rational manner. In addition, he openly belittled the concept that government should be managed like a business. "Can we afford to say that the Government shall never do anything for the general welfare unless each agency can earn a profit?" he asked the Indianapolis Chamber of Commerce in 1915. It was clearly a rhetorical question, as he immediately launched into a story about how the Treasury Department (which then included the Public Health Service) had helped San Francisco exterminate rats after an outbreak of the bubonic plague was detected in the city. "We spent hundreds of thousands of dollars for the extermination of the rats and the plague. We shall never see that money again, but we saved San Francisco. Would you have had the Government leave the people of San Francisco in peril until it could be assured of a profit on dead rats?"[10]

The Crisis in American Shipping

The outbreak of hostilities in Europe during the summer of 1914 presented McAdoo and other members of the Wilson administration with an immediate crisis regarding international trade, but the underlying problem predated the war. America's commercial shipping industry had been in the doldrums for decades. In the aftermath of the Civil War, American-registered vessels carried 30 percent (by weight) of American commerce. By the turn of the century, the proportion had dropped to under 10 percent, which was where things stood at the time of Wilson's inauguration.[11] British ships were moving approximately 60 percent of American cargo, with German and Austrian ships responsible for another 15 percent.[12] Wilson's secretary of commerce, William Redfield, likened the country to "a department store without a delivery system."[13]

Redfield was hardly the first political leader to decry the country's dependence on foreign carriers. The Republican Party's national platform of 1900 had warned that a "European war would seriously cripple our expanding foreign commerce."[14] Congress took the situation seriously but was unable to develop a policy response. Efforts to explain the source of the problem, let alone reach agreement on how to rectify it, exposed some of the deepest fault lines in American politics. Republicans sided with industry figures who emphasized the high prices of U.S.-built ships (drawing particular attention to labor costs) that American shipping companies were legally required to use. They called for federal aid for these companies to level the playing field with foreign competitors, whom, they charged, were being subsidized by their governments. Democrats, beginning to form an alliance with unions, opposed to protectionism, and still bitter over the federal largesse they believed Republicans had squandered on the railroads during the post–Civil War era, discounted industry claims. They blamed poor management and proposed that commercial shippers be allowed to buy vessels produced anywhere.

According to business historians, both sides had a case. The higher costs for American ships and labor did put American shipping companies at a disadvantage, and some nations were in fact offering financial support to their own merchant marines. Meanwhile, American tariff walls raised steel prices 40–75 percent above what shipbuilders in Britain and Germany paid. Another important factor, although it received little attention in Congress, was the backwardness of the shipbuilding industry. Foreign firms were making cost-cutting innovations typical of modern large-scale enterprise that not even the best capitalized U.S. firms attempted. For example, modern steel ships were being put together in American shipyards using the same craft processes as had been used to build their wooden predecessors, without recourse to new technologies, such as pneumatic tools and large-scale cranes, which would have vastly simplified assembly. Whatever the sources of the lackluster performance of American commercial shipping, however, no public intervention of any kind seemed possible given the stalemate in Congress. Republicans regularly introduced bills for direct aid to shipping firms and these were just as regularly defeated by Democrats. Meanwhile, Democratic proposals that foreign-built ships be allowed to register under the U.S. flag were voted down by Republicans.[15]

War broke the deadlock. Fear of the British navy sent German and Austrian cargo ships scurrying for safe ports once the conflict started in early August 1914. Simultaneously, Great Britain withdrew carriers from normal commercial service in order to move troops and munitions. With the shortfall in ocean transport, a bumper wheat crop started piling up on docks along the Atlantic and Gulf Coast seaboards. By the end of the month, Galveston and New Orleans were so clogged that railroads stopped incoming shipments. Soon, the largest cotton crop in American history would be ready for harvest. With cotton still king of the South's economy, panic gripped the region. The prospect of not being able to sell abroad was devastating, since overseas customers accounted for 60 percent of the market. Prices plunged to half the level of the previous year (and well below the cost of production). The administration was under enormous pressure to act. Core Democratic constituencies, export-oriented farmers of the South and West, faced ruin. Indeed, the country's entire financial structure—linked as it was to international trade—was threatened. The New York Stock Exchange closed at the end of July, not to open again until December.[16]

The Plan for a Federal Fleet and Its Reception

McAdoo, the most forceful member of the cabinet—and well situated by having recently become the president's son-in-law—took the initiative. In mid-August he came up with a plan for a government-owned fleet of merchant ships. Wilson signed on enthusiastically, predicting with relish that the proposal was sure to "arouse the hostility of every reactionary in the United States."[17] The first step was to convince skeptical Democratic Party leaders. At a private White House briefing, McAdoo portrayed the trade paralysis as so critical that it required "heroic treatment." By emphasizing the immediate emergency, he was trying to motivate the lawmakers to act. In reality, however, he and Wilson had long-range goals that transcended the moment. Both aspired to expand American international trade beyond prewar levels by developing new markets. A federal fleet controlled by the executive would be a key tool by which to achieve this objective.[18]

Both Wilson and McAdoo had long been committed to trade expansion. Wilson's convictions regarding the moral and material advantages that would accrue to the world at large through the extension of American trade relationships are well known. On the campaign trail in 1912, he described "a great merchant marine" as "absolutely indispensable."[19] Like Wilson, McAdoo's southern roots sensitized him to trade questions. The South's economy had always rested on export trade. Now, as the treasury secretary saw it, the economy of the entire nation was moving in the same direction. At one point in the campaign for a federal fleet, McAdoo told American Federation of Labor (AFL) president Samuel Gompers that acquiring "our share" of world markets was essential, because the country was producing more than it could consume in manufactured products as well as agricultural staples. Enlarging international commerce was the key, McAdoo believed, to avoiding "extremes of prosperity and business depression."[20] In other words, McAdoo saw trade expansion as a macroeconomic stabilizer.

Given such views, the long-coveted markets of Latin America, previously dominated by the British, must have looked particularly alluring in August of 1914. This was the month the Panama Canal opened. So perhaps it was not by coincidence that the day after the first ship sailed through the canal, McAdoo awoke at dawn and jotted his initial ideas for a fleet corporation on a notepad next to his bed. That same day he sent Wilson the draft of a bill that would authorize a federally owned fleet, explaining that the disruption of normal trading relationships in the Southern Hemisphere offered Americans an "unusual opportunity." But he emphasized that "without ships we can do nothing." The president agreed. With his trademark mixture of moralism and appeal to material advantage, Wilson conceptualized it as both "our duty and opportunity" to supply the South Americans now that their normal European trade partners were otherwise occupied.[21]

With Wilson giving strong support, congressional Democrats introduced the bill McAdoo had drafted. The proposed legislation called for a shipping board to oversee a corporation authorized "to purchase, construct, equip, maintain, and operate merchant vessels in the foreign trade of the United States." The board, to be composed of the secretary of the treasury, the postmaster general, and the secretary of commerce, would set policy. Full-time directors would handle day-to-day operations. The corporation would be initially capitalized at $10 million, with the government as majority, or if necessary, sole stockholder. If more funds were needed, the corporation would be able to use the proceeds from the sale of up to $30 million in federal bonds that had previously been authorized to construct the Panama Canal. Representative Joshua Alexander (D-MO), chair of the Committee on the Merchant Marine and Fisheries, introduced the measure in the House. In the upper chamber, Senator James P. Clarke (D-AK), head of the Senate Commerce Committee, presented it.[22]

McAdoo, Wilson, and the Democratic congressional leadership expected opposition, but they were taken aback by the ferocity of the response. The eastern media was apoplectic. The *New York Sun* called the plan an "economic and political monstrosity." To the *New York Times*, it was simply "preposterous."[23] McAdoo later recalled how "a swarm of lobbyists, representing shipping concerns, descended on Washington." The infestation was no doubt related to windfall profits that the industry was suddenly enjoying—in some cases shipping rates leaped over a 1,000 percent.[24] J. P. Morgan, who controlled the International Mercantile Marine Corporation, called on McAdoo at the Treasury to warn that "the government's entrance into the [shipping] field would be a menace." McAdoo was unimpressed, commenting later that the only menace was to the "absurdly high rates" the shipping companies were then enjoying.[25]

Two basic objections were raised. The first was that government ownership of merchant ships would exacerbate the already tense and murky situation with regard to American maritime rights as a neutral nation. Some feared that if one of the belligerents were to capture or attack a cargo vessel owned by the government, it would precipitate a diplomatic crisis severe enough to drag the country into the war. The second argument was ideological. In the words of Republican Senator Elihu Root, a federally owned fleet represented a major step toward "state socialism."[26] According to the Philadelphia Board of Trade, Congress needed to defeat the measure "because Government management of any business is more expensive than private management." As an alternative, the board urged the solution it had "always advocated," which was "direct ship subsidies."[27]

McAdoo tried to counter both lines of opposition in his testimony and speeches during the two years the issue was under consideration in Congress. Speaking before Representative Alexander's Committee on the Merchant Marine when the first version of the bill was being considered, he argued that by establishing an incorporated agency, legally distinct from the rest of the federal government, to own and operate the fleet, the country would be shielded from diplomatic complications if the ships became involved in any altercations with the warring powers. "The idea in having the Government take the controlling interest in the company instead of operating these ships directly as a Government operation is, of course, to avoid any possible complication resulting from the Government itself going into the shipping business," he maintained.[28] The congressmen were skeptical, but McAdoo insisted that the government would be in exactly the same position as a private individual who invested in a corporate enterprise: in both cases the investor was legally separate from the corporate entity. This would be true, he assured them, even if, as seemed likely, private investors did not subscribe any of the stock and the corporation became wholly owned by the government. "The question of its sovereignty in prize courts could not arise in any way whatever," he insisted.[29] The federal government would be "merely" a stockholder.[30] In retrospect, this defense seems hypocritical, although possibly it was simply naïve. Arthur Link, Wilson's leading biographer, concludes that the president was "simply refusing to face" the sticky diplomatic questions related to a federal shipping line.[31]

With regard to the second objection, the treasury secretary rejected core assumptions underpinning the position that the government needed to stay out of the economy at all times. Indeed, he consistently made the case that there were important tasks related to a well-functioning and growing economy that private enterprise could not perform on its own. "This is a question," he told Congress, "of the Government doing directly for the people of this country what private capital can not do."[32] A celebrated storyteller, the secretary illustrated his position on the issue to the Chamber of Commerce national convention in 1915 by recounting an old vaudeville routine. He related how a character named Fields proposes to his sidekick, Weber, that the two organize a "skindicate" to go into the shipping business. Weber agrees and asks what his role will be. Fields replies, "Vell, I furnish ze ocean and you furnish ze ships." McAdoo insisted that this was the same situation in which the country found itself. "Private capital has furnished the ocean for 50 years, but who" he asked, "has furnished the ships?"[33]

McAdoo also disputed his business critics at a factual level. Speaking to the same Chamber of Commerce audience, he argued that it was not government entrance into the economy per se, but competition that his opponents feared. He pointed out how, only days after hostilities erupted, the biggest names in American commerce had urged the government to provide insurance to cover ocean carriers, despite the fact that this would insert the government directly into the economy. The concept of federal protection against potential losses proved tremendously popular. The bill appropriating $5 million to establish a Bureau of War Risk Marine Insurance sped through Congress in just a couple of weeks, landing on the president's desk ready for his signature in early September 1914. Years later in his memoirs, McAdoo reflected with some bitterness on what he viewed as hypocrisy on the part of opponents to his shipping program. When it came to insurance, he wrote, everyone approved: big business supported it, "so did little business; shipowners; shipbuilders; exporters—everybody. Why? Because there was a general impression that no money could be made from the business of war risk insurance."[34]

McAdoo's frustration with the way business executives had embraced a public insurance program that would allow private commerce to continue, all the while never slacking in their denunciations of government participation in the economy, reveals much about his vision for the fleet corporation. In testimony to Congress he described how, soon after the war started, he was approached by a representative of J. P. Morgan's International Merchant Marine Corporation with a plan by which the company would buy and operate German freighters then sitting out the war in American ports. The only hitch was securing funds to make the purchase. Would the government be willing to guarantee the company's bonds, as private capital markets would probably shy away otherwise? McAdoo declined, asserting that if the enterprise "must depend upon the credit of the Government to succeed, or to raise the necessary means, the Government might as well do the thing directly."[35]

What was it that McAdoo and Wilson wanted to do "directly," using the instrumentality of a government-owned corporation? Why did they not prefer to subsidize existing firms? Their basic agenda in this situation was to give government the capacity to perform tasks that they believed private enterprise could not achieve alone. They hoped to develop new markets, an endeavor that required regular transport service from the outset. But providing frequent connections before solid trading relationships had taken hold would be a profit-losing proposition that investor-owned companies could not be expected to undertake. As Wilson put it in his annual message to Congress in December 1914: "The Government must open these gates of trade, and open them wide; open them before it is altogether profitable to open them, or altogether reasonable to ask private capital to open them at a venture."[36]

During committee hearings, hostile congressmen pressed McAdoo to explain why such goals could not be fulfilled by granting subsidies to private shipping companies for providing service on government-designated low-profit routes. It was at this point that the secretary did respond with a characteristic Progressive appeal to efficiency—but not that of the private firm. He contended that a program aimed at foreign trade expansion necessarily involved so many unforeseen possibilities that the government needed "control of the situation itself." That way, policy makers could "deal with conditions as they arise and meet them."[37] Here McAdoo was explicitly challenging the long-standing American conviction that public policy could best be implemented by manipulating the incentive structure for business, using policies like grants, loan guarantees, insurance, or tax benefits. He envisioned a proactive government able to set economic priorities in a way that was not possible when its only means of action was through providing supports for private-sector decision makers. This was why he rejected Morgan's proposal for federal loan guarantees and why he wanted to establish a merchant marine owned and managed by the government.

In addition to expanding international trade, McAdoo seems to have conceived of the corporation as a mechanism to force new practices on ship builders. He even seems to have envisioned using the corporation as a macroeconomic stabilizer. As previously mentioned, American shipyards had not rationalized production to the same extent as many other industries. On the eve of the war, American ships were still being individually assembled rather than manufactured. McAdoo did not stress this issue during his campaign for the shipping corporation, but it seems clear that reforming production was integral to his plan for the new agency. He often said that government management was better than grants, because giving the industry money would underwrite existing inefficient procedures. He usually left these unspecified, although in one major address he did go further, telling the Indianapolis Chamber of Commerce in October 1915 that "under this plan" ships contracted for by the government "could be made to set the pace in merchant-marine construction." In this same speech, he also pictured the corporation as a mechanism the government could use to moderate downturns in regional labor markets. He described how during the "dull winter months" the corporation could contract with Great Lakes shipyards to manufacture standardized parts that could be transported for fabrication elsewhere. This would "give employment to many of our workmen in those parts of the country where they would otherwise be idle."[38]

Why a Corporation, instead of an Ordinary Agency?

In his campaign to build support for a federally owned merchant marine, McAdoo gave only scattered hints as to why he wanted to organize it as a government-owned corporation. Possibly he thought that going into specifics would only further antagonize those already upset by the idea of public enterprise. Alternatively, he may not have fully conceptualized, in his own mind, how the kind of administrative arrangement he proposed would function to accomplish his larger goals. As we will see in later chapters, lack of attention to the long-term implications of choices about organizational structure has been a continual weakness of proponents of activist government in the United States.

His remarks to the Indianapolis Chamber of Commerce in the fall of 1915 represent one of the few times the treasury secretary addressed the administrative aspects of the plan at any length. On this occasion, McAdoo noted three distinct advantages that would flow from the format he was proposing.

First, this organizational form would mean that managers would be "unaffected by political influences." Although this statement might seem to indicate antidemocratic bias, this is not really the case. McAdoo was not trying to wall off the agency from democratic input along the lines of an independent regulatory commission guided by supposedly nonpartisan experts. On the contrary, his design integrated the fleet corporation into the core of an elected executive, with cabinet members serving as directors. Voters unhappy with the policies of the agency would be able to indicate their displeasure at the polls. The political influences that he wanted to discourage were favors solicited and promised between congressmen and bureaucrats in the context of the yearly budget process. The distractions of having to constantly lobby for appropriations and never knowing how much money Congress would decide to allocate from year to year were incompatible with any kind of long-range planning. McAdoo's vision involved insulating the agency from interference in its internal operations, not from political accountability for its overall program.

McAdoo's second point can be summarized as an argument for the virtues of isomorphism. "The corporation can sue and be sued," he explained, "and a [private] shipper will have no difficulty in enforcing his remedy or claim against the corporation." Securing redress from a federal agency was a much more elaborate process, potentially involving going to Congress. In essence, he was saying that the institutional design he had in mind would be able to function more effectively in the economy, because American and foreign businessmen would know how to relate to it. Such predictability would, he maintained, "give confidence to business men."

The third argument he made to the Indianapolis business leaders was that the structure he envisioned would be more flexible and nimble than the standard government agency. This was particularly important for an entity that would need to respond to fast-changing market conditions. Freed from the layers of purchasing, personnel, and budgeting rules that governed standard federal agencies, the federal fleet would be able to respond quickly "to meet any emergency." As an example, he sketched a scenario for helping exporters during peak export seasons when cargo ships were scarce and transportation rates high. "In such circumstances the shipping board could throw a fleet of steamers into the leading ports of the Northwest and South to take care of seasonal demands."[39]

In his testimony on Capitol Hill, McAdoo was more guarded when it came to the administrative innovations of the plan. As noted previously, he maintained during the first set of hearings that giving the agency a legally separate identity would shield the country from diplomatic entanglements if one of the ships got into a dispute with a belligerent nation. Even supporters had a hard time taking this argument seriously, and indeed, McAdoo never made the pretense that this was his underlying motive for wanting to set up the agency as a corporation. The one time the secretary ever put forward anything like a serious rationale to Congress was during the second set of hearings before the House Committee on the Merchant Marine, in the spring of 1916, when he said that his inspiration had come from observing the Panama Railroad and Steamship Company. He told the committee that given the success of this venture, he "simply" wanted to create another entity along the same lines.[40]

As it happened, the format of the federal agency in charge of rail and ship activities for the Panama Canal was an accident of history. The Panama Railroad Company had started life as an investor-owned firm during the nineteenth century. It was absorbed by one of the failed canal companies whose assets came into the possession of the Colombian government. After the Republic of Panama declared independence from Colombia in 1903, the company was transferred to the U.S. government along with rights to the canal. The War Department set policy for the company, but internally it operated like a private concern. Administrators controlled its $7 million capital stock, freeing them from the rigors of the yearly congressional appropriation cycle. Another administrative advantage was that the company, because it was legally independent, did not have to confront the layers of accounting and purchasing regulations that proved so onerous to other parts of the federal bureaucracy. In this situation, good managers were free to run a highly effective organization. At the time the company was acquired, the railroad was reported to be in "unbelievably" bad condition. When the American engineer in charge was told that there had been no recent accidents, he responded that "even a collision has its good points, as it indicates that something is moving." Under War Department supervision the company turned itself around, putting the railroad into "first-class condition." The enterprise provided support for the building of the Panama Canal, operated reliable steamship service between Panama and New York, and actually made money.[41]

The Panama Railroad Company's structure must have looked particularly appealing to McAdoo in the context of the headaches the administration was experiencing as it tried to keep funds flowing for the Alaska Railroad. In 1914 Congress acceded to the Democrats' insistence on direct control of this venture (in contrast to subsidizing private operators as was done in the case of the transcontinental line), and the operation was being run by the Alaskan Engineering Commission out of the Department of the Interior. This meant the commission had to get its budget from Congress on a year-by-year basis.

The "Government Railroad," as it was commonly termed, would eventually link the coastal city of Seward with Fairbanks in the interior, a distance of almost five hundred miles. While the territory's harsh terrain and climate had foiled numerous previous efforts by private companies to establish a working line of any length, the federal construction was generally conceded to have been very competently done. Indeed, a 1919 investigation by the Republican-headed House Committee on the Territories concluded that the line had been built "at the lowest cost consistent with the permanent character of the work performed." The report did acknowledge overruns beyond the cost originally envisioned by Congress but noted that these had been less than the general level of war-induced inflation during the period of construction. For this achievement the committee credited the commission's savvy management skills, particularly with respect to estimating costs and writing contracts. The only critical note in this otherwise laudatory document had to do with how the government's management team had been handicapped by "the system of annual appropriations." Not being able to predict in advance how much money would be available for the following year meant that scarce time had been routinely squandered during the short May-to-October Alaskan working seasons. The committee came to the same conclusion that must have been painfully apparent to McAdoo several years before: that both time and money would have been saved if the entire amount of money ultimately spent had been given to the managers up front "so as to be continuously available."[42]

McAdoo's desire to emulate the format of the Panama Railroad Company was no doubt genuine. What he did not say, but was likely also the case, was that some of his inspiration came from observing similar structures elsewhere. After all, his idea for a fleet corporation came to him during a period of prolific experimentation with new models of public administration all over the world, including other levels of American government, based on the legal device of the government-owned corporation. It is implausible that the cosmopolitan treasury secretary was unaware of at least some of these new institutional forms coming into existence in this era.

Internationally, one of the most influential examples was Ontario's Hydro-Electric Power Commission, established in 1906. A publicly controlled enterprise set up to generate and distribute electrical power from the Niagara River, Ontario Hydro was the forerunner of a myriad of government-owned "crown corporations" in Canada. Historian Thomas K. McCraw has described how the "Hydro," with its "almost unbelievably low residential rates," had a big impact on politicians in the United States. Al Smith and Franklin Roosevelt both campaigned to establish a state power authority in New York, a venture finally approved by the legislature not long before Roosevelt left for the White House.[43] Such initiatives were popular throughout the British Commonwealth. In England, the Port of London Authority was created on the corporate model in 1908 to operate harbor facilities, while the South African government set up a Land and Agricultural Bank in 1912 to make loans to individual farmers and agricultural cooperatives. Australia was particularly active in this area. Both Victoria and New South Wales established corporations to run their railroads in the 1880s, and Victoria set up a State Savings Bank in 1897. In 1911 the national government joined in, creating the Commonwealth Bank of Australia, which became the country's central bank in 1920.[44]

Meanwhile, a similar movement was proceeding at the state and local level in the United States. Beginning in the late nineteenth century, states and municipalities in the United States had been trying out a variety of new institutional arrangements that would allow them to respond to constituent expectations for services and amenities while avoiding barriers to public-sector activity such as voter resistance to higher tax rates, legal ceilings on borrowing, or lack of fit between logical boundaries for service areas and existing political jurisdictions. Chapter 3 explores this line of development, but for now a few examples will suffice. As early as 1869, Illinois incorporated three park districts just outside the existing city limits of Chicago that continued to operate independently even after the territory they covered was annexed by the city in 1889. Massachusetts established the Boston Transit Commission in 1894 to build the nation's first subway system. Ohio set up the Miami Conservancy District in 1914 to "floodproof" the Miami River Valley by building a series of enormous water retarding basins. And New York created river regulation districts in 1915 that were termed "public corporations" in the enabling legislation. Although some of these entities were not formally organized as corporations, all had significant administrative and fiscal independence from other units of government, supporting themselves, at least in part, from user fees and/or proceeds from bond sales.[45]

At the national level, the corporate device had long been a familiar instrument of public administration. Despite the enduring myth of American allegiance to laissez-faire, from the birth of the republic through most of the nineteenth century, enterprising citizens "drew almost casually on city, county, state, and federal government credit resources and revenues." It was taken for granted that public involvement in the economy was a legitimate (and perhaps the only practical) means by which both to encourage and regulate economic development. In the early days of the republic, the national government, along with states, invested in what today would be described as "private" companies—in the sense that the majority of the stock was owned by individuals. The best known were the First and Second Banks of the United States, but there were a number of others, including the National Road (1806), the Chesapeake and Delaware Canal Company (1825), the Louisville and Portland Canal Company (1926), the Dismal Swamp Canal Company (1826), and the Chesapeake and Ohio Canal Company (1828).[46]

President Andrew Jackson strenuously opposed this kind of activity. He insisted that such initiatives were an unconstitutional expansion of the "limited and specific" powers of the national government intended by the framers (although as historian Richard R. John points out, his "antidevelopmental agenda" more likely grew out of fears that a strengthened central state could threaten the interests of his slaveholder base than concern for legal niceties). While it is true that Congress did markedly less in the way of incorporating and directly participating in economic ventures in the years following Jackson's vetoes of bills to authorize federal investment in the Maysville toll road (1830) and to recharter the Second Bank of the United States (1832), these incidents do not mark as complete a break from federal involvement in the economy as generally imagined.[47] For instance, as economic historian Robert Fogel points out, throughout the decades-long debate over the question of a rail line that would span the trans-Missouri West, almost all participants took for granted "the necessity and inevitability of governmental intervention." The legislation of 1862 and 1864 ceded much to private capital, but the Union Pacific Railroad was still, in Fogel's words, a "mixed enterprise." Federal incorporation and subsidies were combined with a provision for some of the directors (ultimately five out of twenty) to be appointed by the president. That the government directors did a poor job of restraining the spectacular financial chicanery for which the Union Pacific became notorious does not negate the reality of its legal structure.[48]

Another example of the way sentiment against federal participation in the economy has been overstated is provided by the political support for setting up a government plant to manufacture steel plate for naval warships. The high and suspiciously similar prices charged by the major steel companies aroused widespread antimonopoly sentiment in the late nineteenth century, and in 1897 Congress appropriated funds for setting up a government-owned manufacturing operation. The venture was cut short by the outbreak of the Spanish-American War, but Josephus Daniels, Wilson's secretary of the navy, took up the cause "almost from the day he took the oath of office" and succeeded in getting congressional approval for a second time in 1916. A year later, ground was broken for a government facility to manufacture naval armor in Charleston, West Virginia. Due to war shortages, the plant did not become operational for steel-plate production before the Democrats lost the presidency, and the Harding administration abandoned the endeavor. Nevertheless, construction did proceed to the point that the plant was producing artillery shells during the war.[49]

Meanwhile, throughout the nineteenth century Congress continued to give corporate charters for educational and charitable endeavors. For example, the Smithsonian Institution was established as a corporate entity in 1846. Other instances include the Columbia Institution for the Deaf (1857; now Gallaudet University), the National Academy of Sciences (1863), the National Home for Disabled Soldiers (1866), and Howard University (1867). While each of these was organized somewhat differently, all were supported at least in part with funds coming from the federal government, either directly or through the District of Columbia, and in every case there was some provision for public supervision.[50]

McAdoo himself had participated in the revival of corporate mechanisms for public administration, even before putting forward his plan for a fleet corporation, when he helped design the Federal Reserve System during the first months of Wilson's administration. The Federal Reserve Act of 1913 established twelve regional "banker's" banks, which were structured as corporations. The government pledged to capitalize them to the extent that private banks failed to fully subscribe their stock. This provision was not needed, which meant the banks were not strictly speaking government instrumentalities. They were, however, supervised by a national board appointed by the president, an arrangement that McAdoo hoped would put "the Government in the saddle." Thus, the Federal Reserve was a hybrid institution with certain elements that prefigured the structure of the public authority.[51]

The Fleet Corporation and Congress

The effort to establish a federal fleet corporation became one of the defining struggles of the Wilson administration. When the bill McAdoo drafted was first submitted to Congress in late August 1914, Democrats controlled both houses. Passage was hardly assured, however, given anxiety on both sides of the aisle concerning the idea of government ownership, compounded by worry about possible diplomatic complications with the Allies if the federal fleet were to include ships previously owned by Germans. A major blow to the bill's chances came early on, when Britain gained surprisingly quick control of the oceans. Dangers subsided for transatlantic commercial ships, as long as they did not try to break the British blockade of the Central Powers.[52]

McAdoo and Wilson had expected that the rapid and effective aid they had delivered to the business community in the early days of the war would at least buy neutrality for their proposal. After all, the administration had pushed through Congress a government insurance program for shippers when private companies withdrew from the market. In addition, the Treasury Department had moved federal funds into American banks that were rushing to fill the hole created by the breakdown of British credit facilities for foreign trade in Latin America. Ironically, however, that help, coupled with the lull in naval hostilities, served to bolster business confidence and thereby encourage resistance to the incursion on private prerogatives that a federally owned merchant fleet represented.[53]

As the weeks went by and the bill's prospects dimmed, Wilson only grew more committed. Ships were crossing the Atlantic, but there were still too few of them, so rates were high. Moreover, shipping companies focused on already-established routes, where profits were sure, rather than pioneering the new Latin American markets that the president and his treasury secretary wanted developed. In the waning days of the Sixty-Third Congress, Wilson framed support as a key test of party allegiance and of loyalty to himself (detractors maintained that he had trouble telling the difference). The president told Democrats that their hope of being the majority party in the future rested with voting the administration line, in order to demonstrate the "solidarity of the Democratic team."[54]

Opposition was most intense in the Senate. The fight over the measure provided weeks of high drama, with the Republican minority mounting a legendary effort to stall a vote. The Democrats first countered by refusing to consider all other business, including appropriations. When this tactic failed to break the determination of the opposition by the end of January 1915, Democrats upped the ante by holding the Senate in continuous session. Undaunted, the Republicans responded by moving cots into the halls of the upper chamber and sending their most indefatigable orators into the fray. In what one filibuster expert ranks as one of the "great feats of physical endurance in the history of the Senate," Senator Reed Smoot of Utah spoke "relevantly and fervently" against the measure for eleven and a half hours straight, without even being allowed the relief of leaning against the arm of his chair. Together, Republicans held the floor for over thirty-six hours continuously, until exhausted Democrats finally called a recess. There were enough Democrats to pass the measure without Republican support, but when Wilson refused to agree that the enterprise would be temporary, the Democratic "team" splintered. Sure to lose, administration allies finally let the Senate adjourn, without ever bringing the measure up for a vote. In the House, the bill ultimately passed, but amended so as to make it a temporary measure.[55]

McAdoo and Wilson were furious, particularly at Democrats who had sided against them. But they took defeat in the spirit of losing a battle, not the war. In the months that followed McAdoo stumped for the plan throughout the Western Hemisphere, extolling its virtues from Helena, Montana, to Buenos Aires, Argentina.[56]

With time the situation changed in four ways that improved the measure's prospects. First, McAdoo switched his public relations strategy, now arguing that marine cargo carriers were "just as essential to a strong and effective Navy as the guns on the decks of our battleships."[57] This was a shrewd move in light of the rising sentiment for military preparedness, especially among Republicans, but reflected no real change of heart on McAdoo's part. He modified his pitch because, as he later commented sadly, he had become convinced that "people as a rule are far more interested in fighting, and in preparations for fighting, than they are in any constructive commercial or industrial effort."[58] A second factor behind the bill's new momentum was the increasing shortage of merchant ships. After initial dislocations during the first weeks of war, American exporters had been able, for a price, to find vessels. This became steadily less true as the conflict wore on, due in part to the increase in trade. By the close of 1915, New York harbor was so backlogged that the railroads embargoed the port.[59] A third factor that worked in the bill's favor was news from the Paris Economic Conference held in June 1916. At this meeting, the Allies announced their intention to create a closed trading block after the war. The plan was ostensibly aimed at Germany, but Americans nervously wondered what it meant for them, as well. Public statements by the Australian prime minister, W. M. Hughes, only heightened American anxieties. Hughes berated neutral nations who were growing "rich while we daily grow poorer" and predicted that the program adopted in Paris would ultimately make those countries "suppliant at [the] feet" of the British and French empires.[60] The final new factor was Wilson's capitulation on the issue of a time limit for federal operation of a merchant fleet.[61]

Of these new circumstances, the increasingly difficult transportation situation probably made the biggest difference. As the war continued, trade opportunities grew. Ships, however, became scarcer. The result was an erosion of a principled stance against government involvement. Not only did business groups lose interest in fighting the proposal, they actually warmed to it. A survey by the National Chamber of Commerce during the summer of 1915 indicated that more than half the businessmen polled supported the idea of a government-owned shipping corporation.[62] In January 1916, the National Foreign Trade Council devoted its annual meeting to "the war after the war." Members were convinced that a fierce struggle for world markets was sure to break out as soon as the shooting stopped. Formerly hostile to the plan for a federal merchant marine, the council now welcomed an administration official who outlined the ways that government ships would provide American manufacturers and raw materials producers with a "continuous" delivery system to new markets. Largely as a result of changed attitudes in the business community, opposition on Capitol Hill slumped. Congress passed the bill, and Wilson signed it on September 7, 1916.[63]

Unfortunately for the president and his treasury secretary the final legislation differed in important respects from the concept McAdoo had sketched out on his bedside notepad two years earlier. Most importantly, the United States Shipping Board (USSB) was assigned the role of regulating the commercial shipping industry, in addition to operating a fleet of merchant vessels it purchased, leased, or built itself. Since the USSB was to function in part as a regulator, its organizational structure was based on the design of previously established regulatory agencies such as the Interstate Commerce Commission (1887) and Federal Trade Commission (1914). These bodies had been set up to function independently of the executive branch based on the logic that experts would be able to make decisions in the public interest if shielded from partisan political pressures. Following this template, the fleet corporation was not embedded in the core of the executive branch with a subset of cabinet members constituting its board, as McAdoo had envisioned. Instead, the president was to appoint, with the consent of the Senate, a board consisting of five individuals who were not to be engaged "in any other business, vocation or employment," with no more than three from the same political party. In addition, any corporate subsidiaries the board decided to establish would have to be dissolved no later than five years after the end of the war.[64]

The Fleet Corporation in Action

On April 16, 1917, ten days after the United States entered the war, the shipping board used its authority to establish the Emergency Fleet Corporation (EFC). German submarines already had sent ships capable of carrying over eight million tons of cargo to the ocean floor, and replacement vessels were urgently needed. Incorporated in the District of Columbia and initially capitalized at $50 million, the EFC received over $2.6 billion from Congress during the conflict. Particularly when one considers that the fleet corporation had to be created from nothing, the organization was extremely effective. In the words of one awed observer: "History records few undertakings which rival it in size and none which approach it in speed of execution."[65] At the peak of activity, the EFC directed operations at 218 different shipyards, having streamlined production to the extent that Americans were launching new vessels in one-third the time British shipbuilders took.[66] When the armistice was declared, less than eighteen months after the corporation came into existence, it had delivered 470 ships, with 1,500 more under construction.[67]

The fleet corporation was remarkable not only for the number of ships it produced, but also by the way it restructured conventional procedures at American shipyards, with regard to both technology and labor relations. It constructed huge new shipbuilding facilities, as at Hog Island near Philadelphia, which were essentially assembly plants for parts manufactured elsewhere. It even experimented with making ships from concrete. Meanwhile, its personnel division trained dozens of employment managers, developed standardized forms for recording work histories, and published a variety of bulletins pertaining to hiring, including "Opportunities in Shipbuilding for the Physically Handicapped." In addition to ships and shipyards, the corporation produced whole new communities. In 1918, Congress authorized the EFC to build housing for workers in crowded shipbuilding centers. The result was over nine thousand permanent family homes in at-

Figure 1.2. Set up a few days after the United States entered the First World War, the Emergency Fleet Corporation (EFC) quickly became one of the largest industrial enterprises in the world, directing operations at 218 existing and newly built shipyards. Employing advanced production methods and innovative personnel policies, the EFC was able to drastically reduce construction time. This poster promotes the agency, which indeed had a lot to boast about.

tractively designed developments that would become famous for their high design standards.[68]

Separate from its own operations, the EFC (advertised in figure 1.2) was noteworthy as the prototype for a number of similarly structured entities that Congress and the president created during the war years: the Food Administration Grain Corporation; the War Finance Corporation; the United States Housing Corporation; the United States Sugar Equalization Board; the United States Spruce Production Corporation; and the United States Russian Bureau, Inc. Like the shipping corporation, these instrumentalities were conceived as temporary, and they were wound down shortly after the war's end.[69] The EFC itself, however, persisted long after the date Congress had set for its expiration. In 1926 it was not only still around, but operating 317 vessels on 71 cargo and passenger lines that served Europe, the Mediterranean, and South America.[70] A year later, it shed its "emergency" appellation when Congress retitled it the Merchant Fleet Corporation. It even outlasted its parent organization, the United States Shipping Board, which was abolished by the incoming Roosevelt administration as an economy measure in 1933. As it turned out, the corporation hung on as a separate entity until 1936, when Congress passed comprehensive maritime legislation that rolled it into the Commerce Department.[71]

Conclusion

Although the fleet corporation turned out to be extremely effective during the war mobilization and so popular that Congress later converted it into a permanent agency, it never became the mechanism for public action that McAdoo tried to forge. Nor did it set a precedent for other administrative structures along the lines that he originally envisioned. As we will begin to see in the next chapter, at the federal level it has been easier to employ these mechanisms to intervene in capital markets than to produce goods and services. This was a disappointment for McAdoo, who wanted to develop alternatives to the federal government's conventional ways of aiding the economy: through providing supports and manipulating the incentive structure for business using grants, loan guarantees, insurance, or tax benefits. The problem with such methods, from McAdoo's perspective, was the way they leave key decisions about economic activity entirely to the private sector, rather than sometimes allowing government to impose its own priorities, with a publicly accountable conception of rationality and/or social justice guiding the kinds and locations for economic development.

If McAdoo desired to create a very different kind of administrative mechanism, how can we explain why the fleet corporation (and by extension, later public authority–type agencies) diverged so far from his initial conception? McAdoo's own conclusion was that he was thwarted by the political power of business. Writing confidentially to Wilson after the much-modified measure finally cleared Congress, he asserted that "shipping interests" were responsible for the "tremendously emasculated" condition of the final legislation. He believed that shipping firms had spearheaded the effort to make cabinet members ineligible for the shipping board, thus distancing the board from executive control. Their objective was to "increase the administrative difficulties," and thereby undermine the project. Now, he warned the president, these same interests were hoping to pack the board with their own candidates.[72]

McAdoo was correct that the shipping companies were threatened by the possibility of a large, permanent, government-owned merchant fleet, and clearly they had tried hard to thwart the plan. But he overlooked the fact that in addition to powerful foes, he had no organized allies outside of Washington, no social movements backing his initiative. As will be described in the next chapter, the lack of a mobilized constituency for a federal fleet stood in marked contrast to the support enjoyed by proposals for a federal mortgage loan program for farmers, which became the other early federal initiative to be organized on the basis of a government corporation.

Another barrier that McAdoo did not recognize was Congress's own institutional reasons for opposing the initiative. Structured as McAdoo desired, the fleet corporation would have been a robust addition to the executive branch, especially with respect to economic policy, a traditional congressional prerogative. This by itself made the plan a red-flag issue for Congress, independent of any ideological abhorrence to public ownership or prodding from business interests. Given the long struggle between Congress and the executive for control over national policy-making stretching back to the earliest days of the republic, it seems almost overdetermined that Congress would reject a proposal that would so obviously have strengthened the presidency.[73] As Stephen Skowronek has argued, Progressives were able to build powerful new administrative structures that resulted in a qualitatively new kind of national government, but the stalemate that developed between different power centers during this period of incremental political change meant that there was no centralized control over the new bureaucratic apparatus. In his words, "the shifting scramble for power and position" was inscribed "into the very structure of the American State."[74] Federal corporations clearly fit this pattern of state development.

As can be seen from this look at the origin of one of the earliest public authority–type mechanisms, the politically insulated structure of the Emergency Fleet Corporation was not the result of conscious efforts by those who first proposed it. While it is true that the self-styled "Progressives" who pushed government expansion and institutional innovation in the early twentieth century were less single-mindedly devoted to democracy and social justice than they or their publicists proclaimed—and were a far more heterogeneous cast of characters than initially recognized—careful investigation reveals that we can better understand why the peculiar government units that came to be known as government corporations or public authorities emerged as they did if we put less emphasis on the personalities and values of politicians (as well as the imputed free-market devotion of the American public). Instead we need to pay more attention to the barriers that impeded attempts to expand the capacity of American government to act independently of, although not necessarily against, private interests.

TWO

The Creation of the Federal Land Banks

The Federal Land Banks, established in 1916, were set up to provide low-interest, long-term loans secured by agricultural property.[1] Created during the same period as the Emergency Fleet Corporation, the land banks manifested the second of the two basic features that would come to distinguish public authorities from conventional government agencies: the ability to raise funds without having to seek legislative appropriations beyond those given for startup. Whereas the history of the fleet corporation shows how these types of agencies acquired administrative independence from democratically accountable parts of government, the story of the land banks demonstrates how these mechanisms gained economic independence. The financial autonomy of these administrative tools would prove to have significant implications. It put public officials in the happy position of being able to initiate new activities without having to ask the electorate for more taxes or authority to borrow. At the same time, financial autonomy restricted the control public officials and the electorate at large were able to wield once these institutions were established. Given the limited accountability of agencies that use the self-financing methodology of the land banks, it is surprising to recall that the banks actually began as an effort to give citizens more control over the conditions of their lives.

As with the fleet corporation, the early history of the land banks runs counter to conventional narratives about the origins of public authority–type agencies. Those responsible for designing the banks were not attempting to insulate experts from political pressures or to bring commercial values into the public sector. Quite the opposite. Senator Henry F. Hollis of New Hampshire and Representative Robert J. Bulkley of Ohio, who drafted what became the Federal Farm Loan Act, were seeking to create mechanisms by which the federal government could facilitate public goals (in this case access to low-cost credit for agriculture) without resorting to the time-honored practice of subsidizing for-profit businesses. They envisioned banks managed by the very people who would benefit from them. The lawmakers were guided by their previous experiences experimenting with ways of extending consumer credit to low- and moderate-income people, beliefs about the value of cooperative and not-for-profit enterprises that were popular at the time, and ideas about how to construct programs that combined decentralized management with centralized control that they developed while helping design the Federal Reserve system.

As with the fleet corporation, the land banks turned out differently from the vision of the instigators. Hollis and Bulkley's hopes for a federally initiated program run by the beneficiaries themselves would be disappointed. Too many powerful actors did not share this vision, and in fact harbored very different views about why and how to reform agricultural finance. Opposition forces gained traction when unforeseen events—war, depression, and a lengthy court challenge—battered the banks in their infancy. Underlying everything else were the usual difficulties faced by not-for-profit enterprises trying to stay afloat within the very different framework of the larger American economy.

Despite the eclipse of important features of the original conception, these institutions had long-range consequences. They pioneered the use of bond sales, as opposed to direct government spending, as a way to fund activities defined as being in the public benefit. They also initiated a methodology the federal government would employ to reorganize financial markets in other sectors that were deemed not to be operating effectively, most notably residential real estate. Perhaps most crucially, they represent a key moment in the evolution of public authority mechanisms because of the fact that they survived a constitutional challenge to their legitimacy (and by extension, the legitimacy of later versions of this type of agency), albeit on narrow, technical grounds that allowed them to exist, but without the Supreme Court's explicit acknowledgment of the government's right to intervene directly in the economy in support of public goals such as fairness or balanced growth.

Dissatisfaction with American Agriculture

Although poor access to credit had been a bane of rural existence since colonial times, it was not until the early twentieth century that the "rural credits" issue emerged on the front burner of the national political agenda.[2] During the presidential campaign of 1912, the Republicans, Democrats, and Progressives all pledged in their party platforms to improve the financial system for agriculture.[3] The following spring, newly elected President Woodrow Wilson promised in his inaugural address that one of his chief priorities would be to help secure "facilities of credit best suited to [agriculture's] practical needs."[4] Over the next three years, members of Congress introduced dozens of bills that aimed to solve the problem.[5]

Once it became clear that some kind of agricultural credit legislation was in the offing, farm organizations mobilized to affect the outcome. Contrary to what has most often been assumed, however, it was not agitation by these groups that forced the issue into the national spotlight. For example, in 1911, the National Grange's list of national legislative priorities included such items as improved roads, a national income tax, a system of international arbitration to prevent war, and opposition to subsidies for shipping lines. In all, the Grange put forward eleven goals for Congress, not one of which touched on getting the government to make farm-mortgage loans more available or cheaper.[6] Early in 1912, the Farmers' Union, the other major farm organization in this period, urged members to contact their congressmen and senators about their feelings on four questions: speculation on agricultural futures, parcel post legislation, direct election of senators, and immigration restriction.[7] Clearly, credit was not a high-profile issue for farmers at this time.

The indifference of farmers cannot be traced to satisfaction with a well-functioning financial system. Rural banking facilities continued to suffer from the same structural inadequacies that had plagued them for decades. With regard to short-term credit needs, the issue was the unfortunate interaction between the character of these small local institutions and the process of agricultural production. Banks in agricultural areas drew their deposits from the surrounding community, which meant that their funds ebbed at exactly the same time of year that farmers most needed to borrow for the coming planting season. Longer-term loans were an even more difficult proposition. These small institutions simply had very little money to lend at any time. As a result, they could rarely afford to tie up their limited capital by making mortgage loans on farm property for periods longer than three to five years. Since investments in agriculture took considerably longer than this to pay for themselves, farmers were caught in an endless cycle of renegotiating loans. In the best-case scenario, this meant constantly paying new fees for new loans. In the worst case, it meant foreclosure.[8]

The underlying problem was that farmers were not connected to national or even regional capital markets, because rural banks had no standardized and trusted security instruments to offer lenders who lacked firsthand knowledge about a specific piece of property. To access funds from outside their locality, farmers had to work through brokers, which drove up costs. In general, credit from whatever source was more expensive the farther one went from the country's financial center. In the early twentieth century, farmers in the South and the West paid as much as 10 percent interest for credit, once commissions were included, while farm owners in the Northeast were paying between 5.5 and 6 percent.[9]

As the foregoing makes clear, the lack of grassroots agitation for agricultural credit reform cannot be explained by a lack of grievances with the status quo. Instead, apathy on the credit question stemmed from the comfortable situation in which farmers found themselves in these years. Not only had the long years of worldwide deflation of the late nineteenth century finally abated, but price levels were actually increasing. Farm families were at last enjoying the inflationary conditions they had urged the government to consciously engineer during the Populist political uprising of the 1890s. Prices for food and land were climbing particularly quickly. Between 1900 and 1910, the overall consumer price level rose by 25 percent, while wholesale prices for agricultural commodities increased by 50 percent.[10] During this same period, prices for agricultural land more than doubled for the country as a whole, with the increase much higher in many regions. In parts of North and South Dakota farms were selling for three times what it had cost to buy them.[11] As a result, farmers were being treated to a pleasing combination of cheaper money (making it easier for them to pay back loans) and higher incomes. Meanwhile, they saw the value of their major asset, land, increasing sharply. Little wonder that in this period American farmers were paying more attention to threats to world peace than to the difficulties of borrowing money!

Rather than emanating from farmers, the campaign for rural credits was orchestrated by a disparate assemblage of business figures, academics, journalists, and politicians who were committed to reshaping American agriculture along industrial lines. This group blamed the high cost and poor terms of farm mortgages for everything from low crop yields, out-migration of population from the countryside, increasing rates of tenant farming, and even the "social disorganization" that they maintained was plaguing rural areas. Most crucially from the standpoint of business figures, the inability of farm owners to mobilize the capital they had invested in land through well-functioning mortgage markets kept them from being able to purchase the machines and chemical fertilizers that would raise crop output.[12]

What gave this critique broad resonance was the contemporary surge in food costs. As historian Meg Jacobs has shown, the price of consumer goods became an increasingly politicized issue in this rapidly urbanizing era. Food was a particular flash point, as it constituted such a large share of the overall cost of living, particularly for people with modest incomes. In this period blue-collar and low-salary white-collar city families were spending approximately 40 percent of their income on groceries.[13] The implication of the arguments being made by agricultural reformers was that it would be in the larger public interest for farmers to produce more, thereby bringing food prices down. But by the early twentieth century, expansion of agricultural production in the United States could no longer be achieved primarily by bringing new land into cultivation, as in the past. Increasing output would require new methods and more capitalization to be able to employ them.

The reformers had a point. The American agricultural sector was not particularly productive in this era. Few farmers outside of the eastern states used fertilizers or practiced crop rotation to increase soil fertility, and crop yields in many regions had actually been dropping since the beginning of the century.[14] Nevertheless, American farmers found the case that they were at fault less than compelling. Mrs. Edith Elliott, president of the Pennsylvania Rural Progress Association and a farmer herself, explained the farmers' position to urban readers in a special 1913 issue of the *Annals of the American Academy of Political and Social Science* devoted to the causes and cures of the high cost of living. According to Elliott, a bushel of beans, for which Florida farmers were paid only slightly more than two dollars, was routinely sold to consumers in distant markets for well over three times that much. Her point was that wholesalers and transportation costs were soaking up a much greater proportion of food costs than producers.[15]

A similar pro-farmer analysis was put forward by James Wilson, the long-serving secretary of agriculture, who had been in the job since the McKinley administration. Secretary Wilson told the press in 1910 that studies by his department comparing wholesale and retail prices demonstrated "that the retailer is the man who has been boosting the prices." A good part of the problem, he said, stemmed from simple inefficiency, such as an overabundance of small grocery stores. The blunt-spoken secretary also made it clear that he believed that many food distributors were illegally colluding to keep prices up, although he disavowed responsibility for following up on such suspicions on the grounds that he had no specific grant of authority to prosecute violations of the Sherman Antitrust Act.

Despite his criticisms of the food distribution industry, Secretary Wilson hardly viewed consumers as innocent victims. Their lack of initiative and demands for locally out-of-season foods were significantly to blame for driving up costs, according to the crusty secretary. A proponent of self-help, he looked back nostalgically to the days when he "was a boy living on a farm in Vermont [and] we went about among those living in the towns and villages taking orders for all the stuff we produced." Given that Wilson was born in 1835, living patterns had changed considerably since the childhood he so fondly recalled, a fact he seemed to recognize, if regret. In a more practical vein for the era in which he now lived, he described efforts by employees in his department to establish a consumer cooperative in Washington, DC, for bulk purchasing of groceries.[16]

Whatever was causing food prices to rise, farmers were not inclined to make radical changes in their standard practices at a time when their incomes were increasing. Understandably enough, the prospect of producing more for less failed to galvanize the nation's farmers. However, for practically everyone else in this period of rapid urbanization, overall inflation, and the high cost of food, the prospect had tremendous appeal.

European Models and Cooperation

President Theodore Roosevelt's Country Life Commission demonstrates the way in which concerns about food costs came to be linked with a critique of the agricultural credit system. Roosevelt, who told Congress in his 1904 annual message that the health of American manufacturing depended "primarily on cheap food," convened a panel to study conditions in rural America. Liberty Hyde Bailey, dean of the College of Agriculture at Cornell University, chaired the commission, which consisted almost entirely of academics, journalists, and government officials. The one exception was Charles S. Barrett, the president of the Farmers' Union, who was added after the membership was first officially announced (presumably as a last-minute effort to include at least one person linked to actual farmers).[17] The Country Life Commission turned in its report early in 1909, just before Roosevelt left office. Among the discouraging features of contemporary rural life reported by the commissioners was the "lack of any adequate system of agricultural credit." They pointed to European cooperative credit organizations as possible models for emulation, describing approvingly how "in other countries credit associations loan money to their members on easy terms."[18]

Over the next several years, the success of European cooperative credit facilities in channeling low-cost capital into agriculture was publicized by influential mainstream organizations, including the National Monetary Commission, chaired by old-guard Republican Nelson Aldrich; the American Bankers' Association; the U.S. State Department; and the Southern Commercial Congress.

All gave particular attention to the German *Landschaften*, described by one analyst as "public corporations under state supervision." These not-for-profit organizations were comprised of farmers who wanted to obtain long-term loans collateralized by their property. Funds to make the loans were obtained by issuing bonds secured by pools of farm mortgages. The *Landschaften* had been in existence for over a century, and during that time their bonds acquired a high reputation for safety based on three distinctive aspects of their operations: the members of each association assumed unlimited liability for every bond issued; each association's business practices were scrutinized by government officials; and loans were amortized. The last feature meant that borrowers paid off principal along with interest during the life of the loan. Amortization made it easier for borrowers to discharge their debt, which benefited investors, because such loans were less risky. *Landschaften* bonds were considered so safe that they attracted capital at interest rates in the range of 3.5 to 4 percent, comparable to what German cities paid on municipal bonds. In one telling example of the prestige these organizations were acquiring in the United States, President William Howard Taft, on the eve of the election in 1912, distributed a report to the governors of all the states specifically recommending "the formation of cooperative mortgage-bond societies along the line of the Landschaften societies of Germany."[19]

Of all the efforts to build support for the idea that the federal government should organize a national agricultural credit program in the United States, the most extensive and effective was the campaign undertaken by the Southern Commercial Congress led by Florida senator Duncan U. Fletcher. In the spring of 1912, Senator Fletcher led an overseas study tour of seventy official delegates (joined by dozens of staff and family members), representing twenty-nine states, the District of Columbia, and four Canadian provinces, to learn about European agricultural practices. Once abroad, tour members fanned out for three months, interviewing leaders of agricultural cooperatives, bankers, and government officials all over Europe, with some of the more energetic venturing as far as Russia and Egypt.[20] On their return, participants waxed enthusiastic about all they had learned, particularly with respect to better methods of capitalizing farmers. An executive summary of their nine-hundred-page official report noted that only thirty years earlier European agriculture had been in a "bad way." The opening of vast new tracts of land in the American Great Plains and South America had all but decimated the European farm sector. Yet in the space of a single generation, European farmers had become prosperous. According to the American observers, the transformation had come about because of "education and cooperation." Farmers had "formed a habit of doing collectively what [they] had been doing singly and alone."[21]

The fervor of American business leaders for cooperative enterprise can seem perplexing until we recall the amorphous quality of the cooperative idea. Popular throughout Europe, the United States, and Canada by the late nineteenth century, the concept had no settled meaning. Cooperation, in the words of Daniel Rodgers, was "unstable at both its socialist and capitalist edges."[22] American business leaders grasped the capitalist edge. According to the Southern Commercial Congress, cooperatives were basically "groups of individual units," that represented "a more profitable way of doing business than the old way of every man for himself."[23]

The capitalist appropriation of cooperation can be seen in the thinking of Benjamin Franklin Harris, a leader in the movement to get farmers to "apply business principles."[24] A past president of the Illinois Bankers Association, who would go on to edit the agricultural finance newsletter of the American Bankers Association, Harris spoke to the Chicago Bankers Club in 1912 about "Problems of Rural Life from the Banker's Standpoint." A major stumbling block to progress, he informed his audience, was that farmers did not think in collective terms. In the same breath that he bemoaned the lack of "co-operation" among farmers, he complained about the dearth of "money saving combinations" in the American countryside. For Harris the concept of cooperation had to do with melding atomistic family-owned farms into larger economic units capable of holding their own in an environment increasingly dominated by large corporations. His message was that bankers needed to take the lead in this effort, as farmers seemed content to continue with their long-standing methods. Rhetorically he asked his banker audience, "Who is a better, abler, friendlier aid" to the farmer? Answering his own question, he told them it was "the banker—the farmer's big brother."[25] Clearly, the kind of cooperation envisioned by Harris was something different from the noncommercial, democratically run enterprises so often associated with the idea of cooperation.

Rural Credit as Part of National Financial Reform

To appreciate why rural credit reform acquired so much momentum in this period, the campaign needs to be viewed as part of the larger movement then under way to upgrade the country's overall financial architecture. The subject of national financial reform had been under discussion ever since

1893, when the banking system seized up and pitched an already weakened economy into full-fledged depression. But it took the panic of 1907, an even more frightening liquidity crisis that threatened to bring down the country's entire financial structure, to truly concentrate the minds of the business and political elite on the need for change. The consensus that emerged about the necessity of integrating the reserves of the nation's banks and creating a more flexible money supply did not, however, translate into agreement as to how to achieve these goals. Three contentious questions stood in the way: what degree of control would be given to the government; whether there would be a single central bank (presumably in New York) or several regional reserve institutions; and to what extent the new system would be structured to respond to the credit needs of agriculture, in addition to those of commerce and industry. Neither the Democrats nor the Republicans coalesced around a single constellation of answers to these questions. Both parties were splintered internally—and feelings ran high.[26]

Wilson came into office determined to break the deadlock. Such an achievement, having eluded Republicans even when they had held the presidency and enjoyed majorities in both houses, would dramatically demonstrate the Democrats' ability to govern. No longer would their party be denigrated as "the organized incompetence of the country."[27] Despite the fact that the new president's party controlled both the House and the Senate, his task was far from easy. Wilson still had to marshal the "centrifugal forces that constituted the Democratic party" behind a workable bill with wide political appeal.[28]

To secure the support of William Jennings Bryan and the Democrats' critically important agrarian base that he headed, the administration's bill for what would become the Federal Reserve System called for decentralizing the system and instituting, at least in theory, substantial government control. These features appalled northeastern business leaders. The *New York Sun* charged that the measure was covered in "the slime of Bryanism." Even so, Democrats with rural constituencies demanded more. They insisted that if the federal government was going to get involved in upgrading the financial infrastructure for industry and commerce, then agriculture deserved attention, as well. Responding to this pressure, the administration agreed to allow member banks to make personal loans to farmers that ran up to six months, twice the length of time permitted for other businesspeople, and even went so far as to allow for loans collateralized by agricultural land for up to five years. With respect to pressure for longer lasting farm-mortgage loans, however, Wilson simply would not capitulate. If banks were to tie up their money in long-term mortgages it would defeat a basic goal of the whole package, which was to inject greater liquidity into the financial system. In the end, the president promised to bring forward a separate bill aimed at improving credit opportunities for agriculture. With this promise, Wilson was able to garner the votes he needed for passage of what is widely regarded as his single most impressive legislative achievement: the Federal Reserve Act of 1913.[29]

The Administration and Farmers Clash

True to his word, as soon as negotiations for the Federal Reserve were essentially over, the president began pushing for legislation to improve access to credit for the agricultural sector. As it turned out, however, Wilson's conception of a good program was at odds with that of most farmers. In December 1913, the president devoted approximately a quarter of his first annual message to Congress to the "urgent necessity" for rural credits legislation. Insisting that farmers "ask and should be given no special privilege," he assured his listeners that no one was contemplating anything as extreme as "extending to them the credit of the Government itself." In line with the consensus in the business community that cooperation, in the sense of pooling risk, was the key to solving the agricultural credit problem, the president explained that what farmers needed was "legislation which will make their own abundant and substantial credit resources available as a foundation for joint, concerted local action."[30] This position was in accord with his New Freedom conviction that the purpose of economic reform was to level the playing field for all parties, rather than to offer help to any specific group based on its particular situation. On this point, Wilson was particularly adamant with respect to farmers. Since his overarching goal was to transform the Democrats into the majority party, he wanted to avoid any suggestion of favoritism toward the sectional interests with which his party had long been identified. Secretary of Agriculture David F. Houston bluntly broke the news to farmers at the annual meeting of the National Grange, telling the delegates that any government program for agriculture that would loan money "at a rate of interest lower than the economic conditions would normally require" would be "special legislation of a particularly odious type."[31]

Senator Fletcher, whose leadership of the Southern Commercial Congress had done so much to make rural credits a national issue, introduced the administration-endorsed bill in the Senate in January 1914. The same bill was introduced into the House by Representative Ralph W. Moss of Indiana, another leader in the movement to improve agricultural credit.

Popularly known as the Moss-Fletcher bill, the measure called for federal incorporation and supervision of federally chartered, voluntarily organized, freestanding, investor-owned credit institutions for agriculture called "national farm-land banks." These would offer self-amortizing mortgage loans on farm property, lasting as long as thirty-five years. To raise capital, the banks would issue bonds backed by pools of mortgages they held. A profit stream would be generated by the difference between the rate of interest paid to buyers of the bonds and the slightly higher rate charged to farmer borrowers. The safety of the bonds offered by the banks would be assured by federal inspectors, who would oversee the business methods of the banks and the value of the mortgages they securitized.

Besides federal oversight, the plan provided investors with a number of other inducements. For example, farm bank bonds were designated as legal holdings for trust funds, estates, insurance companies, and postal savings banks. Another major advantage was the decision to make the bonds "exempt from Federal, State, and local taxation." With the first federal income tax having gone into effect only three months before, this provision meant that the government would be subsidizing the banks' access to private capital through the federal tax code, as well as extending to them the immunity of federal agencies from state and local taxation that has been in effect since the Supreme Court's decision in *McCulloch v. Maryland* in the early nineteenth century.[32]

The Moss-Fletcher bill focused primarily on developing investor-owned, for-profit banks that could be defined as "cooperative" in the sense that business leaders and the president defined the concept, that is, that they would combine the land wealth of a number of different farmers to create an asset that provided more security than a mortgage on a single farm. As the *Wall Street Journal* expressed it, the aim was to replace the credit of individual farmers with "the credit of the agricultural unit, which in this case is a land-bank association under Federal supervision." To satisfy those who understood cooperation in a different way, there was a provision for banks in which all investors would have a roughly equal voice in management and profits would be used to reduce the debts of the borrowers, rather than being divided among shareholders proportional to their investment. Such noncommercial institutions were not the main objective of the bill, however.[33]

Clearly, the legislation drew, albeit selectively, from European examples, but the general approach was not a foreign import. In the nineteenth century, American private entrepreneurs had tried to establish a market for bonds secured by farm mortgages. Such efforts never succeeded, however.

Too many investors guessed in advance or learned from bitter experience that no checks existed on tendencies for overly optimistic, even fraudulent, appraisals of the property backing the bonds. Thus, the Moss-Fletcher bill can be seen as an attempt by the Wilson administration to resurrect a flawed business model and overcome its defects through federal oversight. However, as some observers pointed out at the time, even more important than investor confidence in the underlying soundness of the mortgages on which the bonds were based was investor faith in the government's implicit guarantee against default, given its level of involvement. In the words of one contemporary analyst who advocated a more private market approach: "Investors in the securities of institutions created or assisted by the State look to it, and not to the land or its owner, for the return of their money."[34]

Advocating the bill in hearings before a special joint Senate and House committee established to investigate rural credits, Senator Fletcher described himself as "a great believer in the principle of self-help and self-reliance." It was for this reason that the farm-land banks were to be organized on a voluntary basis, not set up by the government. Fletcher expressed confidence that private entrepreneurs would step forward to capitalize these institutions. He emphasized that the right kind of program was one that did not involve "Government aid." In his eyes the bill met this test, despite both the tax exemptions and federal supervision that were built into the legislation.[35] Fletcher (and Wilson) believed that there was a critical difference between direct disbursement of government funds and the kind of indirect support through the tax code that later policy analysts would term "tax subsidies."

The beauty of the administration's plan for dispensing government aid indirectly through profit-making business firms was lost on the leaders of farm organizations. They vehemently opposed what one National Grange officer referred to as the "Mossbacked Fletcherized monstrosity."[36] The day after the bill was introduced, the Grange announced a national publicity campaign against it, sending out a mass mailing to sixty thousand farmers around the country.[37] One reason for hostility was that farmers turned out to be considerably less concerned about self-reliance than Senator Fletcher and the president were on their behalf. The prospect of a government program aimed specifically at their needs did not strike them as unfair, let alone "particularly odious," as the secretary of agriculture had characterized it. On the contrary, farmers saw a program focused on agriculture as only fitting, given that they perceived their own well-being to be synonymous with the wider public interest. In the words of T. J. Brooks, a professor at the Agricultural and Mechanical College of Mississippi and a member of the National Farmers' Union, "When you allow agriculture to go down it takes all others with it, and everybody's welfare is at stake, the welfare of the Republic is at stake, and the perpetuity of free institutions is at stake, and civilization is at stake."[38]

The farmers' main objection to the Moss-Fletcher bill had to do with its delivery mechanism. According to T. C. Atkeson, head of the West Virginia State Grange, it was "folly to trust a private corporation to carry out a great Government policy." He predicted that "the creation of a private banking scheme" would not succeed, because for-profit enterprises would "never handle their business for an altruistic purpose."[39] The president of the Arkansas Farmers' Union, H. S. Mobley, concurred, warning the subcommittee that if the aid to farmers "has to come from a commercial bank, you are going to discredit the system in the South."[40]

For farmers, the alternative was clear. As Mobley informed the committee, "We would like to have aid direct from the Government."[41] The farmers' position was most closely embodied by bills introduced by Representative Elsworth R. Bathrick, a Democrat from Ohio. Bathrick's bills provided for a farm-mortgage program run by a bureau in the United States Treasury, which would both make and service loans for farmers throughout the country. As with the administration bill, the loans would be amortized, and funds to make the loans would come from sales of bonds backed by pools of mortgages, although in this case the Treasury itself would do the securitizing. Also in common with the administration, Bathrick relied on tax expenditures as a financing mechanism. While he drafted the first version of his bill before the federal income tax went into effect, later variants called for the mortgage-backed bonds to be exempted from federal taxation. Major agricultural organizations, including the Grange, the Farmers' Union, and the American Society of Equity, enthusiastically endorsed the Bathrick bills.[42]

Since Wilson's response to the farmers' plan was essentially the same as theirs to his, the result was stalemate. Even with the president's demonstrated ability to get his balky Democratic congressional majority to do his will, he realized there was no way he could get his preferred legislative solution enacted over the unwavering opposition of farm organizations. Not only were farmers the single best organized group in the country at this time, but their strength in Congress was way out of proportion to their numbers in the rapidly urbanizing and industrializing nation because of the way the Constitution apportioned legislative seats on the basis of territory. As political scientist Elizabeth Sanders has pointed out, the rules of the political game gave farmers, as a cohesive group based in the nation's periphery, "exaggerated influence." Although legislators with rural constituencies may not have been able to override Wilson's firm resistance to their preferred solution, they could definitely stymie his.[43]

New Actors Enter the Picture

Despite what seemed to be an unbridgeable impasse, it was only slightly over two years later that Congress passed and Wilson signed a rural credits bill into law. The successful legislation was crafted by Senator Henry F. Hollis of New Hampshire and Representative Robert J. Bulkley of Ohio, both newcomers to Capitol Hill. As members of the banking committees of their respective chambers, the two had impressed party leaders with their contribution to crafting the Federal Reserve legislation. In recognition of their efforts they were put in charge of a joint subcommittee on rural credits.

To break the deadlock between farm groups and the president, Bulkley and Hollis came up with what one contemporary policy analyst described as a "revolutionary" approach that "boldly set aside American traditions in the farm mortgage business." The proposal provided no role for the for-profit bankers and brokers already working in rural areas, and it aimed to have much of the new system be managed by the farmers who would benefit, rather than by government bureaucrats.[44] While it would be easy to assume that the individuals who came up with such an unconventional approach had emerged from backgrounds far from the mainstream, this was not the case. Both hailed from prominent families, graduated from Harvard College and, before entering politics, had established themselves as successful lawyers.

Robert J. Bulkley grew up on Euclid Avenue, Cleveland's "Millionaires' Row." His father, who built the family's wealth through real estate investment, co-owned the *Plain Dealer* newspaper and served as the first head of the city's Park Commission. Despite Bulkley's privileged background, as a young man he gravitated to the circle of talented idealists around Tom Johnson, the famous urban Populist mayor. Johnson was a Democratic politician who promoted both the single tax and public ownership of basic services, such as mass transit, electricity, and gas.[45]

Bulkley never became the enthusiast for public ownership or the single tax that his mentor had been, but decades-long service as president of the Morris Plan Bank of Cleveland suggests a strong interest in economic innovations that, while in no way socialistic, pushed the envelope of conventional economic principles in order to benefit low- and moderate-income people. Morris Plan banks originated in 1910 as the brainchild of Norfolk,

Virginia, attorney Arthur J. Morris, who sought to fulfill his vision of the "democratization of credit" by creating a profitable method of making small unsecured loans to low-income people so as to give them an alternative to loan sharks and pawn shops. Morris based his plan on character and earning power, rather than collateral. To obtain a loan borrowers were required to provide evidence of a steady job and produce two cosigners who in the case of default would be responsible for repayment. According to Morris, his banks were a purely business proposition, and indeed his financial ventures made him personally wealthy. In truth, however, the banks were hybrid institutions, given that, although they did make money, they were not structured to maximize investor profit. In addition, they were subsidized. In 1914, at a critical early point in the life of his business, Morris secured an infusion of $5 million from a group of wealthy philanthropists, including Julius Rosenwald and Andrew Carnegie. Created in an era when standard banks were not interested in providing consumer credit to anyone, let alone to blue-collar workers, and credit unions were just getting started, Morris Plan banks spread rapidly. Morris set up his first bank in 1910, and by 1931 there were 142 Morris Plan banks in cities around the country providing loans of over $200 million annually. Conventional bankers took notice of the new market, and in the mid-1920s began offering small consumer loans themselves.[46]

Bulkley entered Congress as part of the Democratic sweep of 1910, when the party picked up fifty-six seats in the House to take control of that body for the first time since the depression of the 1890s. (In the Senate, Democrats gained ten seats, and in 1912 won another nine, achieving a majority in that body as well.)[47] Bulkley interpreted his own victory and the rising fortunes of the Democrats generally to a political backlash against the rising prices of the era. He and other Democrats had successfully convinced many traditional GOP supporters that Republican-backed tariffs were fueling the inflation that was eroding urban living standards.[48] In addition, Bulkley's campaign benefited from divisions among Republicans emerging at this time.

Turmoil within the Republican Party also helps explain Henry Hollis's election as senator in New Hampshire two years later. In the spring of 1913 when the newly elected Senator Hollis arrived in Washington to take up his duties, he was already something of a star. Not only was he the first Democrat the Granite State had sent to the Senate since before the Civil War, but his two-month-long, cliff-hanger battle for election in New Hampshire's deadlocked legislature early in the year captured the country's attention as people waited to find out the extent of the new Democratic majority in

Congress's upper chamber after twenty years of Republican rule. Already a political maverick by choosing to align himself with the Democratic Party—his Republican paternal great-grandfather had been chief justice of the New Hampshire Supreme Court and his maternal grandfather had served as assistant secretary of the treasury in the Grant administration—Hollis took positions that were unconventional for a person of his class even within his adopted political home. Proclaiming himself an "ardent admirer and disciple" of William Jennings Bryan,[49] Hollis championed women's suffrage, labor rights, and aid to farmers. In addition, he took a public stand against colonization of the Philippines by becoming a national vice president of the Anti-Imperialist League.[50] A militant foe of corporations, he worked to dislodge business control over his state's Democratic Party, and his anticorporate animus even informed his professional life. He bragged that he had never accepted a corporate retainer, and his successful legal practice was based in good part on personal damage claims against corporations. His specialty was undermining the credibility of expert witnesses during low-key cross-examinations, and the $24,000 that he won for his clients from the Boston and Maine Railroad set a state record.[51] Given his background it is no wonder that, even after the Progressive Party delegation in the state legislature threw its weight behind his candidacy, it took President Wilson's pressure on a handful of conservative New Hampshire Democrats for Hollis to finally squeeze out his senatorial victory.

While other restive political activists in New Hampshire (including his own brother) attempted to use the Progressive Party as a beachhead for challenging business interests that dominated the state, Hollis threw in his lot with the Democratic Party. He was convinced that the Democrats could succeed in becoming the majority party nationally if they distanced themselves from their Wall Street–friendly wing (associated with Grover Cleveland). Shortly after arriving in the capital, the new senator told the Young Men's Democratic Club of Washington that the party should make its appeal "to the men who work hard, obey the laws, pay their bills, protect their wives, educate their children, and sit in their homes after supper and read in the newspapers what their representatives have done in the State legislature and in Congress." As Hollis sized up the political situation, the Democrats and the "Bull Moose" Progressives were in a contest to see which would become "the great progressive party of the nation." To win, the Democrats needed to align themselves with the "forgotten millions."[52]

Hollis's economic views placed him on the left edge of the Democratic party. He was markedly less economically orthodox than his counterpart in the House, Representative Bulkley, who was solidly in the party's progressive wing. For example, even though it was Bulkley who had started his political career with Mayor Tom Johnson, the great proponent of municipal ownership, it was Hollis who talked about social control of production. While a senator, Hollis went on record that he expected that the time would come "when the federal government will take over everything and distribute it at cost among the people." In addition, he urged Democrats to endorse minimum wage legislation.[53]

Like Bulkley, Hollis was involved in an alternative banking endeavor, in this case making no profits instead of limited ones. Since 1895 he had served as a trustee for the New Hampshire Savings Bank, a mutual savings bank. Mutuals were entities peculiar to the Northeast. They had been created in the early nineteenth century to provide people of modest incomes the opportunity to save and borrow small sums. These institutions were not profit-making concerns, but neither were they cooperatives in the sense of being participant controlled. Depositors were the formal owners, and all profits went to benefit them, but they had no role in management. Instead, self-perpetuating groups of directors (called trustees) operated these institutions on behalf of the people who used them.[54]

Overall, Hollis's politics were an example of what historian Arthur Link described as "advanced progressivism," in that Hollis was not only dedicated to developing methods of regulating the new nationally integrated economy dominated by giant corporations, but also committed to reaching out to groups that were disadvantaged in this environment.[55] Shortly after taking office in the spring of 1913, the new senator was excoriated by the *Christian Science Monitor* for advocating that farmers and labor unions be exempted from the antimonopoly provisions of the Sherman Antitrust Act. In shocked tones, the paper reported that Hollis openly acknowledged his support of "class legislation," a position he justified on the grounds that "capital, having admittedly controlled courts and Legislatures to protect its interests, the situation now 'should be evened up' by making concessions to 'labor.'"[56] Hollis's conviction that the government had the right, indeed the duty, to aid groups that had been marginalized during the corporate reorganization of the economy was reflected in the rural credits legislation that he and Bulkley drafted, and which became the basis of the final legislation.

The Hollis-Bulkley Plan

Hollis and Bulkley's basic strategy, in common with the other major proposals, was to encourage private capital to flow into agricultural credit markets by giving investors special inducements: immunity from taxation, a known and standardized investment vehicle, and implicit federal guarantees. In terms of structure, the two lawmakers rejected both the farmers' desire that the program be run directly by the government and the administration's preference for waiting for private parties to come forward (or not) to set up freestanding, profit-making banks, each of which would independently make farm mortgages and issue bonds. Their alternative, not surprisingly given their earlier work, was based on the format of the Federal Reserve. The difference was that instead of tying together preexisting, investor-owned banking institutions, as the Federal Reserve had done, their national agricultural credit system would integrate a set of farmer-controlled, not-for-profit borrowing cooperatives that did not yet exist.[57]

The system had three layers. At the helm was an agency called the Federal Farm Loan Board, based in the Treasury Department. As the two initially conceived it, the board was to be very much a part of the executive branch, similar to how Secretary McAdoo had envisioned the United States Shipping Board. It would have three members. Two would be cabinet members (the secretaries of treasury and agriculture), and the third, the director, would be appointed by the president with the advice and consent of the Senate. No term or provision for removal was specified for the director, implying that this person would serve at the pleasure of the president.

The job of the board was to charter and oversee the second layer of the system, a set of twelve regional Federal Land Banks. Eventually, the farmers who participated in the program were to own and manage the banks, but in the beginning these institutions would be administrative agencies of the federal government. Unlike conventional bureaucratic units, however, they were to be incorporated, making them legally distinct from the standard bureaucratic structure of the executive branch and homologous to private-sector entities. For example, they were to have the ability to make contracts on their own and to sue or be sued independent of the government. If at the outset, sufficient private investment did not materialize to subscribe the required capital stock, the federal government was charged with buying the remainder. The banks would not make loans. Rather, their responsibility was to pull resources into the system by selling bonds secured by bundles of farm mortgages they purchased. The goal, in Bulkley's words, was to create "a national security . . . without the risks attendant on the possible mismanagement or failure of individual farmers." As noted earlier, the interest income on these bonds would be exempted from taxation, which meant that like the other major proposals the Hollis-Bulkley plan called for indirect subsidies through the tax code. It was assumed that these features would propel the bonds of land banks into popularity in national capital markets, resulting in streams of low-cost, long-term credit flowing into rural America. However, in the period before the bonds caught on with investors, the secretary of the treasury was instructed to purchase any that failed to find private buyers.[58]

The base of the program consisted of farmer-borrower cooperatives, termed National Farm Loan Associations. The associations were to be noncommercial, incorporated institutions, voluntarily formed by farmers who wanted to borrow money against the collateral of their farm. To join, the farmers would buy shares of stock proportionate to the size of their loan. Governance of the associations was based on cooperative principles (with elections organized on a modified one-vote-per-person basis, as opposed to the one-vote-per-share format of a commercial joint-stock company). The associations were to be responsible for considering loan applications and approving those that seemed sound. The idea was that firsthand knowledge of local conditions would be superior to the judgment of outside assessors when it came to making accurate evaluations, although the regional land banks were empowered to make their own independent appraisals before purchasing loans from the associations. With each sale of a mortgage loan to the regional land bank, an association was required to buy shares in the bank proportionate to the size of the mortgage. As these stock purchases increased the capital stock of the banks to over the legal minimum, the government was to be refunded its initial investment. In this way the banks would eventually be completely owned by the associations and would cease to be government agencies. As this shift of ownership took place, the associations would take on a greater role in managing the banks, although the government would always exercise oversight, as with the Federal Reserve system in relation to privately owned member banks. In the words of one contemporary policy analyst, the borrower co-ops "were intended to be the active part upon which the ultimate success of the system would depend."[59]

The noncommercial dimension of the proposal, while anathema to businessmen, reflected sentiments that enjoyed strong representation in Congress, especially among legislators from rural districts. These included hostility toward bankers and the belief, dating back to the Populist campaigns of late nineteenth century, that many economic functions—especially interstitial ones, such as transportation, communication, and banking—should be run by government. Such pro-public ownership ideas were still strong among congressional Democrats, as one can see from the insistence, previously described, that the government have a major role in the Federal

Reserve system established in 1913; passage of the Alaska Railroad Act in 1914, through which the federal government took direct responsibility for building a line deep into the interior of the territory; and Congress's appropriation of funds in 1916 to establish a government-run steel plant to manufacture armor for naval vessels.[60]

At the same time, public opinion throughout the country was widely, if diffusely, supportive of cooperative enterprise. Cooperation was commonly viewed as an appealing and viable method of coping with deficiencies in a market economy, although not necessarily as an alternative to it. It helped that the concept was vague enough that different groups were able to project their own quite different (even conflicting) hopes and values onto it. As we have seen, leading figures in business and politics touted producer cooperation as a panacea for American agriculture. Meanwhile, the pressure of inflation on white-collar salaries had given the idea of consumer cooperatives traction among the urban middle classes, as demonstrated by the effort on the part of Agriculture Department employees to establish a grocery co-op.[61]

While the local borrowing associations Hollis and Bulkley designed were obviously intended as a way to minimize costs and risks, thereby making agricultural credit as inexpensive as possible, the two lawmakers had more in mind when they conceptualized these organizations. By setting up a framework for people to come together on a basis of equality to make decisions that affected their lives in important ways, the legislators were trying to strengthen what later political theorists would call "civil society." Defending the plan against criticism that American farmers were too individualistic to want to participate, Bulkley insisted that "the actual operation of the system will provide such an object-lesson in the benefits of farmers' co-operation" that in time objections would "fade into insignificance."[62]

It could easily be argued that the borrower co-ops, which gave participants real responsibility for managing the federal program, constituted the truly radical aspect of the proposed legislation. Yet this aspect of the plan provoked no serious opposition, only skepticism as to whether farmers would actually participate. Nor did the provision for indirect aid through the tax code attract any real hostility (which was not surprising, since this feature had been taken for granted from the beginning and included in the most conservative proposals). The provisions that proved controversial were those for direct government financial involvement in the form of guarantees that the Treasury would make up any failure in the required initial capitalization of the banks and would purchase any bonds that failed to find private buyers. Not only was the American Bankers Association up in arms, but the president was also antagonistic. By spring 1914, it was clear the bill would easily move through both houses of Congress if put up for a vote, but even though Wilson found the measure less objectionable than the Bathrick proposal, he did not like it. Writing to Carter Glass, chairman of the House Banking Committee, the president expressed his "very deep conviction that it is unwise and unjustifiable to extend the credit of the Government to a single class of the community." Reporting the president's communication to Glass, the *New York Times* correctly predicted that rural credits legislation would be "shelved."[63]

Wilson's veto threat kept the Hollis-Bulkley plan languishing for over two years, even though it had overwhelming support in Congress. Farm organizations still preferred a system of direct loans handled by the Treasury, along the lines of the Bathrick bills, but having concluded this would be politically impossible, they threw their support behind the Hollis-Bulkley bill. The standoff lasted until the spring of 1916, when Wilson had a dramatic change of heart. Looking ahead to the presidential election in the fall, he saw the need to expand the national Democratic coalition, given that the Republican party was knitting itself back together. He became convinced that in order to win the Midwest farm vote, he needed to secure rural credits legislation. Once he made his decision known, the bill moved quickly through both the House and the Senate, and he signed it into law on July 17, 1916.[64]

The final bill did have some changes from the original proposal. In keeping with Congress's usual disinclination to strengthen the executive branch, the Federal Farm Loan Board was made more distant from presidential control than Hollis and Bulkley had envisioned. The redesigned board consisted of the secretary of the treasury and four other individuals. The president could chose these four, with the advice and consent of the Senate, but no more than two could be from any one party; they were to serve fixed terms; and the president was not allowed to remove them on the basis of policy differences, only for malfeasance in office. Another change applied to the associations at the base of the system: to encourage prudence in evaluating each other's loan requests, association members were held liable for losses up to double the value of their shares.

The Land Banks in Operation

Once established, the Federal Land Banks turned out to be successful at improving credit opportunities for farm owners, especially in the South, Great Plains, and Mountain West where the financial infrastructure was sketchy.

Even more consequential than the low-cost capital channeled into these outlying regions was the way the program created a more stable architecture for agricultural credit markets generally. The key innovation was the introduction of the long-term, self-amortizing farm mortgage, which became standard practice for all institutional lenders.[65] Amortization made a real difference for farm families who borrowed money for capital improvements. Now they could step off the treadmill of anxiety and expenses associated with continually having to renegotiate the three-to-ten-year, interest-only mortgage loans that previously had been the only form of long-term financing available.[66] Given that principal was not paid off through the term of the loan, the process could go on interminably. And even though renewal was more or less automatic in good times, it could not be counted on, given that small local banks lacked the resources to extend credit during periods of economic contraction. By comparison, the land banks offered farmers the security of loans that ran five to forty years, with the program's directors encouraging farmers to go for the longer timeline.[67]

The appeal of this new type of mortgage was demonstrated by how quickly farmers began forming the cooperative loan associations that served as their gateway to the program. In the first two years after the Federal Farm Loan Board started offering charters, farmers organized 3,529 of the local borrowing co-ops (see figure 2.1 for a map of their locations).[68] By 1929, farmers had borrowed $1.6 billion through the program, and with the stock purchases required to get their loans, had repaid almost the entire $9 million the Treasury had originally invested to capitalize the system.[69]

Despite these positive indicators, the program fell short of fulfilling one of the drafters' key hopes: that the land banks would evolve into "nongovernmental credit institutions owned and controlled by their farmer-borrowers."[70] Instead, management of the system stayed firmly in the hands of the government. Observers differed as to the reasons, although pretty much everyone ignored structural problems with the program and blamed the ideological predilections of various actors. Some pointed to what they saw as the innate individualism of American farmers, which made them disinclined to get more involved than the minimum required to secure their loans. According to one critic who from the start had opposed making borrowers' co-ops the basic building blocks of the program: "Farmers as a class are not possessed of a coöperative spirit."[71] On the other side, partisans of cooperative economics also focused on individual motivation, in this case, that of the top-level federal appointees who were assumed to have lacked sympathy for "the democratic control idea."[72] From this perspective, the fact that rank-and-file farmers did not take over management

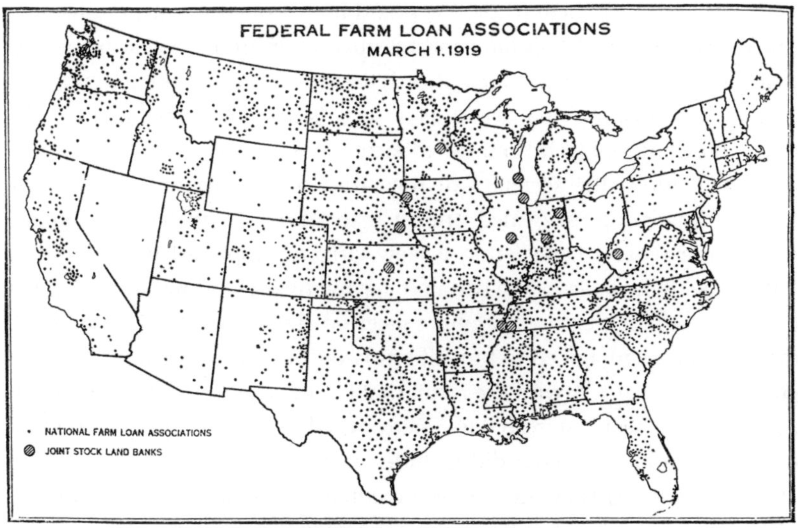

Figure 2.1. This map shows the location of the 3,529 National Farm Loan Associations in existence in early 1919. The popularity of these local borrowing cooperatives among farmers is indicated by the fact that the Federal Farm Loan Board had been chartering these organizations for only two years when this map was made. Just twelve for-profit Joint Stock Land Banks had been formed, reflecting the way the legislation favored noncommercial lending institutions over for-profit ones.

of the banks flowed from the lack of commitment on the part of the program's national administrators, whose attachment to conventional notions of hierarchical organizations kept them from undertaking the "missionary and educational work" required to convince American farmers of "the advantages of teamwork."[73]

What was lost in this debate was both the actual record of the program and its institutional realities. With respect to what actually happened, it should be noted that at the outset, the Federal Farm Loan Board promoted the program vigorously and encouraged farmers to get involved. Indeed, starting early in 1917, it staged a veritable media blitz, placing accessibly written pieces in general interest and more specialized periodicals. Board member Herbert Quick's "Borrowing from Your Uncle," published in the *Saturday Review*, and "Farm Loan Questions Answered," written by board secretary W. W. Flannagan and appearing in *Ohio Farmer*, are cases in point. In addition, the board produced and distributed hundreds of thousands of instructional pamphlets, with titles such as *Farm Loan Primer*, *How Farmers May Form a National Farm Loan Association*, and *Killing off Mortgages* (by which was meant refinancing burdensome loans through the federal land bank system). Meanwhile, the board inaugurated its own publication called *The Borrowers' Bulletin*, sending out two million copies in the first year alone. The *Bulletin*, which shortly began appearing on a bimonthly basis, carried inspirational accounts of successful local cooperative associations and testimonials from satisfied farmer borrowers.[74]

J. D. Darlow, the secretary of the farm loan association of Grenada County, Mississippi, provided one such testimonial. His letter, originally sent to the Federal Land Bank of New Orleans, appeared in the January 1918 issue of the *Bulletin*. On behalf of his members, Darlow wrote to thank the bank "for the treatment we have received at your hands." He explained that the bank had agreed to buy all but two of the thirty-six mortgages his group had forwarded, with the result that the interest payments paid by his members had been cut from 8 to 5 percent. While the sentiments expressed were not unique, the letter did include one unusual piece of information. Darlow noted: "This association is a colored association. Every member is a colored person. I do not know if you knew that or not."[75]

The mailing of the August/September 1919 issue of the *Borrowers' Bulletin* marked the end of the board's ambitious outreach efforts. A lawsuit filed that summer on behalf of private farm-mortgage bankers contesting the constitutionality of the land banks put the program in limbo as the case worked its way through the federal court system. The Supreme Court first heard the case in early 1920 but did not render a verdict for over a year. As investors waited for a decision before buying more bonds, the land banks ran out of money and loan operations halted.[76] The legal cloud finally lifted in February 1921 with the court's declaration that the program was constitutional, but by this time the economy was in depression. With Warren Harding's election in 1920, the Republicans took control of the executive branch, and for the next decade capable administrators appointed by Republican presidents managed the program effectively along business lines, but this leadership, in the words of historian David Hamilton, did nothing "to build a more genuinely cooperative system."[77]

To be fair to the program's cautious administrators in Washington, the basic design of the land bank system made it extremely fragile. According to the rules set down in the original legislation, all operating costs were to come from the small spread between the 6 percent maximum that could be charged to farmers for their loans and the 5 percent maximum interest that could be paid to investors who bought the land bank bonds.[78] In other words, the banks were designed to be run on a shoestring, with rigid guidelines that gave managers little leeway to respond to changing market conditions. Moreover, the effort to create uniform interest rates did not take into account the regional differences in risk. Hollis and Bulkley had set out to make the banks self-supporting within a capitalist framework and at the same time able to supply low-cost capital on an equal basis to farmers everywhere in the country, regardless of very different conditions—goals that were not necessarily compatible.

Given the banks' structure, consistently maintaining solvency would probably have proved challenging whatever the larger economic environment, but the period in which they were launched was particularly volatile. On April 4, 1917, only a few days after the first local borrowing cooperative received its official charter, the Senate voted to enter the war in Europe.[79] Treasury Secretary McAdoo's Liberty Loan campaigns, started shortly afterward, crowded out other securities from private capital markets.[80] With the end of the war came a brief inflationary boom, followed by a short but nasty depression in which industrial production plunged by 35 percent. Most sectors bounced back by late 1921, but not agriculture, which continued to struggle throughout the "prosperity decade."[81] Especially given the disgruntled attitude of rural constituents during this era, represented in Congress by the bipartisan "farm bloc," it is little wonder that no one in Washington was enthusiastic about handing over control of this politically crucial, but not terribly sturdy, program to amateur management, as had been envisioned in the original legislation. In 1923 Congress amended the Federal Farm Loan Act to tip the scales in favor of government control by specifying that the farm loan board in Washington, rather than the local cooperatives (as the legislation had originally specified), had the power to fill the majority of seats on the boards of directors of the regional land banks.[82] Thus, contrary to the original plan for the program, the banks were never spun off by the government and run by private citizens as not-for-profit institutions. Rather, they evolved into government-owned and managed noncommercial business enterprises that functioned to fulfill a purpose that Congress had designated as being in the public interest.

The Land Banks Are Ruled Constitutional

Not everyone agreed that the land banks served a valid public purpose, however, and some felt that this novel form of intervention into the economy by the national government was not legitimate under the Constitution. Private bankers in the farm-mortgage business, naturally enough, were particularly skeptical, and they initiated the court challenge referred to earlier that went all the way to the Supreme Court.[83] The suit turned on the complaint of Charles E. Smith, a mortgage banker from Fort Worth,

Texas, against the Kansas City Title and Trust Company, of which he was a shareholder. Smith objected to the Kansas company's plan to invest funds in farm loan bonds. He maintained that the bonds were not a valid investment instrument, because the Federal Land Bank System was unconstitutional. Congress had no right to capitalize and subsidize, through tax exemptions, institutions that would "lend private capital on farm mortgages." Such an activity could not be considered one of the "express national purposes" of the federal government as defined by the Constitution.[84]

While it was true that the original legislation stated that in addition to providing capital for agricultural development, the purpose of the banks was "to create Government depositories and financial agents for the United States," Smith's suit charged that these responsibilities had been added as a kind of fig leaf to provide Constitutional cover.[85] Ever since Chief Justice Marshall's ruling in *McCulloch v. Maryland* over a century before, activities undertaken to carry out tasks that the Constitution had expressly assigned to Congress, such as regulating the money supply and collecting taxes, had generally been accepted as legitimate for the national government.[86] Smith's lawyers argued, however, that the true intent of the statute was not to carry out such constitutionally sanctioned activities, but rather to set up credit facilities for owners of farm property. Such an activity, particularly when subvented with public funds, set up in competition to businesses organized by private investors, and aimed at aiding one particular group, was most definitely not constitutional, according to Smith's legal team. The supposed duty of the banks to aid in the fiscal operations of the government was a pretext that was being used to legitimate an unwarranted and dangerous expansion of federal power.

The case was clearly regarded as consequential at the time, as evidenced by the high-powered legal talent that participated. Arguing for Smith was William Marshall Bullitt, a wealthy corporate lawyer and important figure in the national Republican Party, who had served as solicitor general under President Taft.[87] Representing the land banks was Charles Evans Hughes, formerly governor of New York State, associate justice of the Supreme Court, and Republican presidential candidate in 1916. (Hughes would go on to serve as Chief Justice of the Supreme Court from 1930 to 1941.)[88] Others who filed briefs in support of the land banks included Westel Woodbury Willoughby, a founder of the American Political Science Association, and William Gibbs McAdoo, former secretary of the treasury, current presidential hopeful, and progenitor of the fleet corporation.[89]

In defending the banks, Hughes made two arguments. First, that aiding "agricultural development" was a public purpose; and second, that Congress had the final say on what agencies were needed to carry out its fiscal responsibilities.[90] Frustratingly, for those (at the time and afterward) who sought a definitive legal ruling on the question of whether Congress had the right to create quasi-autonomous agencies by which to intervene in the economy, the Supreme Court declined to respond to Hughes's first point and decided the case on the formalistic second point.

Justice William Rufus Day wrote the majority opinion. Appointed to the court by President Theodore Roosevelt, Day is best known for his opinion striking down the Keating-Owen Child Labor Act of 1916, Congress's attempt to regulate the labor of children on the basis of the Constitution's commerce clause.[91] Keating-Owen made it illegal to ship goods manufactured by children under the age of fourteen across state lines. Writing for the court, Day stated that even though the Constitution's commerce clause gave Congress the authority to regulate commercial relations between the states, this was not the act's purpose. In reality, the act "aim[ed] to standardize the ages at which children may be employed . . . within the states."[92] While Day was not opposed in principle to placing restrictions on child labor, he believed that the structure of federalism set out by the Constitution gave the authority to regulate production to the states, not the national government. While insisting that the court had "neither authority nor disposition to question the motives of Congress in enacting this legislation,"[93] he maintained that statutes had to be evaluated on the basis of their "natural and reasonable effect."[94] In this instance, even though regulating commerce was the ostensible goal, regulating child labor was its "effect."

Day's decision in *Smith v. Kansas City Title and Trust* was announced in February 1921. Somewhat surprisingly, given the views the justice had expressed when he struck down Keating-Owen, his opinion in the *Smith* case resolutely avoided the Farm Loan Act's "natural and reasonable effect." This was not because the parties to the suit skirted the issue. The appellant's counsel specifically urged the court to look past the pretexts Congress had used to justify its actions and to focus on what the banks actually did. In addition, as previously noted, Hughes, in defending the land banks, did not deny that the legislation's true purpose was to improve farmers' access to credit. Rather, he asserted that establishing agricultural credit facilities *was* a constitutionally sanctioned activity for Congress to undertake, because a strong agricultural sector was in the national interest.

Despite the encouragement, Day ducked the key question of whether it was legitimate for the national government to form a business enterprise in which it owned all or part of the capital stock and to support the operation directly or indirectly with public funds. He ruled that the banks were constitutional because they had been *designated* as facilities that Congress could use for carrying out its constitutionally mandated duties. Establishing them was therefore "within the creative power of Congress."[95] In response to the appellant's argument that the true meaning of the act should be gauged by looking at how the banks actually operated, Day acknowledged that they indeed had never been used as federal depositories and had only briefly and marginally functioned as fiscal agents (when three of the banks had disbursed federal loans for seeds during a drought in 1918). Nevertheless, he insisted that Congress's power to do something for which it had authority under the Constitution was "not determined by the extent of the exercise of the authority conferred under it." In this case, rather than dealing forthrightly with the way the legislation impacted the real world, Day insisted that it was "not the province of the judicial branch of the government to question [Congress's] motives."[96]

Why the court was willing to sanction, even if it did not endorse, the considerable expansion of the federal government's reach into the economy represented by the land bank system will probably never be known with certainty. Perhaps the banks seemed the only practical solution to an otherwise intractable problem within the existing economic structure, but the justices shrank from describing the situation as one of market failure, for fear such a characterization in this instance would raise a host of questions as to whether other markets might need government intervention to function optimally. Whatever the motivations, the effect of the Supreme Court's decision in *Smith* was to give a green light to the expansion of federal power into the economy. Although the basis for this expansion was not legitimated very clearly, the decision provided constitutional and legal shelter for the operations of quasi-public agencies from that time forward to today.

Conclusion

While the world of the early twentieth century, when a third of Americans lived and worked on farms, seems remote today, the agricultural credit program designed by Hollis and Bulkley remains significant for several reasons.[97] The ability of government-created agencies to secure funding from private capital markets by issuing bonds, instead of from legislative appropriations, plays a major role in contemporary public finance. Although Hollis and Bulkley's ingenious concept for a program that would ultimately be managed by the beneficiaries themselves—who might as a result be mobilized to participate actively in the public realm more generally—failed to take hold as a paradigm for later government programs, it is noteworthy as a demonstration of the democratic aspirations (contradicting stereotypes) of many early U.S. statebuilders.

Another aspect of the land banks that has important implications for the larger story of American political development is the particular way they survived the challenge to their constitutionality: by being designated as tools for controlling the money supply. From here on, federally launched authority-type agencies could intervene in capital markets without fear of challenge.[98] This would not be true with respect to corporate agencies that did not intervene in the financial sector. Such a distinction was already manifest in the fact that the Emergency Fleet Corporation had to be justified as a short-term response to an emergency, while the Federal Land Banks were conceptualized and approved as permanent institutions, to deal with what was perceived to be an endemic shortcoming in the nation's financial structure. This difference in ease of legitimation is an important reason that federal intervention into the American economy came to be focused predominantly on providing financial incentives for desired activities, rather than on undertaking them directly.

THREE

Municipalities Struggle to Meet New Needs

Well before officials at the national level began developing new tools for public economic activism, local government officials had been searching for ways to expand public services. These explorations sometimes led to publicly owned and operated enterprises, but more often to agencies similar in structure and function, however they were labeled, to public authorities. Although they have become so ubiquitous that they are commonly assumed to have been inevitable—or at least to embody powerful interests and values—these institutions took a surprisingly unplanned and circuitous route over several decades to arrive at their present form.

Even more obviously than was the case with national-level quasi-public instrumentalities, these mechanisms at the local level did not emerge from conspiracies by antidemocratic elites, nor in response to popular suspicion of government. On the contrary, the public authority took shape as elected officials pursued ad hoc experiments to escape the constraints that prevented local governments from performing tasks the public demanded. While the format for the public authority did not fully crystallize until the federal government stepped in during the Great Depression, the basic elements of this institutional model were generated over the previous three decades at the local and state level as officials struggled to solve the dilemmas of local public action.

The Campaign for Public Ownership

In 1914 Daniel Hoan, the socialist city attorney of Milwaukee, pronounced regulation of public utilities a "complete fizzle." Hoan's conclusion was based on years spent battling the imperious Milwaukee Electric Railway and Light Company with the limited legal tools at the city's disposal. He argued that even in Wisconsin, where regulatory agencies were at their most efficient and honest, it was impossible for public utility commissions to force good service at moderate cost from investor-owned companies. Commissioners would only push so far, realistically fearing they might drive private capital out of state. Thus, in Hoan's opinion, the only sensible course was "to secure the democratic control of collectively owned property." Despite this conviction and his astonishingly successful political career—spanning thirty years as an openly socialist public official, including twenty-four as Milwaukee's mayor—he retired from politics in 1940 having socialized only a stone quarry and the city's street lights. As with many other local socialist officeholders in the United States, Hoan left a robust legacy of honest, efficient, and humane administration. But when it came to expanding public ownership his record was meager.[1]

How can we explain Hoan's lack of success in effecting a program so dear to his heart? Most historical writings on American socialism conclude that Americans were too wedded to capitalist values to support any real overhaul of the U.S. political economy. According to this view, the socialist electoral breakthrough, which saw over one thousand victories in town and city races between 1910 and 1912, represented simply a protest against the corruption and incompetence of the major parties. Socialists never had the electoral base to function as anything more than the left wing of Progressivism. Rationalizing public administration by mandating competitive bidding or instituting modern cost accounting systems was fine, but the head-on assault on capitalist property relations that public ownership represented crossed the line of political acceptability. With socialist officeholders able to do little more than fine-tune the system, the major parties found it easy to co-opt their issues and defeat them. This is why it was only in exceptional places, such as Milwaukee or Bridgeport, that socialists held power after the late teens.[2] Thus, the failure of socialists in the electoral arena is construed as a reflection of the public's deep-seated and coherent attitudes toward government and its role in the economy.

What this interpretation neglects is the public appeal of the urban vision that reformer Frederic C. Howe articulated as cities "that owned things and did things for people."[3] A key reason for this oversight has been the almost single-minded focus on the fate of the self-described socialists who ran for local office in the early twentieth century. Although the so-called sewer socialists faded as credible contenders for political power after a brief surge in the early teens, that outcome cannot be taken as an accurate barometer of public attitudes regarding local government activism, given the structural barriers within the political system to class-based electoral challenges.

The parliamentary path to socialism was probably preordained to failure by the same factors that doomed other class-based electoral challenges in the United States. As Richard Oestreicher has explained, the institutional structure of American politics systematically muffled class sentiment, while privileging the expression of ethnocultural loyalties. Political insurgencies of all kinds, including those with a class base, smashed into the three practically insurmountable barricades of American politics: the entrenched position of the two major parties; the winner-take-all election system that gave newcomers little chance of establishing a foothold in the electoral arena; and the division of government into local, state, and federal layers. To these obstacles must be added the myriad of voter registration requirements, instituted by northern as well as southern states in the late nineteenth and early twentieth centuries, that contracted the electorate. Alexander Keyssar estimates that "millions of people—most of them working class and poor—were deprived of the right to vote in municipal, state, and national elections." One result was that "third-party insurgencies were deprived of a potential electoral base." For all these reasons, the electoral success achieved by socialists in these years provides an unreliable guide to the popularity of their programs.[4] In reality, the idea that local governments would take on production and distribution of goods and services—a concept expressed by the term "public ownership"—was actually quite popular both before and after municipal socialism crested as an electoral challenge.

Municipal socialists were important actors in the early stages of the development of government activism in the United States, but they were far from the only advocates of government expansion. The ideology to which people like Daniel Hoan subscribed was but one part—albeit the most explicit and systematic—of a broader political tendency in the late nineteenth and early twentieth centuries. Populists, union activists, and mainstream Progressives shared with socialists an aspiration for the community to take greater self-conscious control of economic life, in order to achieve goals that market forces could not. Thus the agenda of public ownership was central to what might be called the "broad left" of late nineteenth- and early twentieth-century America. Many others, including business owners, had no general desire to reduce the sway of the market but felt that there were times when private enterprise did not step up to the plate and public action was needed.

Widespread public support for government economic activism is evident from looking at what happened when voters were given the opportunity to express their opinions directly. The urban electorate often backed referenda on the kind of programs socialist candidates put forward. In part, this was because of familiarity with the idea of public ownership. As Daniel Rodgers has explained, reformist intellectuals in the Progressive Era zealously publicized the wide-ranging activities of European cities in an effort to legitimate and inspire a similar "politics of municipal supply" on this side of the Atlantic. But the impulse had native roots as well. The widespread antimonopoly sentiment of the late nineteenth century flowed easily into support for public production and distribution of basic goods and services, as demonstrated by the 1892 Omaha Platform of the People's Party, with its well-known proclamation that "the time has come when the railroad corporations will either own the people or the people must own the railroads."[5]

While broad proposals for public ownership had long been a staple within opposition circles, it was labor leaders who began explicitly linking such ideas to local politics. Events during the long depression of the 1870s—most notably the response of public officials to the nationwide railroad strike wave in 1877—convinced many labor groups of the need to enter politics directly. In 1878, labor-backed candidates won fourteen seats in Congress, numerous statewide races, and a large number of local offices, including mayoralties in Scranton, Utica, Birmingham, and Toledo. That same year the *Atlantic Monthly* reported that the "active, capable" workingmen who led the labor parties favored government ownership of national and regional transportation systems. In the years following, presumably as a result of hands-on experiences in local government, labor groups began to advocate municipal takeover of parts of the urban infrastructure. The Mechanics' Assembly of San Francisco, for instance, called in 1881 for municipal ownership of gas, water, and street-sweeping machinery, in addition to making more traditional labor demands, such as the eight-hour day in public employment and higher pay for teachers. In 1886, when labor organizations throughout New York City came together to draft the platform on which Henry George was invited to run for mayor, they included a plank advocating public ownership and operation of urban mass transit.[6]

In the following years, voter behavior demonstrated the popularity of such proposals. Examples include the 1894 New York City referendum on whether the city should build a subway, which carried almost three to one; the 1894 Detroit advisory vote on whether the city should operate, as well as own, its street railways, which was supported by a four-to-one majority; the 1902 Seattle election that asked voters to approve a bond issue to construct a municipal power plant, which they did by a margin of nearly seven to one; and the 1902 Chicago referendum on public ownership of the city's mass transit system, which voters approved four to one.[7]

By the late nineteenth century, public ownership was popular enough to start getting picked up by major party politicians, albeit mavericks. Probably the best known was Tom Johnson, the Democratic mayor of Cleveland. In this era, Cleveland was a cauldron of militant working class politics, with public ownership on the agenda before Johnson arrived on the scene. In response to the 1892 Homestead steel strike, the city's Central Labor Union advocated "governmental absorption and ownership of such great corporations as that of the soulless Carnegie." In 1899, independent Republican Robert McKisson appealed for support among working-class voters in a tight mayoral election by coming out for municipal ownership of all public utilities.[8] During Johnson's administration (1901–1909), the city took over garbage disposal, set up a free tuberculosis sanitarium, established public bathhouses, and acquired a small municipal electric-light plant when the city annexed a nearby village.[9] Johnson failed to municipalize the street railways, as he hoped to do, but his efforts did lead to lower fares, and five years after he left office the city-owned Municipal Electric Light Plant ("Muny Light") went online, realizing one of his fondest hopes.[10]

Other examples of major party advocates of public ownership include two big-city mayors who went on to the governorships of their respective states. Republican Hazen S. Pingree, a wealthy Detroit businessman, simply wanted honest, lower-cost government when he was pressed to run for mayor by the city's elite in 1889. Soon after taking office, however, Pingree espoused public ownership out of outrage at the corruption and unresponsiveness of the local streetcar, gas, and electric companies. By threatening municipal takeover, he got concessions, even if he was unable to socialize any of these operations. He did manage to establish a city-owned electrical generating plant, which went into operation in 1895, that provided power for streetlights and public buildings. Technologically advanced and professionally managed, the Detroit facility provided improved service for lower prices and became a prime exhibit for advocates of public ownership elsewhere, much to the chagrin of the electric industry. Pingree's former friends ostracized him and his family socially, but the majority of voters supported his initiatives enthusiastically, electing him mayor four times in a row before sending him on to the governorship of Michigan in 1896.[11]

Like Pingree, Democrat Edward F. Dunn of Chicago was a mainstream party politician and public ownership advocate who went from the mayoralty of his state's biggest city to the governor's chair. Dunn was not as successful as Pingree, either at instituting his program or building an enduring majority coalition, but the circumstances of his mayoral victory are telling with respect to political sentiment in early twentieth-century Chicago. Public ownership of the hated street railways was so popular that Dunn's 1905 campaign pledge of "IMO" (*immediate* municipal ownership) carried him to a solid 54 percent victory over a reform Republican rival who also advocated "MO," but at an unspecified later date.[12]

Meanwhile, often with little fanfare, cities moved into revenue-producing activities as one part of their overall transformation into what urban historian Eric Monkkonen has called the "service city," the form of municipal government we are familiar with today.[13] Public provision of water led the way. In 1870 slightly less than half of cities with networked systems of water supply and distribution (as opposed to individual wells) owned their waterworks. By 1924—with the total number of integrated systems having grown by a factor of forty—publicly owned waterworks comprised 70 percent of the total.[14] By this time, public ownership was, in the words of one contemporary public administration expert, "taken almost for granted in the field of water supply."[15]

Mundane as it might seem, providing water represented a sharp break for cities, which had previously confined themselves to supplying things traditionally regarded as indivisible public goods, such as police and fire protection, that did not lend themselves to the commodity form—that is, to being socially defined as discrete objects bought and sold in markets. Water, by contrast, was generally charged for in some relationship to use. In a sense, then, water opened Pandora's box. The widespread reliance on municipal provision of this vital substance enhanced the plausibility of following the same course in other areas. In addition, there were other goods and services that were logically connected.[16] For example, once cities began pouring massive quantities of water into the urban fabric, provision of sewer systems by local governments was practically taken for granted. Cities generally paid for these sophisticated and expensive engineering achievements, at least in part, by charging property owners.[17] Supplying water also opened up the question of public power when water sources lent themselves to hydropower exploitation, as for Los Angeles and Seattle.[18]

In addition to water, cities supplied other goods and services. Such activities were generally described with inoffensive rubrics such as "public services" and "public utilities," although not everyone shied away from more inflammatory terminology. In his 1915 public finance textbook, Berkeley professor Carl C. Plehn, a skeptic when it came to public ownership, bluntly labeled much of what cities were doing as "semi-socialistic." By this he meant that they were providing residents with "things which they might—and for a long time did—provide for themselves, or which might be provided by private enterprise." As examples, Plehn listed, along with water: electric power; gas; street railways; markets and scales; cemeteries; crematories; meeting halls; ferries; toll bridges; lunchrooms; farms; newspapers; belt railroads; harbor management; liquor agencies; and even, in one city, a municipal organ.[19]

What happened to the momentum for public ownership evident at this time in American history? Daniel Rodgers and Morton Keller, two historians who have recognized the intensity of this sentiment in the early twentieth century, argue that it petered out in the face of the "democratized corruption" that often characterized American local government in this period. They argue that despite the widespread abstract appeal of the "self-owned city," when it got down to cases, voters shrank from the prospect of the patronage and graft they feared would come along with expanding the range of moneymaking activities politicians controlled.[20]

Whatever truth this interpretation may have, it is incomplete. Institutional more than attitudinal factors hindered the development of public ownership. Direct government involvement in the economy often had wide support, but legal barriers stood in the way. Public pressure for affordable services did not dissipate, however, and officials were forced to devise alternative methods for securing at least some of the desired results. To overcome the roadblocks, government officials faced two institutional tasks: establishing the legality of new kinds of public activity and finding the money to capitalize the new ventures.

The First Institutional Task: Establishing the Legality of Municipal Enterprise in the Courts

Advocates of municipal activism often held up the example of local governments abroad. Frederic C. Howe, an indefatigable publicist for public ownership starting from his days working with Cleveland mayor Tom Johnson, extolled the achievements of cities in Britain and Continental Europe in a series of influential books and articles. For example, in *The City: The Hope of Democracy*, published in 1905, he described how numerous British cities were operating their own water, gas, and light-rail systems "with scrupulous attention to maintenance, replacement, and adequate sinking-fund appropriations so that the property is kept at its original efficiency." At the same time, costs to the public dropped, service improved, and the overall morale of urban residents increased. Glowing reports such as this were frankly aimed at inspiring American readers to push their own cities to take on a greater range of tasks.[21]

The only problem, as Howe candidly admitted, was the more restrictive legal context in the United States. European cities were generally allowed to do anything their central governments did not specifically forbid. But for cities in the United States, the situation was almost the reverse. American courts treated cities as administrative subdivisions of the states that created them. They had no inherent powers, only those explicitly assigned to them in charters or state laws. That perspective, codified by the influential jurist John Dillon in his 1872 treatise on municipal law and generally referred to as "Dillon's Rule," held that local governments could claim only those powers that had been expressly granted, were clearly implied, or were absolutely necessary to accomplish goals established by the legislature. Any doubts as to whether a locality had the authority to act, according to Dillon, should be "resolved by the courts against the municipal corporation."[22]

Yet even as the courts invoked the ultimate authority of state legislatures, American jurists were working to assert their own primacy over urban affairs. They insisted that legislatures could only authorize local governments to undertake activities that had a public as opposed to private character, and that they, not legislatures, had the final call as to whether an undertaking qualified as "public." Thus, under this principle, even a municipal activity explicitly authorized by the state legislature might be deemed unconstitutional. As legal historian Hendrik Hartog points out, judges were able to utilize the doctrine of strict construction of legislative intent as a way "to interpose judicial authority between the legislature and the city."[23]

This authority, when combined with the generally narrow view of the proper scope of government activity held by most judges, made the courts a tremendous barrier to new municipal undertakings. As time went by, however, the judiciary became open to broader conceptions of "public" purposes, giving credence to William J. Novak's contention that American courts, despite their reputation as an obstacle to statebuilding, actually "embraced change."[24] The saga of the municipal ice cases illustrates the dynamics of this transformation in one sector of the economy.

Before the spread of electric refrigerators, affordable ice was a public health issue in urban environments. For that reason, numerous localities attempted to establish facilities for the production and distribution of low-cost ice in the early twentieth century. Some of the attempts were not contested in court. A few, even in the early years, were adjudged legal. In 1910, for example, the Georgia Supreme Court upheld the constitutionality of a 1907 state law allowing the town of Camilla to operate an ice plant.[25] In general, however, early efforts by cities to provide ice ran afoul of the courts. The attempt of the socialist administration of Schenectady to enter the ice business provides a dramatic example.[26]

Running for mayor in the fall of 1911, George Lunn, a crusading pastor turned Socialist Party member, highlighted the high price of ice in a "natural ice zone" like upstate New York as a particularly egregious example of the workings of private enterprise. "Save the babies of the working class" became a rallying cry of his campaign. Lunn triumphed in an election that swept a majority of socialists onto the city council, but he warned his supporters that "the handicap of laws framed to establish and sustain the capitalists' system" severely limited what his administration could accomplish with respect to public ownership. Nevertheless, after consulting with his special council, the lawyer and national Socialist Party leader Morris Hillquit, the new mayor decided to establish a municipal ice business. Hillquit advised him that such an operation should be legal, reasoning that the city was expressly empowered by its charter and state law to furnish water. And wasn't ice simply water in frozen form?[27]

Shortly after taking office in early January, Lunn directed his public works commissioner to begin harvesting ice from the nearby Mohawk River (a task for which the city provocatively hired workers who were striking the American Locomotive Company, which along with General Electric, was one of the city's two biggest employers). When hot weather arrived a few months later, the city began selling the ice, offering it for approximately 40 percent less than private distributors charged. Needy families were supplied free of charge. Soon after, an outraged local grocer with a small ice trade went to court proclaiming the endeavor to be "illegal, wrongful, unlawful and improper and not within the corporate powers and functions of the city." On the eve of the Fourth of July, a state court judge issued a sweeping injunction that took effect immediately, prohibiting the city from continuing to sell ice, or giving it away to the indigent.[28]

Lunn and his fellow socialist officeholders were infuriated, assuming that the order, coming just before the big summer holiday when their new customers were particularly counting on getting ice, was "timed to place the Socialists at the greatest possible disadvantage." They obeyed in form, although not in spirit, by organizing themselves overnight into a self-financed, nonprofit company and continuing the next day with scheduled service. Despite harassment by private ice dealers, the "irregulars," as the socialist officials dubbed themselves, continued their business through the summer. Unable to use city vehicles, they had to buy their own equipment, but they kept the operation going with donations out of their own pockets, help from the local Socialist Party chapter, and sales to the public of red "Ice at Cost" buttons. Shoestring financing finally undid the enterprise, however. Unusually warm weather the following winter meant the river failed to freeze, and the operation folded for lack of funds to purchase ice from outside vendors.[29]

Other localities were stopped by state courts when they tried to go into the business of producing and selling ice in the early twentieth century, even when they did not rhetorically challenge the prerogatives of private enterprise. Nonetheless, city ice operations became increasingly common as time went on. By 1915, Harvard University's Municipal Research Bureau reported that ice plants were producing good quality ice at reduced prices in a number of cities, including Weatherford, Oklahoma; New Britain, Connecticut; Lafayette, Alabama; and Fernandina, Florida. In addition, the bureau noted that the League of Kansas Municipalities was in the process of lobbying the state legislature for a general grant of power for local governments to enter the ice business, and a similar push was under way in Illinois. Meanwhile, Cleveland's cold storage plant, operating in conjunction with its new municipal market, was renting refrigerated lockers to individual customers, as well as retailers, making it possible for residents "to buy at the municipal market any amount of provisions, when they are cheap and plentiful, and to store them there for a nominal charge, to be used when prices have risen."[30]

In some communities, private business groups still fought such ventures in the courts, but by the late teens legal challenges were meeting with less success. Judges were finding it increasingly difficult to reconcile their traditional conceptions of the public good with contemporary reality. The 1919 Missouri Supreme Court decision in *Kansas City v. Orear* illustrates the way this shift of judicial attitudes was occurring. The case concerned a bond referendum passed in the fall of 1918 by voters in Kansas City that authorized the city to borrow $400,000 to build a facility to manufacture ice. Irate local businessmen in the ice trade took the city to court, maintaining that the city's charter did not expressly grant it the power to operate an ice plant. Furthermore, they added, even if the state legislature had given such an authorization, it would not have been constitutional. Making and selling ice was simply not a public purpose, and "not even the sovereign Legislature, much less a municipal corporation, can, by fiat, make that public which is in fact private."[31]

Ultimately, the Missouri Supreme Court concurred with the private ice vendors' position, but it was not an easy decision, nor was it unanimous. One justice penned an impassioned dissent, graphically describing the human suffering caused by summer heat in the densely packed neighborhoods of big cities. Contrasting the situation in small towns and rural areas, with their pure air and abundant shade, he argued that the new urban environment required that ice be readily available for refrigeration. Otherwise, he warned ominously, rotting food would breed "microbes, bacteria, disease and death," causing "babies to die like flies." In the eyes of this jurist, changes in living conditions had elevated ice to a "prime necessity." Thus, its provision had become a public purpose.[32]

While the other justices did not accept this conclusion, they clearly found it no easy task to reconcile traditional conceptions of the public good with current realities. The majority's decision noted that "bread, clothing, shoes, water, light, fuel, ice, drugs, and medicines and transportation may be enumerated as some of the things now deemed to be absolute necessities for the human race in the latitude of this state." Yet while it had become conventional for a city "on its business side" to furnish some of these things, others, "by common consent," were not considered legitimate for a city to provide. What was the difference? Ultimately, the court could find no way to draw a sharp distinction. The justices concluded that "the rule to be invoked in determining whether the business in question . . . is public or private, is *whether such business is sanctioned by time and the acquiescence of the people as being public or private.*" Even though the court finally categorized ice as a private, rather than a public, good—and on that ground ruled that a bond issue would contradict the state constitution—it conceded forthrightly that the distinction between public and private had become a "twilight zone." The fluidity of the situation became even more apparent the following year when Missouri's new state constitution of 1920 made explicit provision for municipalities to borrow for ice plants. (It also allowed debt financing for city-owned water, light, and gas works; street railways; telegraph and telephone operations; and heating facilities.)[33]

By 1929, a decade after the Missouri Supreme Court wrestled with the question of what was legitimate public activity, the private ice dealers of Denton, Texas, discovered that the legal tide had shifted definitively in favor of a broad conception. Initially, the owners of the Denton Home Ice Company had reason to be confident that they could stop the city from entering their field of business. Almost immediately after discovering that bids were being collected for construction of a municipal ice plant, they were able to get a court injunction against the city. A few months later, however, a higher court ruled flatly against the company, as did the Texas Supreme Court, when the case was appealed the following year. The higher courts were responsive to the city's argument that it was not exceeding its powers, based on a 1925 state statute that authorized cities "to manufacture [their] own electricity, gas, or anything else that may be needed or used by the public." In response to the plaintiffs' charge that the city was using too expansive a definition of the statute, the Supreme Court asserted that "things 'needed and used by the public' change to suit industrial inventions and developments. Ice is now so generally needed and used that it is a public necessity." Clearly, much had changed in the ten years since the Missouri Supreme Court had anguished in the "twilight zone," trying to draw a clear line between ventures that governments should and should not undertake and eventually coming down with a restrictive ruling.[34]

The ice cases provide an example of how cities gradually pushed over the wall that had once neatly separated local government from the private sector in the eyes of the courts. After the mid-1920s, none of the challenges that private ice producers took to the courts succeeded.[35] The fabric of legal certitudes regarding the proper role of government in the economy, fraying a decade earlier, was now in tatters. Courts seemed anxious to exit this arena, leaving the question to state lawmakers, who—as the liberalized borrowing provisions of the new Missouri Constitution of 1920 and the broad authority to institute new public services authorized by 1925 Texas statute indicate—were growing increasingly favorable to public production of goods and services. At this point the principal barrier was no longer legal but financial; that is, once a city had support from the state legislature for establishing a municipal enterprise, and the courts acquiesced, it was difficult to obtain the funds to put the plan into practice.

The Second Institutional Task: Overcoming Restrictive Public Finance Rules

In 1896 Cleveland's Republican mayor Robert McKisson articulated the crux of the municipal financing dilemma when he complained about not being able to borrow what he needed to upgrade the city's water, sewer, and garbage disposal systems, despite the fact that "probably no other city of any considerable size in the State has as small a relative indebtedness or has been administered on more safe and conservative financial lines." The source of McKisson's problem was not resistance from the courts. All the activities he wanted to undertake were by then seen as standard city functions. Nor did he face public opposition. As we have seen, Cleveland was a place where expanding the local public sector had real voter appeal. Municipal production and distribution of electricity—finally realized when "Muny Light" came on line in 1914—had been a live political issue since

1890. Successful politicians such as Tom Johnson, Newton Baker, and McKisson himself regularly assembled political coalitions by advocating more public services. Rather, the problem McKisson faced was state law limiting municipal debt, which meant he had no way to finance the infrastructure improvements he wanted to make.[36]

In Ohio, as in practically all states, laws established the amount local governments were allowed to borrow by fixing the total at a certain percentage of the value of the municipality's taxable real property. These percentages tended to be quite low, typically 5 percent, which was the limit in Ohio.[37] In addition, many states mandated that voters approve bond issues by supermarjorities. These restrictions were the result of nineteenth-century voter backlash in the wake of failed economic development schemes pursued by states and municipalities that left high debt loads to be paid off by angry taxpayers. The legacy of these tax revolts endured in numerous laws, and (even more formidably) in amendments to state constitutions. The nineteenth-century tax revolts had been precipitated by economic slumps, but what made these uprisings especially virulent was that even in good times, property taxes were widely perceived as unfair. Since the affluent tended to hold a large part of their wealth in forms other than real estate, they paid proportionally far less than people of more modest means. Not unreasonably, therefore, property taxes were regarded as regressive. In addition, the generally arbitrary and inconsistent methods by which property taxes were assessed and collected did nothing to endear them to small-property owners. In the words of one scholar of antitax movements, taxing real estate was a procedure seemingly "designed to incite rebellion."[38]

McKisson took on the problem of debt limits directly, energetically publicizing statistics that illustrated Cleveland's low debt load compared to other large cities in the country. After winning over local elites, he gained the approval of the legislature, which raised the city's debt limit from 5 to 7 percent. McKisson's campaign was successful, but the victory proved ephemeral. The city council strongly opposed the change, and the legislature later restored the lower cap.[39] Thus, it is not surprising that most local politicians did not follow McKisson's lead in explicitly challenging the institutional structure of local public finance. Instead, they developed indirect methods to achieve the same ends. These methods would become the building blocks of the public authority.

The search for ways to circumvent institutional barriers to borrowing resulted in two basic strategies. The first was to create new government entities not bound by existing debt restrictions. The second was to devise new methods by which to borrow. The energy and creativity put into crafting these institutional innovations attest to the pressure felt by politicians in this era to provide more and better government services.

Of the two strategies, creating new government bodies was the most obvious, since it drew on existing precedents. States had been setting up specialized local government structures since before the American Revolution. The Maryland Assembly, for example, set up tax-supported county-level commissions to administer almshouses in 1768.[40] In the nineteenth century, as reformers won battles in state legislatures for free public education, independent school districts, with their own elected boards and powers to tax, became the administrative mechanism of choice in rural areas.[41] In urban America, specialized units that operated outside the regular structure of government also become a standard feature of the political landscape during the nineteenth century, as historian Robin Einhorn has explained. To defray the cost of physical upgrades, officials routinely divided cities into what were called "special assessment" or "special taxing" districts. Within such areas, property owners were given the option of incurring the costs of such improvements as street paving and sewers. Einhorn concludes that although special district financing did produce a lot of infrastructure with a minimum of corruption, it "segmented" the city, preventing the redistribution of resources and excluding those without real estate from input.[42]

Whatever the drawbacks of special districts, they proved an expedient way to handle problems that otherwise might have proven politically intractable. In the late nineteenth century, as Sarah Elkind has described, states turned to them to provide networks of services over areas that made sense functionally, but that overlapped existing jurisdictional boundaries. This is the origin of such well-known agencies as the Metropolitan Sanitary District of Greater Chicago, established in 1889 to protect the local water supply from sewage contamination, and the East Bay Municipal Utility District, set up in 1923 to provide water for the eastern section of the San Francisco Bay Area.[43] Today, when people think of special districts, it is these behemoths that usually come to mind.

Less recognized is the way public officials latched onto special districts as a way to solve the debt limit problem identified by Cleveland's Mayor McKisson. This was what happened in 1917, when the Indiana legislature established a park district and a sanitary (sewage disposal) district that covered virtually the same territory as the city of Indianapolis. The legislature bestowed independent borrowing powers on the two new entities, specifically mandating that their debts not be a legal obligation of the city. As the *American Political Science Review* was quick to point out at the time,

Indianapolis, which already had an independent school district, had become "four separate, legally distinct municipal corporations over what is for all practical purposes the same area." In effect, these overlapping political units meant that Indianapolis had quadrupled its borrowing power. Although the journal was apprehensive that the "legal stratagem of separate corporate existence" was limited only by "legislative discretion and good sense," it was upbeat about the potential for the newly created government units to construct infrastructure previously impossible to finance.[44] The special district formula for expanding the public sector proved extremely popular, so much so that some questioned whether legislatures were always showing "good sense." The phenomenon reached its zenith in Cook County, Illinois, where 419 separate taxing districts operated in 1933.[45]

The enthusiasm for special districts can be explained by the fact that, in addition to providing a fiscal escape hatch, they possessed other appealing qualities. For example, local elites and state-level politicians used them to wrest control of particular functions from urban machines, either to obtain greater professionalization of management or to secure patronage possibilities for themselves. But whatever other elements contributed to their appeal, special districts gained favor principally because they provided a relatively easy way of circumventing the regulations relating to municipal finance, regulations that not only made it impossible to borrow the amounts required for modern infrastructure, but that in many instances were even hard to determine with confidence because of the haphazard way they had accumulated over the decades in state statute books and constitutions.[46]

The expansion of special district debt provides a rough gauge of the growth of these nonstandard government units. During the thirty years before the Great Depression, the debt of special districts (excluding school districts) exploded. Starting from a mere $5 million in 1902, it stood at $1.3 billion in 1932. As a proportion of total local borrowing, this represents an increase of from 0.3 percent to 9 percent—a thirty-fold increase in the importance of this form of public activity.[47]

In one sense, special districts were only one step removed from general-purpose government. They had the power to impose mandatory levies, within their geographic jurisdiction, that were somewhat similar to property taxes. They usually had some kind of elected governance, although electoral power was not necessarily distributed on a one person, one vote basis. Public authorities represented a more radical institutional break, one made possible only by the second strategy for escaping the yoke of borrowing limits.

This strategy was revenue-bond financing, which was based on the doctrine of the "special fund." According to this doctrine, revenue from income-generating operations should be considered separately from a city's general funds derived from taxes. Projected fees from such operations would be available as collateral against which to borrow, and such borrowing should be allowed to take place outside the city's debt limit. The rationale for not counting bonds issued on behalf of projects that made money against the city's legal debt cap was that these particular financial instruments would not be backed by the city's "full faith and credit"—that is, its taxing power. Instead, the principal and interest would come exclusively from a particular project's stream of revenue. The promise to pay represented by such bonds did not put the citizenry in debt; if the enterprise failed to produce the expected revenues, citizens would not (in theory) have to make up the deficiency. These kinds of financial instruments became known as "revenue bonds."

Spokane is credited with pioneering the revenue-bond idea when it convinced the Washington Supreme Court in 1895 that city bonds designated as payable exclusively from the income of its waterworks should not be considered a general obligation of the city, and therefore should not count against its debt limit.[48] After the legislature explicitly authorized this method of financing, the state's largest city picked up the ball and ran with it. Starting in 1916, Seattle issued millions of dollars' worth of revenue bonds to develop the vast publicly owned utility empire known as City Light, and to purchase the local street railway system from eastern investors.[49]

Special districts and revenue-bond financing proved useful devices for funding public-sector activities, but setting them up was laborious. Without general authority to create these mechanisms, municipal officials needed to seek specific approval from their state legislature for each new endeavor. Otherwise they could go through all the steps of putting together a complex financial arrangement, only to see it crumble in the face of a lawsuit. Even in the increasingly lenient judicial atmosphere, this still happened. For example, in 1930, Iowa's Supreme Court scotched the plan by the small town of Sidney to acquire an electrical plant through a variant of revenue-bond financing. Officials in Sidney proposed to use an earmarked account, funded by charges to residents for electricity, to pay a private company for generating equipment. The court voided the town's contract with the company, ruling that, although the legislature had granted cities and towns authority to own and operate their own electric plants, no "express power" had been granted to Sidney to use revenue-based financing.[50]

Conclusion

Thus we see how even after legislatures and courts had stopped enforcing narrowly traditional notions of the proper role of government, politicians ran up against regulations governing public finance that thwarted their plans for expanding the public sector. Rare was the public official who dared to confront the issue of debt limits head-on; rarer still one like Cleveland's Mayor McKisson who did so and succeeded, if only temporarily. The typical response was to craft workarounds, via special districts and revenue bonds. In the emergency conditions of the Great Depression, federal officials would meld the two strategies together, opening up new avenues for activist government, albeit of a kind quite different from that which municipal socialists and other early twentieth-century advocates of activist local government had envisaged. The next two chapters move back to the national level, tracing first the history of federal corporate agencies, and then an even more consequential story: how the federal government contributed to standardizing and disseminating the institutional template of the modern public authority, allowing this institutional form to grow rapidly after the Second World War.

FOUR

The Truncated Career of Autonomous Federal Agencies

At the same time as quasi-public agencies were gaining traction at the local level, parallel structures, inspired by the organizational innovations represented by the Emergency Fleet Corporation and the Federal Land Banks, were being created at the national level. Chartered by Congress or incorporated under the laws of a state, these new federal agencies became known as government corporations, and they were extolled as the optimal means to carry out economic activities. The Wilson administration employed such agencies extensively to mobilize the economy during the First World War. In the interwar period, groups from across the political spectrum called on the federal government to launch corporate agencies to carry out goals the group espoused. By the mid-1930s a helter-skelter array of these entities had been created, with more to come during the Second World War.

At the same time, many people became suspicious and even alarmed by the expanding use of the government corporation format. This reaction was not to socialistic rationales for corporate agencies by those who employed them—there were no such rationales to react to. In contrast to Great Britain, where those who advocated using these mechanisms contended that they would provide the optimal administrative machinery for running socialized sectors of the economy, proponents in the United States justified their use with legalistic and technical arguments. No conspiracy to cloak true intentions was involved. American liberals were not closet socialists, although they did harbor an inchoate vision of a more activist national government. In common with groups across the political spectrum, liberals turned to these kinds of agencies on an ad hoc basis to solve specific problems. Yet even those who latched onto them enthusiastically in particular circumstances could be uncomfortable with their use more generally. Such ambivalence—well illustrated by the contradictory relationship both Herbert Hoover and Franklin Roosevelt had with government corporations—combined with the hostility of small government advocates, would ultimately spell their decline.

Herbert Hoover and the Grain Corporation

Entry of the United States into the Great War involved far more than raising an army and transporting it to European theaters. Modern industrial warfare called for the federal government to exert an unprecedented degree of control over the economy. To implement this control, the government needed new forms of what the experienced private-sector administrator Herbert Hoover termed "social machinery."[1] The Wilson administration experimented with a variety of novel bureaucratic structures, calling them councils, boards, commissions, administrations, and corporations. Of these, the seven so-called war corporations departed most from conventional practice. These were the United States Shipping Board Emergency Fleet Corporation; the Food Administration Grain Corporation; the War Finance Corporation; the United States Housing Corporation; the United States Sugar Equalization Board; the United States Spruce Production Corporation; and the United States Russian Bureau, Inc. (The last two were created so close to the end of the war that they never really functioned.) The war corporations were similar to each other in their independence from traditional governmental departmental agencies, but otherwise quite varied in their powers, functions, management, capitalization, sources of income, supervision, and methods of incorporation.

One of the most important of the war corporations was the Food Administration Grain Corporation, and its story illustrates the attractions of quasi-public agencies from the standpoint of federal officials anxious to accomplish tasks that involved the government directly in the economy. The grain corporation was set up by Herbert Hoover, the head of the U.S. Food Administration. Hoover had come to this key position by virtue of his reputation as the brilliant humanitarian administrator who had coordinated food aid for Belgium after the Germans occupied the country. At the time the war broke out the millionaire mining engineer was living in London mulling over ways he could turn his exceptional management talents to public service. The Belgium food crisis provided the opportunity. Hoover's Committee for Relief in Belgium shipped 2.5 million tons of foodstuffs across enemy lines into Belgium and occupied northern France, saving over nine million people from destitution, if not outright starvation. So effective and egalitarian was the distribution system devised by Hoover that studies found child mortality rates in the region to have actually declined during the occupation compared to the period before the war.[2]

A little over a month after the United States declared war in April 1917, President Wilson tapped Hoover to manage the nation's food supply. The challenge was significant: to feed the American military and supply increasingly desperate European allies, while holding down domestic prices—and all this in a situation of short harvests! By spring 1917, the situation was already serious. Belligerents and neutrals alike were bidding against each other in American agricultural markets, sending overall food prices up by 45 percent from prewar levels.[3]

Most worrisome was the spike in the cost of wheat. Wheat was critically important for the allies, because bread made from wheat flour provided the mainstay of working-class diets. With traditional suppliers in Eastern Europe and Russia out of the picture due to blockades and revolution, India and Australia too distant, and Argentina experiencing crop failure, European purchasing agents scrambled to buy up the smaller than normal American wheat harvest. Increased demand, decreased supply, and speculation sent wholesale prices rocketing upward. By April 1917, when the United States entered the war, a bushel of Number 1 Northern Spring Wheat, the premier grade, was selling for $2.43, an increase of 50 percent over the cost in the last half of the previous year.[4] Workers' incomes were rising in the tight labor market, but food prices climbed faster, and consumers became increasingly agitated. Earlier in the year, food protests, sometimes violent, had broken out in several large cities. In New York City in late February, police had used clubs and horses to disperse a crowd of over a thousand women who converged on city hall demanding that the mayor "make prices go down."[5] Pressure mounted to restrict European purchases, an idea that outraged farmers and that Wilson resisted because he hoped to use the threat of an embargo as leverage to get the British and French to accept his plan for a negotiated peace.[6] Meyer London, the lone Socialist Party member in the House of Representatives, proclaimed that the situation demonstrated the failure of the "so-called law of supply and demand," and called for a national commission "to regulate the transportation, marketing, preservation and distribution of food."[7]

Hardly a socialist, Hoover nonetheless agreed with London that the situation could not be left to the free play of market forces and that the government would have to take political control over the agricultural sector, at least for the duration of the war. The question was how to do it. Even before any formal requests were forthcoming from the White House for Hoover to play a role, he let it be known through intermediaries that he would accept the responsibility only if he were given substantial control. New to government and despite an off-puttingly cold demeanor, the tenacious Hoover proved himself an effective bureaucratic infighter.[8] Whereas everyone, including the secretary of agriculture, expected food control would be administered by the Department of Agriculture, Hoover maneuvered to have the operation established as, in his words, "an independent executive organ operating directly under the President."[9] In addition, he successfully badgered a reluctant Wilson into agreeing that executive control of the powerful agency be concentrated in a single person (himself), rather than a board, even though the strong-willed president professed himself to have "a troubled mind" after capitulating on the question.[10] Anxious to establish facts on the ground, Hoover got the Food Administration up and running weeks before Congress finally passed legislation giving the agency statutory authority. He accomplished this by setting up a management team of elite volunteers and paying for clerical help out of his own pocket.[11]

As successful as Hoover had been at getting his way with regard to the structure of his operation, the hard-driving new government bureaucrat set his mind on wresting from the president one more significant concession. He insisted to Wilson that the Food Administration be allowed to employ incorporated agencies. Making his case, Hoover argued that it would be impractical to purchase and sell foodstuffs without, as he put it, "conforming to the usages of the trade," by which he meant that if his agency was going to enter the market directly, it needed to do so on the same basis as private business players. For example, it would need to be able to sue and be sued, which required a separate legal identity. Also, his operation needed to have control over its own finances, including independent authority to borrow, because as he put it, trying to run commercial transactions through the Treasury would be "fatal." Pointing to the recently established Emergency Fleet Corporation, he reminded the president that "this arrangement is not without precedent."[12] Hoover was able to convince Wilson, who after all had helped conceptualize the format for the fleet corporation, but neither talked openly about the plan while the bill to formally establish the Food Administration was under consideration in Congress. Indeed, when the press raised the subject, Hoover publicly denied any intention to set up government-owned corporations, insisting to the *New York Times* that such an idea was "but a rumor."[13]

Wilson and Hoover kept quiet about their plans for employing government-owned corporations because the food control bill, with its grant of practically unlimited power for government over the agricultural sector, was already throwing rural areas of the country into an uproar. Farmers, fearing that they would be sacrificed on the altar of low prices for American consumers in the event of government intervention, objected to interfering with the free play of market forces. Debate in Congress was lengthy and emotional, going so far as to include personal attacks on Hoover. Senator Thomas P. Gore, a Democrat from Oklahoma who chaired the Agriculture Committee, predicted that the food administrator, in restraining the free flow of commerce, could become "a blood clot on the brain of business."[14] Senator James A. Reed, Democrat of Missouri, objected on the grounds that the man who would wield the "despotic and unconstitutional powers" envisioned in the bill was insufficiently American.[15] He charged that Hoover, having been out of the country fairly continuously for practically twenty years pursuing his international mining career, was "quite a stranger here."[16]

After a grueling ten weeks of debate, Congress finally passed the food control bill, and Wilson signed it into law on August 10, 1917. The legislation assigned the president responsibility for assuring "an adequate supply and equitable distribution" of food and other stipulated necessities while the country was in a state of war, and to carry out this task, he was empowered "to purchase, to store, to provide storage facilities for and to sell for cash at reasonable prices, wheat, flour, meal, beans and potatoes." In order to carry out these functions, the statute authorized the president "to create and use any agency or agencies." Based on this grant of authority, Wilson signed an executive order setting up the Food Administration the same day. Four days later he signed another executive order, this time creating what the *New York Times* described as a "Big Corporation to Control Wheat."[17]

Wilson's executive order establishing the Food Administration Grain Corporation explained that the agency would allow the buying and selling activities authorized by Congress to be carried out "in the manner and by methods customarily followed in the trade." The order stipulated that the agency be incorporated under the laws of the state of Delaware, and that it be capitalized with $50 million of the $150 million that Congress had appropriated for food control. Four directors of the corporation were named, including Hoover, all of whom were directors of the Food Administration, as well. The four were to name three more, with the consent of the president. All directors were subject to removal by the president.[18] Although the grain corporation was formally an independent organization, later analysts would agree that "in reality it was so closely identified with the Food Administration which created it that often their joint functions could scarcely be separated." This near unity is unsurprising given that Hoover and the volunteer leadership he assembled ran both.[19]

Hoover's term as food administrator is commonly recalled as a triumph of patriotic enthusiasm, when the country rallied to his calls for "wheatless" and "meatless" meals, and with only minor grumbling, ate "Victory Bread" that included ever-increasing proportions of corn, oats, buckwheat, barley, rice, sweet potatoes, soy beans—and even peanuts and bananas![20] It is true that Hoover's efforts were strikingly successful. Most dramatic was the fact that, although the disappointing wheat harvest of 1917 was barely enough for domestic consumption, the Food Administration was able to export over 100 million bushels of this key commodity to sustain the Allies, while at the same time keeping prices stable at home.[21] Yet despite the stress that Hoover's public relations department put on voluntary cooperation, more was involved in achieving these impressive results than housewives signing pledge cards and school children singing about "The Patriotic Potato."[22] Rather than voluntarism, the key to the Food Administration's success was its program of centralized planning, regulation, and direct participation in agricultural markets through the grain corporation. As Hoover frankly stated in his memoirs, he aimed to control the nation's food supply "from the soil to the stomach."[23]

To accomplish this, Hoover rejected production quotas and rationing, believing such methods would require a huge bureaucracy and in any case had not succeeded in Europe. Instead, his plan was to insert the grain corporation directly into the distribution chain in order to set prices at a level that would placate urban consumers while still motivating farmers. During the bitter debates over the food bill, Hoover had insisted to Congress that "price fixing" was not on the agenda. However, on August 12, 1917, only two days after passage of the legislation, he announced that he intended to establish a "fair price" at which the government would purchase wholesale wheat. At the end of the month, an advisory committee composed of farm organization leaders, labor union officials, and academics set the price at $2.20 a bushel for the highest grade of wheat at Chicago, the largest interior terminal market, with other grades at other terminals prorated down from this basis.

Hoover was disappointed that the committee pegged the price this high, but farmers found it unreasonably low (despite the fact that before the war wheat was selling for less than $1.00 a bushel). Earlier in the month the price had soared to over $2.50 on the open market, and experts predicted that it would settle at $3.00 if no controls were enacted. While technically, Hoover's price did not "fix" the price for all transactions, it essentially was the only one available, given that the grain corporation was the most powerful actor in the wholesale market, either buying or supervising the

Figure 4.1. This humorous depiction of the man in charge of the country's food supply as a military commander hints at a reality that Hoover downplayed. Hoover always emphasized the importance of voluntary cooperation in meeting conservation goals and keeping retail prices from skyrocketing. In reality, however, it was his control of the grain corporation, through which he could force companies to sell grain at a price he determined, that gave him the power to shape markets and achieve his goals. (Reproduced courtesy of the "Ding" Darling Wildlife Society.)

purchase of all the wheat supplied to the U.S. armed forces, the Allies, and neutral nations. Moreover, Hoover warned via press release that if commercial dealers failed to follow suit, he was "prepared to take the whole harvest if necessary in order to maintain a fair price."[24] (Figure 4.1 shows a cartoonist's not entirely positive take on Hoover's style.)

In an effort to conciliate disgruntled farmers whose hopes for windfall profits he had just crushed, Hoover argued that the grain corporation's price should not be considered a ceiling, but rather a floor that would protect them in the event that a sudden end to the war released the vast wheat stockpiles of the Southern Hemisphere onto the world market. Farmers and their spokesmen in Congress were little comforted. The irascible Senator Reed, on behalf of his wheat farmer constituents in Missouri, took to the Senate floor to denounce Hoover's price management program as "a crime against liberty." Despite the dissatisfaction, the price Hoover set turned out to be high enough to encourage increased investment in agricultural machinery and a 30 percent increase in acreage of planting in 1918, leading to one of the biggest crops in American history. To stick with its guarantee, the grain corporation needed an infusion of $100 million, the rest of the congressional appropriation for food control. In addition the corporation borrowed $385 million in private capital markets.[25]

After the war, the public corporation recommended itself to a variety of constituencies. Hoover's grain corporation, along with the other war corporations, demonstrated how well this administrative device could influence the way the economy worked, based on its ability to engage directly in commercial operations. But in addition, observers noted how a corporate agency could provide an escape hatch from the sometimes paralyzing regulatory framework of federal bureaucracy. With the grain corporation, Hoover was able to sidestep civil service rules and hire the personnel of his choice. He was not constrained by the rigid purchasing rules involving time-consuming public bidding required of ordinary units of the federal bureaucracy. In addition, the agency's initial capitalization, plus its ability to retain earnings and borrow, freed it from the cycle of annual appropriations. This meant that Hoover was able to dispense with having to continually cultivate powerful legislators to keep appropriations flowing. Moreover, he was free to plan beyond a particular year's budget and had virtual autonomy over specifics of policy. Yet along with all this freedom, Hoover's grain corporation still reaped the benefits that normally accrued to a government agency, such as freedom from state and local taxation. Given all these appealing features, it is hardly surprising that once the war was over a range of groups advocated the creation of similar bureaucratic instruments by which to advance their own interests.

Some groups lobbied for maintaining particular wartime corporate agencies and in a few instances achieved some success (the most extreme example being the Emergency Fleet Corporation, which as described in chapter 1, continued in existence until 1936). The postwar history of the grain corporation provides a good illustration of this phenomenon. The end of the war brought more large harvests, and although the Food Administration was phased out, Congress extended the life of its affiliated corporate agency, changing the name to the United States Grain Corporation and pumping a billion more dollars into the organization. The corporation continued its buying operations through the spring of 1920, and despite the sharp decline in international demand during its last year, managed to close its books with a net profit of over $27 million (in part because

Hoover insisted on charging purchasers from neutral nations high administrative fees in retaliation for what he deemed their extortionate shipping rates).[26]

The Government Corporation Idea in the 1920s

Farmers, bitter foes of the grain corporation when it seemed to be closing them off from the possibility of bonanza earnings during the war, suddenly turned enthusiastic about the concept of a government-owned agricultural corporation when the market collapsed after hostilities ended. As emphatically expressed by one farm organization leader: "The government grain corporation was used during the war to keep the price of grain down. IT CAN BE USED NOW TO KEEP THE PRICE OF GRAIN UP."[27] It was a sentiment that clearly resonated. Through the 1920s some version of a corporate agency became a regular feature of the legislative proposals put forward to deal with the problem of mounting surpluses and falling prices of basic crops.

The first of these proposals was introduced by Senator George Norris, Republican of Nebraska, in 1921. The Norris bill proposed a Farmers' Export Financing Corporation capitalized at $100 million that would operate as a not-for-profit middleman, buying agricultural staples for cash, shipping them abroad using Emergency Fleet Corporation ships, and marketing them to foreign buyers on credit. The rationale was that, given the disruptions of the war, "the foreigner is not able to pay cash for these products. He is exceedingly anxious to buy, but must have time in order to pay." To support itself, the corporation would sell tax-exempt bonds to private investors. These would be guaranteed by securities provided as collateral when foreign buyers made credit purchases.[28]

Herbert Hoover, by now secretary of commerce under President Harding, opposed the plan, arguing that if the government were to embark on this business venture it would only exacerbate the unfortunate international trend toward "nationalization of all overseas trade." He called on Congress to uphold the country's "tradition of individualism" by passing an administration-sponsored substitute measure that would reorient the War Finance Corporation (WFC) into a government bank for agriculture. The WFC had been established during the war to aid the mobilization by providing financial help to war-related industries and banks connected to them. The administration proposed that instead of Norris's export corporation, which would be a public entity operating directly in the agricultural market, the role of government should be confined to financial support, with all buying and selling performed by private entities, such as livestock dealers, export companies, and financial firms. As it became clear that the administration was going to be successful in quashing his bill, Norris bitterly commented that Hoover's plan put the government in business just as much as his own did, but "the Government is all right in business if the middleman and the banker and the trust company can get their rake-off. If they are eliminated it is a crime. . . . It is populistic."[29]

With passage of the administration bill, in August 1921, the War Finance Corporation became a source of agricultural loans of "intermediate" duration, that is, for briefer periods than loans available through the government land banks, but running longer than short-term credit available from commercial banks. This period was defined in the legislation as up to three years. To give a sense of the extent of its activities in its new role: the WFC ended up lending $383 million to the agricultural sector under its new authority, more than the $306 million advanced under its war powers. Given the demonstrated demand for this kind of credit, Congress in 1923 established the Federal Intermediate Credit Banks as permanent additions to the government-coordinated agricultural credit system begun in 1916 with the Federal Land Banks, discussed in chapter 2.[30] (Later in the decade, the controversial and never-enacted McNary-Haugen bills, aimed at raising prices for farm products, would also propose using a federal corporation.)[31]

Once the concept of an administratively and legally independent, self-supporting agency that could intervene directly in the market was in play, other constituencies besides farmers picked up the idea. The United States Building and Loan League, the national trade group for what are now known as savings and loans, campaigned for a government organized system of "building-loan banks." These were modeled explicitly on the Federal Land Banks. Like the land banks, the proposed institutions would provide a secondary market for mortgage loans, in this instance on urban residential property. The head of the league, testifying before Congress in 1919, began with arguments as to why the plan would promote the welfare of the whole society, but his bottom line was that "if this exemption from taxation was given to the farm loan system . . . [,] we may establish a claim here." In other words, it was only fair that the federal government, having created tax-advantaged credit agencies to direct private capital into one sector of the economy, should do the same for theirs."[32]

Labor joined the chorus of advocates of new government corporations with the proposal for public ownership of the nation's railroads. During the war, transportation snarls that threatened to cripple mobilization efforts prompted the administration to seize control of all the private lines and run them as an integrated system. After the war, a lively debate ensued over whether and how to return the lines to private ownership. Glenn E. Plumb, general counsel for the railway unions, put forward "Labor's Solution of the Railroad Problem," which came to be known as the Plumb Plan. According to this proposal, the federal government would buy all the railroad lines and administer them in a unified way, just as the Railroad Administration had done under Secretary of the Treasury William McAdoo during the war. In this case, a permanent government corporation would be established, which would be directed by a board composed of representatives from three groups: rank-and-file railroad employees, administrative personnel, and the public.[33]

Public power advocates also picked up the idea of corporate agencies in this period. Their proposals emerged during debates over the future of federal facilities on the Tennessee River at Muscle Shoals, Alabama, which included a partially finished hydroelectric dam that was to have provided power for production of synthetic nitrogen to be used in explosives. After the war, Wilson's Secretary of War Newton Baker drafted a bill to create a government corporation to take charge of the property in order to produce nitrates for fertilizer and, if needed, munitions. (As mayor of Cleveland, Baker had presided over the building of the largest publicly owned electrical plant in the country.) Baker's bill was the first of many that envisioned this kind of administrative structure for the property, which as time went by became more prized for its hydropower potential than as a possible source for cheap fertilizer. From 1922 until Franklin Roosevelt's first term, Senator George Norris introduced at least one bill into every session of Congress calling for public ownership of Muscle Shoals. From the start, Norris's bills assumed administration by a freestanding, incorporated agency along the lines of what would eventually become the Tennessee Valley Authority.[34]

Even though the government corporation became a familiar concept in the 1920s, the Republican-dominated congresses of this period were not receptive. Despite their hostility, they did approve two new corporations: the previously mentioned Federal Intermediate Credit Banks and the Inland Waterways Corporation. The latter was set up at the insistence of the War Department, which had been tasked with running barge lines on the Mississippi River and its tributaries that the federal government had operated during the war.[35] The balance shifted once the economy plunged into depression, however, and the pressure to create corporate-type agencies became harder to resist. Both Hoover and Roosevelt set them up, even though both manifested unease about this organizational form, and neither articulated any general rationale for its use.

The Depression Heyday of the Government Corporation

Hoover demonstrated his conflicted feelings regarding government corporations in his December 8, 1931, "Third Annual Message to Congress," which he gave against the background of an economic downturn that after two years showed no signs of bottoming out. In this address he condemned the "large administrative functions independent of the Executive" exercised by the shipping board and recommended that it be absorbed into the Department of Commerce. By now the Emergency Fleet Corporation was so well institutionalized that Congress, in 1927, had renewed the agency's charter and given it the more permanent sounding title of the Merchant Fleet Corporation. As the shipping board and its corporate offspring were so intertwined as to be virtually identical (similar to the relationship between Hoover's Food Administration and the grain corporation), the president was obviously taking on the autonomy of the fleet corporation. Thus, even though he had been adamant during his days as food administrator that he needed to work through an agency outside normal lines of authority of the executive branch, and thus free of standard controls, he was clearly not comfortable with this kind of arrangement as a general rule.

Yet, even as the president implicitly disparaged the fleet corporation for its splintering impact on the executive branch, he pointed to the deflationary spiral that was threatening to bring down the economy and called for putting "some steel beams in the foundation of our credit structure" with a program that included two new kinds of autonomous instrumentalities. His first recommendation was for a "system of home-loan discount banks." These would be structured along the lines first proposed over a decade earlier by the urban home mortgage bankers who had advocated a government-organized secondary market for mortgage loans similar to the Federal Land Banks. The administration's bill to establish a Home Loan Bank System to extend credit to home financing institutions was passed into law the following summer.[36]

Hoover's second initiative utilizing the format of a corporate agency was a government-owned bank "of the nature of the former War Finance Corporation." He had resisted taking this step and did so only when his favored solution, a private credit pool organized by the nation's leading bankers, had demonstrably failed to help struggling banks. From the start, leading bankers had offered only grudging acquiescence to Hoover's proposals for private-sector solutions, leaving him to bemoan the difficulty of securing the cooperation of "the financial institutions of the country who have little cohesion and little leadership." With the economy deteriorating precipitously, the beleaguered president finally abandoned his aspiration for an effective response through voluntary collective action. Bowing to the wishes of the big banks, congressional Democrats, and the conservative eastern wing of his own party, he endorsed the creation of a government bank to extend credit to financial institutions and railroads. Little more than a month after his speech, Congress passed legislation establishing the Reconstruction Finance Corporation (RFC), capitalized at $500 million and authorized to borrow up to $1.5 billion more. The legislation specified that the RFC would be a short-term operation, lasting only two years at most, a provision that presumably helped assuage Hoover's apprehension over launching this new autonomous vehicle. In fact, however, the RFC became so popular that it lived on much longer than its original legislation stipulated, lasting into the early 1950s when it was finally dismantled under the Eisenhower administration.[37]

Despite widespread support for setting up the Reconstruction Finance Corporation, not everyone was enthusiastic. Two kinds of criticism emerged. Some objected because they saw it as aiding the very people who were to blame for the disastrous state of the economy. Representative Louis T. McFadden, a Republican from rural Pennsylvania, vilified the RFC as a "supercorporation," set up "for the sinister purpose of helping a gang of financial looters to cover up their tracks." Others, such as Senator Robert Wagner of New York, were bitter that the RFC legislation contained no provision for aiding localities with the mounting costs of relief. Wagner complained that when the bankers came to Washington, no one preached the value of rugged individualism. Yet, when ordinary Americans "cry out in despair 'Give us work,' we suddenly are overwhelmed with devotion for the preservation of self-reliance."[38]

Under President Franklin Roosevelt, the lack of a clear strategy for employing quasi-public agencies at the federal level became more apparent, even as the momentum for setting them up increased. Eight federal corporations existed in 1933 when Roosevelt took office. By 1939, New Dealers had created twenty-three more. The war period brought another sixteen.[39] (A complete list of these bodies, including their purpose and authorization, is found in the appendix.) In their haste to tackle problems and in the absence of much preexisting bureaucratic apparatus, New Dealers made almost indiscriminate use of this organizational device. They created so many autonomous incorporated agencies so quickly that after only eight months, the *New York Times* would proclaim: "New Deal Rules by Corporations."[40]

New Deal corporate agencies were extremely heterogeneous. Not only was there no consistent format for their structure and powers, there was no consistent basis on which they were legally justified. Of the twenty-three created from the outset of the Roosevelt administration through the end of the decade, ten were established without any explicit authorization from Congress. While some in this latter category were based on executive orders from the president, several were formed solely on the authority of an administrative official.[41]

Almost all the major New Deal figures participated. For example, Secretary of the Interior Harold Ickes and Secretary of Agriculture Henry Wallace joined Federal Emergency Relief Administrator Harry Hopkins to incorporate the Federal Surplus Relief Corporation (FSRC) in October 1933 in Delaware. They created this agency to be a mechanism that would buy, process, and distribute surplus crops to needy people. At the same time, they hoped that removing agricultural surpluses from the market would cause prices to rise. The president publicly gave his approval, telling the press that he believed "the corporation can be organized quickly and in such manner as to become the best agent for decisive action in the emergency." Yet he issued no executive order to this effect (even though he would do so only two weeks later when Wallace set up the Commodity Credit Corporation to make loans on crops subject to production control under the Agricultural Adjustment Act). Thus, Hopkins, Ickes, and Wallace essentially set up the FSRC as an autonomous agency on their own authority, citing as justification several pieces of legislation, including the Agricultural Adjustment Act, the National Industrial Recovery Act (NRA), and the Federal Emergency Relief Act.[42]

While Ickes and Wallace took part in other corporate ventures (Ickes was particularly active in this area), this was the only one in which Hopkins was actively involved. Hopkins did, however, in late 1934, develop a plan for a permanent semiautonomous agency to provide public-sector jobs for the unemployed. The idea created a stir when rumors about it were leaked to the press. In one sensationalized account, the *New York Times* termed his program "EPIA (End Poverty in America)," thus comparing it to the EPIC (End Poverty in California) plan proposed by socialist Upton Sinclair, who campaigned for governor of the Golden State promising to create a California Authority for Land and a California Authority for Production to take over idle farms and factories, run them on a nonprofit basis, and hire the jobless to work in them.[43]

In some cases corporate agencies begot more corporate agencies. The most extreme case was the thirty corporate subsidiaries of the Federal Subsistence Homesteads Corporation (FSHC). Harold Ickes established the FSHC to carry out a program mandated by a cryptic, anomalous section of the National Industrial Recovery Act that authorized the president to spend $25 million "through such agencies as he may establish" to carry out an undefined program described as "subsistence homesteads." The term subsistence homesteads referred to an amorphous idea that had to do with model rural communities. Depending on the advocate, these communities would cater either to unemployed urban workers or poverty-stricken farmers living on submarginal lands. In either case, the communities would demonstrate better land management techniques to inhabitants of the surrounding region. Senator John Bankhead of Alabama, who had inserted the proposal for subsistence homesteads into the legislation, explained that his purpose was to help in "the restoration of the small yeoman class which has been the backbone of every great civilization."[44]

By executive order, Roosevelt transferred the authority vested in him to his secretary of the interior, including "full authority to designate and appoint such agents, to set up such boards and agencies, and to make and promulgate such regulations as he may deem necessary or desirable."[45] Ickes then created a Division of Subsistence Homesteads within the Interior Department to set up experimental communities where residents could combine subsistence farming with part-time wage work. To carry out the kind of tasks the program would entail—including land acquisition, contracting for construction, and making loans to prospective residents—Attorney General Homer Cummings suggested to Ickes that a "Government-controlled corporation" would provide an efficient vehicle. Thus, just as Hoover had established the Food Administration Grain Corporation and the Sugar Equalization Board to be the operating arms of the Food Administration, Ickes incorporated the FSHC under the laws of Delaware to be the administrative mechanism that would carry out the program of the Division of Subsistence Homesteads. As the corporation's general counsel candidly explained, the purpose of setting up an incorporated entity was "to free the program from as many as possible of the procedural technicalities and delays inherent . . . in established administrative procedures."[46]

To M. L. Wilson, the visionary agricultural economist Ickes tapped to run the Division of Subsistence Homesteads, the corporate device presented itself as the ideal institutional structure to foster grassroots democracy. Wilson came up with a plan by which the individual projects would be incorporated as subsidiaries of the national-level corporate entity. The subsidiary corporations would have boards of directors that included representatives of local business groups, labor unions, and state agricultural schools, in addition to some of the homesteaders themselves. As a corporate entity, each subsistence community would be able to undertake the tasks necessary to develop itself on the basis of "ordinary business procedures." Wilson saw this setup as superior to centralizing all control in Washington, the only practical course if each project had to adhere to government procedures for financial transactions—procedures that were not only complex but also best suited to the regularized, predictable activities of government bureaus, not commercial undertakings. With a perspective reminiscent of that of Senator Henry Hollis and Representative Robert Bulkley when they designed the Federal Land Banks, Wilson believed that the experience of actually running the subsidiary corporations would encourage residents to become engaged participants in the program, rather than passive recipients of government aid. Less than four months after the FSHC was incorporated, thirty corporations were established in eighteen different states.[47]

Despite this energetic start, the plan faltered. The obstacle was John Raymond McCarl, the conservative and legalistic comptroller general, whose animosity prefigured a larger backlash to come. McCarl insisted that all accounts of the community corporations had to be audited on the same basis as standard government agencies, meaning that his office had to approve all transactions before they took place. This ruling by the comptroller general meant that the community corporations lost most of the advantages sought by setting them up in the first place. In the scenario Wilson had hoped to avoid, the program was centralized in Washington, with local input advisory only. The few subsistence communities that were set up were not terribly successful, and as the program was always a headache for Ickes, he was probably relieved when President Roosevelt, in 1935, shifted it into the newly formed Resettlement Administration, under Rexford Tugwell.[48]

The comptroller general's opposition was predictable, although seemingly unanticipated by Ickes and Wilson. Ever since his appointment in 1921 by President Warren Harding to head the newly established Government Accounting Office (GAO), McCarl had protested the idea of exempting any federal government expenditures from his oversight. Congress had set up the GAO as part of an effort to provide better financial management of the federal government. The agency, which was to function independently of the executive branch, was charged with auditing its accounts. McCarl interpreted his role broadly, and he worked to control spending before it happened through pre-audits, rather than merely reporting after the fact. In his pre-audits, he sought to determine whether proposed payments were, in his opinion, legal. With regard to the subsistence homestead corporations, McCarl justified his ruling on the basis that these agencies had not been given "specific statutory authority" by Congress. It is true that the comptroller general was a stickler for explicit congressional authorization.[49] He once disallowed $3,000 in travel costs for a committee that President Coolidge had sent to tour the national parks on the grounds that there were no specific statutes in place to justify the expenditure. But ultimately, McCarl's efforts to police government expenditures were not about trying to protect the constitutionally mandated prerogatives of the legislative branch. His real bugaboo was activist government, as he made clear after his fixed term ended and he publicly excoriated Congress for going along with what he identified as the New Deal trend toward "government-run-everything."[50]

Pushback against Federal Corporations

The rapid proliferation of corporate agencies and the seemingly haphazard manner in which they were formed posed questions for friends as well as foes of the New Deal. Republican Senator Thomas Schall of Minnesota probably had little support—after all, he was reputed to be the second most unpopular person in the Senate—when he railed hysterically that the New Deal corporate agencies were part of a conspiracy to effect "world revolution" by subverting constitutional government and "tak[ing] the place of all business activity in the country."[51] Nevertheless, the miscellaneous and obscure character of these agencies did raise legitimate worries, making them easy targets for those who wanted to couch their critique of activist government in legal and constitutional terms.

Various issues were involved. One was what it meant for federal agencies to be chartered under the laws of states—especially those of Delaware, which, as one quip had it, allowed its corporations to do practically anything "except solemnize marriages and hold religious services."[52] More fundamentally, when a corporation was chartered by a state rather than by Congress, it raised the question of whether state or federal rules applied with respect to issues such as taxation and police powers. Separate from the ambiguity of the federal-state relationship was the murky connection between the incorporated agency and the federal government. The fact of incorporation implied that the agency was legally independent, but when disputes arose, would courts agree? Should they? Another issue had to do with whether the powers granted these agencies in their corporate charters were congruent with the legislation on which they were based. Particularly problematic was the fact that charters for several corporate agencies established to carry out purposes of the 1933 National Industrial Recovery Act (NRA) stated that they would be permanent, even though the NRA itself was enacted as a temporary measure with a two-year deadline.[53] Critics found it particularly provocative when Harold Ickes put the word "emergency" into the titles of two of his corporate agencies that he justified on the basis of the NRA—the Public Works Emergency Housing Corporation and the Public Works Emergency Leasing Corporation—and then included in their articles of incorporation the provision that they be endowed with "perpetual existence."[54]

FDR himself was one of those who was troubled by corporate agencies, even though he found them convenient in the short run. Like Hoover before him, Roosevelt worried about the accountability of agencies that operated outside standard departmental structures. He demonstrated his unease by his efforts during his second term to secure legislation that would allow him to reorganize the executive branch.

In 1936 he appointed a committee of public administration experts headed by Louis Brownlow to recommend plans by which the president could take better control of the sprawling, heterogeneous mass of federal agencies he nominally directed. Endorsed by the president and sent to Congress the following year, the Brownlow committee's report highlighted the negative impact of the long-term trend of creating new agencies not connected to regular departments. The report explained that adding so many "administrations, boards, commissions, committees, governmental corporations, and authorities" meant that "there are now in the Government of the United States over 100 separately organized establishments and agencies presumably reporting to the President." The key word here was "presumably." In order to cut back the impossible number of distinct lines of authority leading to the president, the report recommended adding two new cabinet-level departments to the ten already in existence: a department of social welfare and a department of public works. The next step would be to make all administrative agencies, including the government corporations, answerable to one of the twelve departments.[55]

Another recommendation relating to corporate agencies was to raise the quality of the civil service (above its current "dead level of mediocrity," as the committee members said privately). During Roosevelt's first term, in order to fill posts with politically sympathetic, professionally trained personnel, the administration exempted from civil service requirements more than four-fifths of the quarter of a million new people who were hired. Emergency agencies of all kinds, including incorporated agencies, proved a useful device for avoiding the antiquated and slow-moving Civil Service Commission. The report advocated replacing the bickering, ineffectual bipartisan board of the commission with a "well-qualified, nonpolitical Administrator," and providing this person with more and better staff. With greater ability to process trained applicants, the civil service system would be able to function effectively as the central personnel agency of the vast and complex organization the federal government had become. Once this happened, the motivation for setting up nonstandard agencies to get around personnel rules would be significantly reduced.[56]

Roosevelt endorsed the Brownlow committee's report as the basis for reorganization bills introduced in 1937, but the legislation did not pass until 1939, and then only in a watered-down version. Timing proved a major problem, as the bills got caught in the firestorm ignited by FDR's simultaneous effort to expand (detractors said "pack") a Supreme Court that was striking down New Deal legislation. As the court controversy gained traction, critics charged that the president's plan to reorganize the federal bureaucracy demonstrated another instance of his drive to amass "dictatorial powers." While some opponents seem to have been sincere, others appear to have been opportunistic. Former president Herbert Hoover claimed that Roosevelt was trying "to abolish the Civil Service Commission which for fifty years has given fine service" and replace it with "personal political control." What Hoover failed to mention was that while president he himself had recommended replacing the existing bipartisan committee in charge of the civil service with a single "Personnel Administrator."[57]

The uproar over executive reorganization provided political cover for those opposed to expanding the capacities of the national government. Corporate agencies proved soft targets for these forces, which were led by Senator Harry Byrd, Democrat of Virginia. Byrd, who would become a key player in the bipartisan conservative coalition that dominated Congress from the waning days of the New Deal until the coming of the Great Society, grandly pictured himself "the monetary conscience of the Federal Government." In the eyes of his detractors, however, he was simply a reactionary skinflint.[58] During Roosevelt's first term, Byrd had hesitated to come out in open opposition, given the president's popularity back in the senator's home state. Only after Roosevelt had been weakened by the court fight and the first phases of the executive branch reorganization struggle did Byrd go public with his conviction that the New Deal was "the most costly, the most wasteful, and most bureaucratic form of government this republic has ever known."[59] In 1936, promising to develop plans to reduce federal expenditures by 25 percent, Byrd convinced the Senate to establish and name him head of the Special Committee to Investigate Executive Agencies of the Government. This special committee would be the precursor to the Joint Committee to Reduce Non-Essential Expenditures, established in 1941, over which he would preside as "Mr. Economy" for the next twenty years.[60]

As chair of these committees, Byrd pursued his goal of radical retrenchment, although, apart from his attack on corporate agencies, with negligible results. In general, his proposals were either too extreme to be taken seriously—during the Second World War he called for mass firings of a third of the federal workforce—or too minimal to make a difference. In either case, they exhibited no larger vision of government than "cut, cut, and cut again."[61] Even though his nitpicking harassment of programs he disliked failed to make any systemic impact, his campaign to shrink government did earn him the enmity of liberals. Soon after getting to the Senate, Hubert Humphrey charged that Byrd's Joint Committee for Non-Essential Expenditures was itself "nonessential" and urged that it be abolished, a breach of Senate decorum for which the old-guard southern leadership would freeze out the freshman senator for years. Byrd's only large-scale success came in his campaign against corporate agencies, and this only because of the professionalized research assistance he received from the Government Accounting Office and the fact that these agencies were low-hanging fruit.[62]

In the spring of 1943, Senator Byrd told the press that his joint committee had begun a probe into what he described as "a maze of Federal corporations." The committee's *Report on Government Corporations*, appearing in the summer of 1944, leveled a powerful attack on autonomous incorporated agencies. While the report definitely betrayed the conservative viewpoint of the committee chairman (referring at one point to how in recent years the concept of the "general welfare" as a rationale for government action was likely "overemphasized"), the report acquired its power by raising issues that transcended any particular political perspective. In contrast to Byrd's characteristic superficial style of attack, in which he singled out trivial examples of questionable looking expenditures by agencies he disapproved of, this document was a solid overview of a significant sector of the federal bureaucracy, raising important questions and providing a large amount of relevant data. One table presented the enormous growth of incorporated agencies, showing how in 1933 existing corporate agencies had a total net worth of $3 billion, whereas a decade later, with dozens more in operation, the assets of this sector had increased to $16 billion.[63] The report described and documented three major problematic issues concerning these instrumentalities: their extreme heterogeneity in terms of legal basis and structure, their lack of any overall control over their finances, and the incongruity of using state charters to organize them.

Hard to refute, these critiques fueled passage of the Government Corporation Control Act of 1945.[64] Without ever giving a definition of a government corporation, except for listing the entities to be covered, the legislation did two main things. First, it mandated more accountability, primarily by requiring that all corporate agencies be audited each year by the General Accounting Office, with reports sent to Congress. These were to be retrospective commercial audits, not the continuous legal checking (and sometimes disallowing) of financial transactions before they took place that Comptroller General McCarl had used for regular federal agencies and sought to impose on corporate agencies. Second, the agencies with state charters were required to get statutory approval from Congress by June 30, 1948, or else go into liquidation.

The Government Corporation Control Act did not categorically prohibit the use of this bureaucratic device; however, as it turned out, the legislation marked the end of an era. A number of the agencies that already had federal charters lived on, and although Congress reincorporated several that had state charters, several were allowed to go out of existence entirely.[65] Of the 101 government corporations covered by the 1945 legislation, only 75 were operating eight years later. Meanwhile, the pace of creating new ones slowed to a crawl. From the time the act was passed in 1945 through the end of the 1950s, only two new corporate agencies came into existence: the St. Lawrence Seaway Development Corporation and the short-lived Federal Facilities Corporation (FFC), which was set up to manage the tin and synthetic rubber operations the RFC had handled during the war.[66] In addition, the 1950s saw the dismantling of the once mighty Reconstruction Finance Corporation, as well as the sale of the Inland Waterways Corporation into private hands. Starting in the 1960s the pace picked up, but only slightly.[67]

Yet even if rarely employed, the fuzzy template of the federal corporation remains available, and as in its salad days, has been employed for a hodgepodge of purposes. Examples include the Resolution Trust Corporation, established in 1989 to clean up the savings and loan debacle, and the United States Uranium Enrichment Corporation, created in 1993 to operate the two government-owned industrial facilities (in Paducah, Kentucky, and Portsmouth, Ohio) that enriched uranium for use in nuclear power plant fuel. As was the case early on, there is no consistent method of creating a government corporation, nor a generally accepted definition of what one is.[68]

Explaining the New Deal Experience

What accounts for the ad hoc, almost cavalier, manner in which officials went about creating what one critic described as the "New Deal Corporate Maze"?[69] To some extent this phenomenon can be subsumed within the larger improvisational—some would say anarchic—style of administration that characterized the entire New Deal. To many commentators, this penchant for constantly setting up new agencies on an ad hoc basis is seen as reflecting a nonideological "pragmatic" approach to politics on the part of New Dealers. As one group of public administration scholars put it, New Deal officials "were primarily interested in results, not in the theory of administrative relationships."[70] Others have explained the "rambling structure" of the New Deal as rooted in FDR's proclivity for "competitive" administration. According to historian Richard Polenberg, "Encouragement of overlapping jurisdictions may have seemed poor administrative theory, but it often spurred government officials to great achievement."[71]

Arthur M. Schlesinger, Jr., has suggested that the New Dealers' messy administrative style can be explained largely in terms of the personalities of FDR and his talented and lively subordinates, all of whom would have found conventional styles of government organization "claustrophobic." It was the very "looseness of the New Deal," allowing as it did for creativity and innovation, that made public service for these individuals "tolerable and amusing."[72]

In addition to this interpretation, Schlesinger makes the more persuasive point that Roosevelt had little choice but to circumvent the existing bureaucracy. When the new administration took office the old-line departments of Agriculture, Commerce, Labor, and Treasury were staffed by civil service employees who were neither particularly energetic nor able—Tugwell called them the "best of the worst"—and, at the higher classification levels, primarily stalwart Republicans. Thus, Roosevelt had little choice but to create new, experimental institutions to implement his programs.[73]

Certainly there is some truth to each of these different perspectives, but unless one gives a lot of credence to Schlesinger's whimsical portrait of the New Dealers' psychological makeup, which assumes they consciously embraced bureaucratic incoherence, it is hard to understand why, even if they felt they had to develop new kinds of administrative machinery, they went about it in such a slapdash way. One clue is provided by William E. Leuchtenburg, who argues that much of the New Deal can be traced to memories of the mobilization during the First World War, a time when a Democratic administration led the most far-reaching government interventions into the U.S. economy up to that time. As we have seen, the public corporation played a major role during the First World War, so it is not surprising that when liberals faced a new emergency and wanted to respond with alacrity, this institutional form would be called into service again.

Despite the appeal of government corporations for leading New Deal figures, none of them tried to define a long-run strategic role for these kinds of agencies, with the exception of "braintruster" Adolph Berle. Late in the decade, Berle floated the idea that Congress create regional capital credit banks, which would operate along the lines of venture capitalists, actively seeking out worthwhile private and public investment opportunities. Berle's proposal never gained a following, in part because he offered no convincing explanation for why such powerful independent entities could be trusted to operate in the public interest.[74] While it is true that some legal scholars and political scientists wrote about federal-level quasi-public agencies in this period, their studies were largely descriptive accounts of how already-existing government corporations had come into being and functioned and how courts had handled their ambiguous public-private character.[75] In any case, there is no indication that their studies influenced the New Dealers involved in setting up or administering these agencies.

The appeal of the government corporation to New Dealers was essentially as an expedient solution by which to sidestep immediate problems. On the one hand, as the general counsel for the Federal Subsistence Homesteads Corporation bluntly stated, they offered an escape from required procedures and legal rules that constrained standard units of the federal bureaucracy.[76] On the other hand, these kinds of administrative mechanisms allowed some degree of financial autonomy. For example, the "huge reserves and fiscal independence" of the RFC gave Roosevelt the capacity to sidestep laborious negotiations with Congress to secure appropriations for programs. The RFC supplied large sums to, among others, the Home Owners Loan Corporation ($200 million), Farm Credit Administration ($40 million), Regional Agricultural Credit Corporations ($44 million), Federal Home Loan Banks ($125 million), Rural Electrification Administration ($246 million), and Resettlement Administration ($175 million). When Roosevelt created the Works Progress Administration (WPA) on the basis of the 1935 Emergency Relief and Appropriation Act, the RFC gave the new agency an immediate billion-dollar infusion so it could get started without having to wait for funds to start flowing through normal channels.[77]

The tactical and untheorized approach to corporate agencies by New Dealers stands in contrast to the situation in Great Britain, where leading politicians dedicated to a more activist role for government were presenting arguments for establishing semiautonomous public bodies and putting forward proposals for how they should be structured. Both Herbert Morrison and Clement Attlee publicized their ideas about the government corporation as an administrative form based on their experiences in the Labour government of 1929–1931.

Morrison, while minister of transport, initiated the London Passenger Transport Board, a government corporation to provide "one single undivided consolidated ownership" of the myriad, uncoordinated modes of private and public transportation then operating in the greater London region. In his influential book *Socialisation and Transport,* published in 1933, Morrison put forward an in-depth rationale for the government corporation. He argued that outright public ownership of passenger transportation made more sense than regulation, explained why such an endeavor should be run by a public agency situated outside the traditional framework of government, and offered plans for organizing this kind of agency (making clear he saw this format as also appropriate for other sectors of the economy).[78]

Attlee, best known for his later work as prime minister of the reforming Labour government that came to power after the Second World War, was another Depression-era advocate of autonomous agencies. His stint as postmaster general convinced him that the post office was essentially a "nationalized trading undertaking," by which he meant that it generated income in exchange for services, rather than simply administering tax-supported programs. As such it was not well served by being situated within a ministerial department, because Treasury control was "wholly incompatible with the flexibility necessary in the conduct of a business concern." Therefore, it made sense to separate the finances of this kind of operation from the general budget.[79]

The particular institutional structure that Morrison and Attlee advocated during the 1930s—a publicly owned, legally incorporated body operating at arm's length from the government, both administratively and financially—would be used to manage the wave of nationalizations of almost a fifth of the economy carried out by the Labour government after the war.[80] This is not to say that no criticisms were leveled against this model, either from within and outside the ranks of the Labour Party, only that the British politicians tried to develop a coherent rationale and a standardized pattern for setting up quasi-autonomous agencies to pursue public purposes.

It seems only fair to New Deal public officials to note that their counterparts in the British Labour Party did not come up with their ideas about new administrative structures appropriate for government participation in the economy in an intellectual vacuum. Also, progressive statebuilders in Britain did not face the same intensity of conservative opposition. In Britain, discussion about when and how government should participate directly in the economy had been going on since the late nineteenth century. Fabians like George Bernard Shaw, focusing primarily on municipal services, took for granted that administration would take place within the departmental structure of government. But Guild Socialists popularized more participatory conceptions of how socialization would work, and such ideas led to calls for moving administrative units outside the existing bureaucracy. For example, the Miners' Federation bill to nationalize the mines, introduced in Parliament in 1919, envisioned a "Corporation to be known by the name of the Mining Council" that would be legally and financially distinct from government. One half of the corporation's board of directors would be chosen by the union and the other half by the government.[81]

Many in the Conservative Party also warmed to the idea of using an independent organizational form to carry out public purposes in the interwar period, although obviously not out of a desire to promote workers' control of industry. For conservatives, this kind of administrative vehicle seemed more amenable to business principles than an agency directly under parliamentary control. In 1926, faced with a moribund economy and social unrest, Conservative leader Stanley Baldwin's government displayed what historian Charles Loch Mowat described as "the empiricism of Tory policy during these years" by setting up the Central Electricity Board (CEB). The CEB was assigned the task of integrating the nation's fragmented, inefficient, and high-cost electrical industry, which private utility companies had been unable to rationalize on their own.[82] Universally hailed as a success, the CEB "created order out of muddle" by constructing and operating an interlinked system of long-distance transmission lines known as "the grid" that moved wholesale electricity energy throughout the country.[83] As Morrison himself was quick to point out, the financially self-supporting and administratively autonomous CEB foreshadowed his own plan for rationalizing public transportation under the London Passenger Transport Board.[84]

Conclusion

In general, the officials who employed the administrative device of the government corporation had an expansive, if unsystematic, conception of how a more capable federal government would be able to help achieve a more stable, regionally balanced, and equitable national economy. However, with the exception of William McAdoo, Henry Hollis, and Robert Bulkley, who (as described in chapters 1 and 2) provided at least some broad justifications for using the mechanisms they proposed, federal statebuilders who advocated and managed corporate agencies tended not to link their larger substantive goals for government to any particular methodology of public administration. After the template of the government corporation emerged during Wilson's second presidential term, it was employed chiefly as a means of evading the rules governing standard units within the federal bureaucracy. This approach would reach its apex in the New Deal, when what one proponent of government corporations would sadly describe as their "over-enthusiastic and unplanned exploitation" sparked a broad-based counterreaction that all but snuffed out this line of institutional development.[85]

The truncated career of federal corporate agencies does not mean they had no lasting impact on the American state. On the contrary. One of the most powerful of the interwar federal corporations was responsible for kick-starting a related institutional trajectory at the state and local levels. This was the Reconstruction Finance Corporation (RFC), the giant government bank set up by Hoover and expanded by Roosevelt. The RFC, which administered Hoover's public works program, provided the initial incentive for localities to try to set up quasi-public bodies with the characteristics of the public authority so they could take advantage of federal loans. Even after Roosevelt's own public works agency, the Public Works Administration (PWA), was up and running, the RFC was still supplying capital directly to some public authorities, while at the same time providing financial backup to the PWA. Moreover, the PWA, which itself had some of the characteristics of a government corporation, played an instrumental role by routinizing and popularizing the public authority template. This story will be told in chapter 5.

Administratively and financially independent agencies at the federal level were clearly problematic on a number of dimensions. Nevertheless, it seems unfortunate, given the dearth of mechanisms available to the national government for guiding the economy, that supporters of a more robust national government did not at least try to develop them into useful administrative tools for the long run. Even more unfortunate was the fact that interwar liberals did not try to reform the standard bureaucracy so that it had more of the features they were seeking when they set up quasi-autonomous bodies in the first place, features such as freedom from the mass of stultifying legal rules that handicapped responsive action, and freedom to retain funds beyond the yearly appropriation cycle so as to allow long-range planning. With a person like Hoover, who, although not the advocate of laissez-faire portrayed in popular culture, did want private-sector actors to take the lead in designing collective solutions, such behavior is understandable. But the lack of more self-conscious efforts to build the permanent institutional capacity of the national government on the part of New Dealers is discouraging and lends credence to William Leuchtenburg's characterization of mid-twentieth-century American liberalism as an "impoverished tradition." Possibly at some point in the future, the American spirit of experimentation will be linked to a more coherent view of the role of the federal government in economic life.[86]

FIVE

The Federal Government Promotes Public Authorities

During the New Deal the federal government became more active in the economy than ever before. Public authority–type agencies played an important role in this activism. Most visibly, a fleet of government corporations was launched at the federal level. But behind the scenes, the Roosevelt administration also molded the quasi-public sector at the local level, creating the basis for that sector's dramatic growth after the Second World War. In the long run, the New Deal's role in proliferating public authorities would be one of its most significant contributions to American political development.

The Great Depression and American Cities

For practically every American municipality, the economic crisis of the 1930s presented the worst emergency in its history. Skyrocketing demands for relief, traditionally the responsibility of municipalities and counties, threatened to overwhelm local jurisdictions. Yet the basic cause of incapacity to meet local needs—the fiscal straightjacket of localities—long preceded 1929. As we have seen, municipal officials had been struggling since the late nineteenth century to figure out ways to provide public services using seriously inadequate tax systems and in the face of severe constraints on borrowing.

The relief crisis of the Depression laid bare the irrational structure of American local public finance: the fact that municipalities and counties were expected to meet the many needs of their residents, including infrastructure, education, relief, and much more, almost entirely from the property tax. This is a tax with so many drawbacks that most experts readily agree with the characterization of turn-of-the-century political economist E. R. A. Seligman who called it "one of the worst taxes known in the civilized world."[1] From the standpoint of those on the collecting end, the key drawback is that this form of taxation never yields sufficient income to support the local public sector effectively. Revenues rise and fall in tandem with the business cycle, but even in good times they are not enough to fund capital budgets. During downturns, municipalities find their tax yields reduced right at the time that residents require more help. To make things worse, reduced municipal revenue usually means cuts in municipal jobs, thus exacerbating unemployment. This phenomenon was glaringly apparent during the Great Depression. At the bottom of the downturn in 1933, cities suffered an average delinquency rate of 20 percent of their tax levies. Single-industry municipalities like Detroit were hit particularly hard. Just when the closing of car factories presented the Motor City with an avalanche of human need, its tax revenues plunged by almost half.[2]

Borrowing would seem to have been the obvious answer, at least as a stopgap measure. But cities did not have this option, ensnared as they were in the same statutory and constitutional restraints that had crippled the efforts of public officials to borrow for capital improvements during more prosperous times. While restraints took many forms, the most universal—and most crippling—was the debt ceiling defined as a percentage of the assessed value of taxable property in a given political jurisdiction. Procedural rules were also constraining. Many states mandated not only that voters approve bond issues, but do so by supermajorities. In addition, there were many laws on the books specifying long periods of notice before public hearings, elections, and bond sales. These laws had been self-consciously designed to slow the process to a crawl—and they were successful.

The restrictions on borrowing by local governments were the heritage of nineteenth-century tax revolts, and their consequence was that when American cities entered the Great Depression, most were already at or near their legally mandated debt ceilings. In the crisis atmosphere of the time, legislatures were sometimes willing to loosen statutory restrictions, but the limitations on local borrowing in the constitutions of thirty-six states were a more formidable barrier.[3]

The institutional obstructions were real, but cities would have had a tough time borrowing in any case. Investors shunned municipal bonds in the early 1930s. And no wonder: falling property values and mounting tax delinquencies threatened to bankrupt the best managed local governments. At the bottom of the downturn, many cities were collecting only three-quarters of their normal tax revenues, and even with draconian layoffs and cutbacks of services, dozens of municipalities were reduced to meeting payrolls with their own local currencies or "scrip." The most dramatic example was Detroit. Starting in the spring of 1933 and continuing for the next year, the desperate city issued approximately $42 million worth of its own scrip to meet its needs for cash. Before the decade ended, more than a thousand local governments defaulted on their debt obligations at some point.[4]

As cities and towns are essentially creatures of their state governments, it would seem that local officials could have turned to their state legislatures for help. But three obstacles stood in the way. First, the fiscal health of the states was only marginally better than that of their municipalities. As historian James Patterson has pointed out, states were the most active level of government during the 1920s, spending heavily on roads and schools. Although in theory states had access to more diverse streams of revenue than municipalities, in fact, they supported this spending surge almost exclusively with money that was gushing into state coffers from taxes on motor vehicles and gasoline, and by heavy borrowing. Only fourteen states were taxing individual or corporate incomes, and these at low rates. When the economy slowed and tax receipts from automobile use tapered off, states were left with little income and high levels of debt service. The second obstacle to getting state help was political. State legislatures, dominated by conservative rural interests, were less than eager to aid their big cities, particularly since large urban centers were often Democratic strongholds. The third obstacle was legal. In many cases, even if a legislature could have been persuaded to authorize borrowing, the state constitution prohibited it. Stipulations restricting state borrowing written into thirty-three of the forty-eight state constitutions were a particularly daunting barrier, since the amending process typically involved statewide referendums, in addition to action from legislatures. In Pennsylvania, where the General Assembly held regular sessions in odd numbered years, constitutional amendments had to be approved by both houses of the legislature in two consecutive sessions, after which the question was put to the state's electorate in a special election.[5]

Given that local officials found themselves on the cutting edge of the disaster, it is not surprising that they took the lead in trying to change the rules of the fiscal game. A key aspect of the struggle was challenging the powerful idea that federal participation in social welfare was not only unnecessary, but actually pernicious. After all, unlike cities, or even states, the federal government had enormous fiscal capacity, based on its power to tax income (including that from capital as well as wages) and its lack of legal restraints on borrowing. In the summer of 1931, the socialist mayor of Milwaukee, Daniel Hoan, by this time serving his fifth term, wrote to one hundred other mayors around the country urging a meeting to demand that the federal government assume a share of responsibility for aiding the unemployed. Hoan insisted that "throw[ing] the whole burden of relief on local communities" was both unfair and ineffective. It would "only result in further impoverishing the small home owners," while nevertheless failing to provide adequate resources. Providing federal aid was, he argued, "the least that the richest nation on earth can do in keeping with what every other civilized nation is doing to alleviate distress and relieve unemployment."[6]

Hoan's call received no immediate response, in part because the situation had not yet reached crisis proportions. But the following spring, Detroit mayor Frank Murphy, facing his own city's imminent financial collapse, picked up Hoan's idea. This time a gathering did take place, with mayors or other officials from twenty-nine cities coming to Detroit in the summer of 1932 to hear Murphy insist that local governments had done "everything humanly possible to do, and it has not been enough. The hour is at hand for the federal government to cooperate." The group, which would develop into the United States Conference of Mayors, ended its meeting by endorsing a series of resolutions to Congress, including requests for the federal government to fund a $5 billion work relief program and to loan money to cities on the verge of bankruptcy.[7]

While the mayors were calling for a dramatic break from past policy, their proposals were not unprecedented. Federal aid for the unemployed was certainly not a novel idea for Jacob Coxey, who attended Murphy's Detroit gathering in his role as mayor of Massillon, Ohio. Thirty-eight years earlier, during the depression of the 1890s, Coxey led a national march on Washington. "Coxey's Army" came to demand that President Cleveland and Congress institute a federal work relief program. At that time, the concept of federal aid for social welfare seemed so radical that Coxey was arrested merely for attempting to speak on the steps of the Capitol.[8]

The length and depth of the Great Depression provided the mayors a better opportunity to challenge conventional wisdom than had been available to Jacob Coxey and his followers forty years before. Even so, many people, especially in the business community, clung to a traditional concept of American federalism. As late as the third winter of the Depression—when an estimated 24 percent of the labor force was without any job whatsoever and over half those still employed were working part-time—the idea that federal funding of social welfare would undermine the vitality of states and localities and thereby sap the strength of the nation as a whole still commanded a strong following. In early 1932, the National Association of Manufacturers railed that such an intrusion by the federal government would reduce the states to "mendicant provinces awaiting Federal philanthropy."[9] President Herbert Hoover was one of those who believed that direct federal help for relief costs threatened "the roots of self-government."[10] Nevertheless, as economic circumstances became more dire and he struggled to preserve the possibility of a second term, Hoover did move to involve the federal government in public welfare efforts. The program he developed would inadvertently initiate a dramatic shift in the structure of local public finance.

Hoover's Contribution to Building the Local Quasi-Public Sector

As is well known, Hoover preached a gospel of local responsibility in response to growing demands from states and cities for assistance from the national government. Indeed, his many pronouncements on the importance of maintaining "the spirit of charity and mutual self-help through voluntary giving and the responsibility of local government" are commonly cited to explain his resistance to using federal funds to aid local relief efforts.[11] Despite such rhetoric, his bedrock objective seems to have been keeping federal spending in check. Not unreasonably, since private capital was the lifeblood of the economy, the president believed that shaken investors needed to be reassured for recovery to begin. More problematically, given the lack of demand at the time, Hoover assumed that a balanced federal budget would provide that reassurance and generate a spurt of private investment. Whatever the accuracy of his analysis, Hoover never wavered in his conviction that "nothing is more important than balancing the budget with the least increase in taxes."[12]

Despite the president's commitment to his economic principles, constituent pressure rather than abstract theory drove events in the nation's capital. In January 1932, Hoover publicly bemoaned the "flood of extravagant proposals" for emergency aid then under consideration in Congress and exhorted both houses to abandon the "spirit of spending" these bills represented. But in the months ahead, as protests mounted around the country, Congress became only more determined to launch some kind of program to aid the unemployed. In March a hunger demonstration at Ford Motor Company's River Rouge plant resulted in the deaths of four participants and injuries to sixty. Days later thousands of angry Detroit residents joined a huge funeral procession that moved through the city to the strains of the "Internationale." In May veterans from across the country began their so-called Bonus March toward the Capitol. This was the third march on Washington since December, an unprecedented expression of discontent given that the only previous demonstration of the kind in the nation's history was the advance of Coxey's Army during the depression of the 1890s. That same month, when conservative Democrats in Congress withdrew support for the administration position, Hoover decided he had to come forward with his own proposal for local aid, if only to head off what he perceived as disastrous alternatives.[13]

Yet even when forced to capitulate on the principle of keeping the federal government out of public welfare activities, the president was still not prepared to abandon his core commitment, which was no new federal outlays. His solution, ultimately embodied in the Emergency Relief and Construction Act (ERCA) of July 1932, was a plan by which the federal government would lend, with interest, money to states and localities. Two kinds of loans were authorized. The first, for which $300 million was allocated, was directed at the states, so they could provide relief for the needy and destitute. The relief loans would be repaid by deductions from future annual state highway grants to which the federal government had already committed. The second kind of loan, authorized for up to $1.5 billion, was for income-producing public works initiated by government entities of any kind. These loans would be repaid entirely from income generated by the facilities the loans had financed. Hoover described such loans as "self-liquidating," by which he meant they would pay for themselves.[14]

The president had high hopes for his public works plan. He envisioned it stimulating a "huge expansion" of economic activity, while not pushing the federal budget into deficit (at least, not technically). Clearly delighted by the cleverness of the scheme, Hoover practically gushed in a letter to the American Society of Civil Engineers that the program "requires no Congressional appropriation, does not unbalance the budget, is not a drain upon the Treasury, does not involve the direct issue of government bonds, [and] does not involve added burdens upon the taxpayer either now or in the future."[15]

The Reconstruction Finance Corporation (RFC) was to make the loans. As noted in chapter 4, the RFC was the government-owned bank Congress had chartered early in 1932 at the president's urging. Hoover had conceived of the RFC as a temporary expedient, loaning money to railroads and financial institutions unable to secure capital through normal channels, and then going out of business after a couple of years at most. Instead, starting with Hoover's relief and public works legislation and continuing through the Second World War, Congress and the president would continually find it practical to assign the Reconstruction Finance Corporation new tasks, increase its capital, and extend its existence. With the passage of the Emergency Relief and Construction Act, the RFC's mandate expanded to include making loans to entities within the public sector.

Given the fierce opposition that in earlier years had greeted efforts by local governments to undertake activities that involved buying and selling, Hoover's public works program provides tacit but powerful evidence that such activities were no longer controversial in principle. The plan not only assumed that municipalities would engage in commercial ventures, but actually pushed desperate local governments to embark on them as the basic condition for receiving emergency help. ERCA program officers could not even consider projects that resulted in traditional public goods freely available to everyone, such as parks and schools, but only initiatives that would result in saleable commodities. By 1932, neither the president nor anyone else seems to have found that dimension of the plan even worthy of comment, much less criticism.

What did provoke criticism was that ERCA hardly functioned. By the end of November, four months after going into effect, the program had advanced less than $1 million of the $1.5 billion that had been earmarked for it. At the end of its eleven months of existence—it was taken over in June 1933 by the New Deal's Public Works Administration (PWA)—Hoover's initiative had managed to disperse only $30 million, a mere 2 percent of its allocated funds. Observers were livid. The *New Republic* lambasted RFC lawyers for "stick[ing] all the pins they can through every project submitted," while Senator Robert Wagner bemoaned the "mile after mile of red tape." Despite the program's overall sluggishness, the RFC did approve two multimillion-dollar projects in California on the eve of the presidential election. Livid political opponents accused the administration of "Buying California for Hoover."[16]

In truth it was not finicky lawyers, too many forms, or partisan politics that prevented federal money from flowing to the local level. Hoover's public works legislation turned out to be unworkable for two entirely different reasons: first, the nature of public services at the local level, and second, the institutional realities of public finance. With regard to the first, a high proportion of facilities needed and desired by citizens, such as public school buildings and parks, were not easily adaptable to a fee-for-service model, and others that could readily commoditize at least some of their services could never pay for themselves entirely along the lines of Hoover's conception of "self-liquidating" public works.

Actually, few public construction projects fit the model envisioned by Hoover's ERCA, as Paul V. Betters, executive director of the recently organized United States Conference of Mayors, tried to explain to Congress a few months after the law went into effect. Testifying in early 1933 before the Senate Committee on Banking and Currency, which was considering ways to rework the ERCA into a functioning program, Betters used the example of municipal water systems. At first glance it would seem that these operations would be perfect for running on a commercial basis, since users could be asked to pay for the amount they consumed. But in fact, waterworks could not be run in this fashion, since they had to be engineered to provide water not just for domestic and business consumption but also for firefighting. If homes and businesses were charged enough to defray the costs of water mains large enough for this purpose, rates would be exorbitant. Thus, the prevailing practice was to charge off part of the cost against general tax revenues. Milwaukee, for example, billed customers for only about 70 percent of the total cost of the water department. Cities with fewer customers calculated a higher proportion of overhead for fire protection. Betters said that in smaller Wisconsin cities, where he had precise figures, customers routinely paid for as little as half the cost of municipal water systems. The general tax levy covered the rest.[17]

The second reason that Hoover's legislation did not work was that it had been drafted with an insufficient understanding of the legal situation at the local level. The ERCA specified that the Reconstruction Finance Corporation make its public works loans by buying bonds backed by the future income of the capital improvements to be funded, in other words, revenue bonds. But few local governments, even if they managed to write plausible proposals, could legally offer such bonds. When Congress passed Hoover's urban aid package, only nineteen states had legislation on their books that allowed revenue-bond financing, and most of those statutes had been passed with specific projects in mind.[18] Nor could states rectify the situation quickly. In general, their legislative bodies were ineffectual. Turnover of elected officials was high, professional staffs practically nonexistent, and in any case, most state legislatures were simply not in session much, meeting for only a few weeks once every two years. In 1932 more than half never convened at all.[19]

The two giant California projects that received early ERCA funding from the ERCA program, the San Francisco–Oakland Bay Bridge and the Metropolitan Aqueduct, illustrate the situation. Each was being constructed by a parent organization that had been granted explicit approval by the state legislature to borrow on the basis of projected income long before Hoover ever thought about initiating a federal public works program. The California Toll Bridge Authority, in charge of the Bay Bridge, was authorized to issue revenue bonds at the time of its creation in 1929. The Metropolitan Water District of Southern California, builder of the Metropolitan Aqueduct (also known as the Colorado River Aqueduct), had been granted the right to tax and borrow in 1927. Contrary to the claims of outraged Democrats, it was preexisting borrowing authority, not partisan machinations, that explained why those projects received federal funding while other applications languished.[20]

Yet even as Hoover's public works program was stymied by the existing legal environment, it started to transform that environment. Lured by federal dollars, state legislatures began liberalizing their public finance laws. Quite promptly, considering the impediments to action, states began passing statutes that gave municipalities broad grants of power to finance projects using anticipated income as collateral for borrowing. During 1932 and 1933, fourteen states put statutes authorizing the use of revenue-bond financing on their books for the first time, while many of the nineteen that had previously allowed such financing in specific situations passed general enabling laws permitting local governments to issue bonds for specified categories of projects without having to ask the legislature for permission in each instance.[21]

This movement followed a fairly consistent pattern, even in states that were otherwise dissimilar. For example, in April 1933, soon after the Michigan legislature convened for the first time after the passage of Hoover's public works program, Republican state senator Felix Flynn cosponsored a bill specifically designed to take advantage of ERCA loans. Flynn told the press that he had "personal knowledge of projects involving an expenditure of $3,000,000" that would be possible if the bill passed. The bill authorized any political subdivision of the state (including cities, townships, counties, special districts, and school districts) to build projects and "to issue self-liquidating revenue bonds, payable solely from the revenues derived from the operation of such project[s]." The list of acceptable endeavors was long and varied, including housing, garbage disposal plants, sewer systems, public markets and storage buildings, merchandise marts, yacht basins, harbors, docks, wharves, terminal installations, "bridges over, tunnels under, ferries across rivers, streams and/or channels," stadiums, convention halls, auditoriums, dormitories, hospitals, parks, and recreation facilities. The legislation stipulated that the revenue bonds issued for these projects would "not be subject to any limitations or provisions provided by the laws of the state," which meant that the debt caps or procedural requirements that a government unit would normally have to deal with when floating a bond issue did not apply. Flynn's bill moved through the legislature with dispatch. At the end of May, the *Detroit Free Press* reported its passage on page one with the headline CITIES WILL GET CASH FOR JOBS.[22]

In South Carolina the response to the possibility of ERCA loans was quite similar, despite that state's very different political and economic environment. Here, too, the legislature eagerly embraced its opportunities. A bill passed in May 1933 authorized localities to "adopt ordinances providing for the issuance of revenue bonds." The South Carolina legislation allowed for all the kinds of projects enumerated in the Michigan bill and more—even specifically mentioning ice plants, which as we saw in chapter 3 were a flash point for municipal enterprise before mechanical refrigeration.[23] As in Michigan, South Carolina specifically exempted revenue bonds from any legal constraints that applied to full-faith and credit borrowing.

The New Deal's Contribution to Building the Local Quasi-Public Sector

The New Deal's Public Works Administration (PWA) took over Hoover's program and made it work. Title II of the National Industrial Recovery Act authorized the president to set up the PWA to take over public works from the Reconstruction Finance Corporation, which Roosevelt did in the summer of 1933.[24] While the PWA became the lead agency in the field of public works, the Reconstruction Finance Corporation never left the field entirely. The RFC continued to oversee projects originally green-lighted under ERCA, and it functioned as something of an investment banker for its replacement agency by selling bonds the Public Works Administration acquired as collateral for loans, thereby refreshing the PWA's budget so it could continue to initiate new projects without having to seek new budget appropriations from Congress. This was possible because in 1934 Congress granted the PWA the power to operate its budget as a revolving fund, which gave it some of the financial autonomy enjoyed by corporate agencies.[25]

That the PWA was more successful than ERCA is not surprising. The PWA's enabling legislation allowed it to offer terms that were not just more generous, but more realistic. In contrast with its predecessor, the PWA was not constrained to offer loans only for projects that were able to pay for themselves completely. Along with making loans, the PWA was allowed to provide outright grants of up to 30 percent. A rule change in 1935 made possible grants of 45 percent. As we have seen, many local projects, while generating revenues, were not fully adaptable to a fee-for-service model, so the provisions for grants allowed them to be funded. Moreover, PWA loans came with lower interest rates. Whereas the RFC began by setting minimum rates at 5.5 percent, eventually settling on 5 percent for most loans, the PWA charged 4 percent.[26]

Even more significant than the better financial incentives, the PWA was administered by people with a greater understanding of the institutional environment in which the program had to function. Harvey Couch, who headed the ERCA program under the RFC, was a brilliant Arkansas businessman who had built a financial empire in telephones, electricity, and railroads from almost nothing. Yet he possessed little familiarity with the legal intricacies of local government. By contrast, Harold Ickes, the PWA administrator, was a lawyer who came to Franklin D. Roosevelt's cabinet with close to four decades of experience fighting for municipal reform in Chicago. With this background, Ickes quickly recognized the need for a large legal division with particular expertise in public bonds. Ultimately he assembled a legal staff of 170 lawyers—more than any federal agency outside the Justice Department.[27]

Ickes's focus on the need for legal talent was not misplaced. Although critics of the PWA's slow pace have generally offered psychological explanations—specifically the self-described Old Curmudgeon's tendencies for defensive micromanagement—in truth, Ickes faced the same daunting institutional barriers that had stymied Hoover's administrators. While the possibility of securing money from the federal government spurred a few state legislatures to revamp their restrictive debt laws effectively, most lacked the expertise for what was truly a daunting task. A 1932 report by New York's State Tax Commission described the accumulated additions to that state's tax code over the years as "a veritable hodge-podge of cumbersome exemptions and exceptions, one sentence alone containing more than 400 words. Furthermore, many of these new provisions were inserted without recasting the other clauses, thus complicating the whole structure so that it is difficult to read and more difficult to understand."[28]

As if the statutory thicket was not enough of a challenge, those states with borrowing limitations written into their constitutions faced a seemingly insurmountable barrier to accessing federal loans. Enterprising public officials in Washington State did come up with one creative solution. In 1933 the legislature passed a $10 million bond issue on the basis of a constitutional provision that permitted overriding the debt limit in case of public danger. In the words of one skeptical public finance expert, "Nothing can be more sure than that the dangers of depression were not present in the minds of the framers of this exception." Nevertheless, the state's supreme court went along, declaring that "any rational mind" would agree that it was "better to cure insurrection or incipient insurrection by promoting prosperity rather than by the use of bullets." Washington's "bonds instead of bullets" approach did not turn out to be a universal panacea, however. Colorado's high court turned back a similar attempt by its legislature the same year, ruling that since no attack by force of arms was imminent, no borrowing was necessary "to defend the State." In the end, no other state was successful with the Evergreen State's strategy.[29]

For its part, the PWA also explored innovative methods by which states and municipalities could borrow. At first the PWA tried ad hoc tactics, such as accepting tax anticipation warrants and special assessment bonds from municipalities that could not borrow by issuing general-obligation bonds, arrangements that state courts were sometimes willing to allow. In other cases the PWA employed a leasing strategy, as when it loaned $1.5 million to Wayne County, Michigan, to build four trash incinerators needed by the city of Detroit. Since Detroit was already over its legal debt limit, Wayne County served as the borrower of record, planning to rent the facilities to the city. The arrangement set off a legal battle, however. Taxpayer groups challenged the deal all the way to the Michigan Supreme Court, and while the court ruled in favor of the city, the litigation postponed construction and cost the PWA valuable staff time. The difficulties involving the Detroit incinerators illustrates why the PWA was anxious to find methods for enlarging state and local borrowing capacity that were less potentially vulnerable and more routinized.[30]

Revenue bonds were the preferred strategy. The RFC, just on the basis of the types of loans it offered, had already started the ball rolling with regard to reshaping the legal landscape for municipal borrowing. But revision of bond codes needed to happen fast for the states to be able to participate in the emergency public works program, and many states had little professional expertise on which to draw. So rather than wait, Ickes threw his legal team into action. PWA lawyers partnered with state attorneys and municipal corporation counsels across the country to frame bills easing restrictions on borrowing, primarily through permitting the use of revenue bonds.

By 1937, PWA lawyers had drafted nearly five hundred suggested bills, and every state but two had adopted some or all of the recommended legislation. These bills were not formulaic one-size-fits-all products: each state required an extensive investigation of its constitutional and statutory law and judicial precedents so that the laws would pass muster in the courts.[31] PWA administrator Ickes was not exaggerating when he told Congress that "the Public Works Administration has probably been the most important single factor responsible for the recent trend toward the use of revenue bonds as a method of financing municipal public service enterprises."[32]

Another way in which the PWA greased the wheels for revenue-bond financing was by helping to develop the market for new and unfamiliar financial products. This was a self-conscious strategy. As one PWA report noted, the success of these instruments would be determined not only by the earning record of the facilities financed by them, "but also by the extent to which bond dealers become interested in purchasing and distributing such issues."[33] PWA activity publicized the revenue-bond mechanism, and the agency's reputation for rigorous oversight legitimated these financial instruments in the eyes of bond dealers and investors who had previously shown little interest. As the *American Political Science Review* reported in 1935, the PWA

> retained the right to approve in detail all the plans and specifications for the projects undertaken, and insisted upon rigid inspection of the work and auditing of the accounts and financial transactions. The government insisted through these contracts not only that the projects should be sound from an engineering point of view, but that the contract prices paid should be reasonable and that the cities should get their money's worth.[34]

Not surprisingly, this kind of minute supervision spurred investor confidence. When the RFC put the securities the PWA had accepted as collateral up for sale in the open market, purchasers readily stepped forward. Often there was a tidy profit, as for example, when the RFC got $104,000 for Evanston, Illinois, waterworks revenue bonds that the PWA had purchased for $77,000.[35] (By 1950 the RFC had cleared a net profit of $53 million on the $651 million worth of bonds it had purchased from the PWA.)[36] In effect, PWA supervision transformed revenue bonds into a standardized commodity, of known and uniform value, which therefore could be widely traded.

Revenue bonds were a methodology by which to achieve desired outcomes, first and foremost the evasion of legal constraints on borrowing. As useful as they were, they had limitations. The biggest was that some states counted any bond issues, including ones for self-supporting projects, against the debt limits of sponsoring governments. Thus, to achieve the desired results, it was sometimes necessary to create whole new government units, not just funding instruments. To meet the limitation of debt ceilings applying even to revenue bonds, the PWA and President Roosevelt personally promoted the template for what would become known as the public authority. In 1934, Roosevelt sent a letter to all forty-eight governors urging them to draw on the expertise of the Public Works Administration's Legal Division to liberalize municipal finance laws so they could take advantage of federal credit "at least for the duration of the existing emergency." The president's first recommendation was for a simplification of regulations so that municipalities could borrow more freely. But where this was not feasible, he suggested that they set up legal machinery to permit the creation of what he called "municipal improvement authorities" or "non-profit benefit corporations," which he defined as legally independent instrumentalities that could finance themselves by issuing revenue bonds.[37] In essence, Roosevelt and the PWA were endorsing an organizational template that combined the funding strategy of revenue bonds with the organizational structure of special districts stripped of their power to levy taxes. Given that public authorities were legally separate from the governments that created them and had no taxing power, these institutional structures—it was successfully argued in the courts—should not be constrained by constitutional or statutory limitations on traditional government borrowing.[38]

Some such mechanisms did exist before the Depression. As described in chapter 3, starting in the late nineteenth century, local public officials had developed the basic building blocks of public authorities—special districts and revenue bonds—as they experimented with various ways of circumventing the fiscal constraints that blocked their ability to expand urban services and amenities. For example, in 1921 these features were combined in the New York Port Authority, which gained widespread recognition by virtue of its ability to mount major infrastructure projects without recourse to government taxing power. Its most dramatic early achievement was the George Washington Bridge. Completed ahead of schedule and under budget, the bridge was almost entirely self-financed with revenue bonds. At the dedication ceremony for the bridge, in 1931, Governor Roosevelt praised the Port Authority as a "model for government agencies throughout the land." Roosevelt was being sincere. To oversee one of his key priorities, noncommercial development of hydroelectric power along the St. Lawrence River, he proposed a government corporation designed along the lines of the New York Port Authority. The legislature approved the establishment of the New York State Power Authority in 1931. By this time, these kinds of semiautonomous units, set up outside the regular structure of government and authorized to borrow against future earnings, were being established in other parts of the country.[39] The California Toll Bridge Authority and the Metropolitan Water District of Southern California, mentioned earlier, are two examples. Indeed, such units were common enough that the Hoover administration-sponsored Emergency Relief and Construction Act of 1932 included "public corporations, boards, and commissions" in its list of local and state public bodies eligible for self-liquidating loans.[40]

The efforts of Buffalo, New York, to upgrade its sewer system demonstrates how and why the public authority device gained traction during the New Deal. Starting in the nineteenth century, with the construction of its first sewers, Buffalo had been dumping its raw waste straight into Lake Erie, where it subsequently drained into the Niagara River and then Lake Ontario. A 1909 treaty with Canada committed cities around the Great Lakes to treat their sewage before discharging it, and by the 1920s, Chicago, Milwaukee, Toledo, Cleveland, and Detroit had taken steps to comply. But Buffalo, given its debt cap, could not raise the estimated $15 million to construct the required treatment facilities. In the early 1930s, Governor Franklin Roosevelt, the New York State Health Department, and the Canadian government all clamored for Buffalo to take action. Still the city failed to act, blocked by what the *New York Times* described as the "the ogre of limitation of bond indebtedness." Even an outright grant of $6.7 million from the Public Works Administration could not vanquish the ogre. The city was too close to its constitutional debt ceiling to be able to borrow enough to close the gap.[41] Offering revenue bonds to the federal government, rather than standard municipal securities, was not a solution. A recent state law had cut off that work-around with the unequivocal directive that "a city shall have no power to issue obligations to which it has not pledged its faith and credit for payment of the principal and interest thereof."[42]

To solve the problem, PWA lawyers worked with Buffalo's corporation council to draft legislation creating an entirely new government agency, independent from the city, that would not be subject to state laws limiting municipal borrowing. In April 1935 the New York State Legislature chartered the Buffalo Sewer Authority as a "public benefit corporation" authorized "to provide an effectual means for relieving the Niagara river, Buffalo river and Lake Erie from pollution by sewage and waste." The authority was given the power to borrow up to $15 million against future income. It would be managed by a board of five members appointed by the mayor and confirmed by the common council. As envisioned in its enabling legislation, the Buffalo Sewer Authority was to be a temporary expedient. It would exist for "only five years," after which it would pass "all its rights and properties" to the city of Buffalo, except in the event that it took longer than five years to meet its liabilities, including paying off its bonds.[43]

That public authorities would later become ubiquitous was not obvious during the 1930s when the template was first gaining a foothold nationally within the nurturing legal and financial environment created by the PWA and RFC. Some doubted these entities had any future at all once the federal government stopped its loan programs. But in the postwar period, public authorities stepped out on their own.

Toll roads provided the transition. The pioneer was the Pennsylvania Turnpike, which received support from the PWA and RFC. It opened in 1940 and achieved higher-than-expected usage. Private investors snapped up its bonds. Following this success, other states set up their own authorities to build and operate limited-access highway systems, and these bonds also fared well in capital markets.[44] Meanwhile, private investment in authority bonds of all kinds was encouraged by changing patterns of taxation. Wartime increases in the income tax (and changes that enhanced its progressivity) increased the appeal of holding the debt instruments of authorities, since interest income from public authority revenue bonds, like that from state and municipal bonds, was exempt from federal taxation. (Earlier there had been some question about whether the federal exemption would always be in place, but after court decisions in the mid-1940s quashed the efforts of the Roosevelt administration to tax the interest on securities of the New York Port Authority and the Triborough Bridge Authority, the immunity of income from public authority bonds has been accepted as settled law.)[45]

The Ambiguity of Government-Sponsored Economic Activity

Under the pressure of the Great Depression, the federal government opened the floodgates for the kind of democratically unaccountable government units that would become a large, if little-understood, sector of economic activity in the United States. Casting around for a way to aid localities that would be cost-free to the federal government, Hoover unintentionally initiated a movement that would markedly change the institutional structure of subfederal public finance. This was a movement that the PWA would carry forward with energy and expertise, not in order to carry out a federal public works program cost-free, but in order to carry one out at all.

The public authority strategy may have been the only realistic alternative the New Dealers had for aiding local governments quickly, but it is also the case that elements of Hoover's vision appealed to them. While President Roosevelt and leading members of his administration did not share Hoover's vision of a fee-for-service public sector, the reality is that many of them—including the President—were sincere fiscal conservatives, as historian Julian Zelizer has pointed out. As such, they preferred alternatives to direct spending whenever they could find them. Roosevelt's willingness to run deficits during the Depression came out of a sense of responsibility to alleviate mass suffering, not out of any idea of compensatory fiscal policy.[46] Thus, a public works program that would provide employment and build needed facilities, while at least partly paying for itself, had real appeal.

By this time, as described in chapter 3, the legality of municipal enterprise had been established, and the main institutional barrier to public ownership of economic enterprises was a procrustean bed, laid down decades earlier, of ad hoc regulations against borrowing. The other big obstacle was access to capital markets. Local governments had never had an easy time selling their bonds in national markets where investors had little information about the security of such investments. And during an economic downturn, what private parties in their right mind would want to invest in bonds backed by taxing power as property tax levies plummeted? The solution to both problems was an adaptation of Hoover's scheme: independent revenue-producing bodies that would pay for themselves by borrowing against their future earnings streams. On the one hand, such bodies could evade legal rules that constrained municipalities from borrowing in any situation; on the other, they could mobilize private capital, when conditions improved, by offering standardized, tax-advantaged debt instruments with which investors were familiar and comfortable.

Thus it was that in the 1930s, spurred by the most extreme economic collapse the country had ever experienced, the federal government initiated institutional changes in the structure of state and local government that would have far-reaching and problematic impacts. While the public authority made it possible for subfederal governments to break free of their fiscal straightjackets and provide financing for capital expenditures that provided jobs and needed infrastructure during the Depression, this mechanism also opened the door to a byzantine world of public finance that both increases the costs and undermines the accountability of government activity. This is the story that will be traced in the next chapter.

SIX

Public Authorities since the Second World War

After the Second World War, trends in the use of authority-type agencies diverged markedly at different levels of American government. At the federal level, the number dropped, although it can be said to have held roughly steady if one counts the new legally independent entities that serve similar purposes. At the state and local level, however, the number exploded. This chapter explores the reasons for and consequences of these two trajectories.

Authority Structures at the National Level

Government corporations lost popularity in the postwar era. The shift happened quickly. From a high of forty-seven during the war, the number dropped to thirty by 1960.[1] The devolution consisted primarily of dismantling incorporated administrative units set up specifically to support industrial mobilization during wartime and looks like a normal post-emergency phenomenon. It is the lack of interest in setting up new agencies—only two were created in the 1950s—that is puzzling.

Why did federal-level incorporated agencies fall out of favor? One factor was the constraints that had been placed on these institutions. As described in chapter 4, Roosevelt made efforts during his second term to better integrate government corporations into the executive branch by bringing them under general management rules, and the Government Corporation Control Act of 1945 mandated more congressional oversight, including the requirement that all corporate instrumentalities be chartered by Congress, rather than being incorporated in a state. Thus, in the postwar era federal officials found it more laborious to set up and operate corporate agencies. But the new controls were not particularly onerous, nor were they rigorously applied; they would not have stopped the formation of new corporations if there had still been a strong desire to use them. Why the lack of desire?

One reason was the advent of more attractive options for achieving many of the same ends. The new possibilities emerged from experiences during the Second World War. The government's strategy of assembling teams of scientists and engineers to pursue military research at national laboratories such as Oak Ridge and Los Alamos had been highly successful. The national laboratories were government-owned, but contractor-managed, which meant they were not constrained by civil service rules or general management regulations that applied to the executive branch. Afterward, the military services were loath to part with the kind of expertise that had been available at these installations and came up with the idea of setting up private, nonprofit corporations as a way of creating permanent scientific establishments. By working through these organizations, the services could better compete with the private sector in terms of ease of hiring, pay, and working conditions for top scientific and technical talent.[2]

The RAND Corporation became the prototype for this new class of organizations, termed Federally Funded Research and Development Centers (FFRDCs). Project RAND (an acronym for research and development) began in 1946 as a division of Douglas Aircraft Company, where it was supported by a $10 million contract from the air force to research the possibilities for intercontinental warfare based on advances the Germans had made in long-range missile technology. Later RAND would become best known for its work in systems analysis, a branch of applied mathematics used in policy development. Within a short time after it began, Douglas's Project RAND became controversial. Other weapons manufacturers complained that they were being put at a competitive disadvantage, and in 1948 the operation was spun off as a nonprofit corporation under the laws of California.[3]

This organizational template—the privately owned but government-funded corporate entity that performed tasks exclusively for its sponsoring federal agency—was quickly adopted by other parts of the military establishment. Meanwhile, civilian agencies, primarily but not exclusively the Department of Energy and its predecessor the Atomic Energy Commission, followed suit. By 2010 the universe of FFRDCs included such varied entities as the National Astronomy and Ionosphere Center, sponsored by the National Science Foundation; the Jet Propulsion Lab, sponsored by the National Aeronautics and Space Administration; Fermi National Accelerator Laboratory, sponsored by the Department of Energy; and the Center for

Advanced Aviation System Development, sponsored by the Department of Transportation and the Federal Aviation Administration; in addition to a myriad of military-related research organizations. Clearly, military purposes dominate the FFRDCs, but perhaps less than first appears, since some have taken on diverse functions. The Los Alamos National Laboratory, for example, is now a leading center for research on HIV, and the Lawrence Berkeley National Laboratory has not taken on classified research since the 1970s.[4]

In many ways the FFRDCs can be seen as the functional equivalents of government corporations, providing administrators the ability to pursue projects over multiyear periods without the uncertainties of the annual congressional appropriation cycle, to hire for and manage projects without having to deal with a rigid regulatory scheme designed for more routine bureaucratic activities, and to launch new projects without first obtaining cumbersome legislative approval. Also, the legal form of federally sponsored nonprofits is similar to the early federal corporations chartered under state law.[5] Even though the 1945 Government Corporation Control Act required federal officials to get congressional approval to establish corporate instrumentalities, Congress did not object to the practice of incorporating such centers in the states. Indeed, Congress gave the FFRDCs little oversight until the 1980s, when some rules were imposed on the creation and use of these entities.[6] Because of these similarities, the rise of FFRDCs may go far to explain the declining use of traditional government corporations in the federal establishment after the Second World War.

As for federal corporations themselves, the decline has continued. By 2009, the Congressional Research Service counted only seventeen. However, in this same year, the National Science Foundation, which keeps statistics on FFRDCs, listed forty-one.[7] Thus, the total number of quasi-government agencies at the federal level is not dramatically different from what it was in the 1930s and 1940s—albeit with a more military slant than in the 1930s.

Even though corporate agencies are no longer a growth category within the federal bureaucracy, they do not seem poised for extinction. Most analysts—however they evaluate these institutional mechanisms—tend to agree with the conclusion expressed in the 2006 study by the Congressional Research Service: "The future of government corporations . . . appears generally bright." The enduring strength of these structures stems from their ability to achieve objectives not easily obtainable by other means. This remains true even as the institutional and ideological environment has shifted.[8]

While alternatives now exist, using FFRDCs and other kinds of contracting arrangements, to escape central management rules such as unrealistically low ceilings on personnel and compensation, the government corporation still offers policy makers unique advantages for evading legal barriers to action. This is particularly the case with regard to the new institutional environment relating to the federal budget. Congressional attempts since the 1960s to cut or at least slow the growth of the federal budget by setting fixed targets means that independent corporate agencies have become convenient devices for moving spending and borrowing off-budget. A good example is the creation by the George H. W. Bush administration and Congress in 1989 of the Resolution Trust Corporation (RTC) and its financing agency, the Resolution Funding Corporation (REFCORP), to deal with the losses incurred by the widespread failures of savings and loan associations. (This intervention was estimated to cost $190 billion in 2008 dollars.) As Harold Seidman, arguably the most influential public administration scholar of the late twentieth century, summed up the situation, "Once a device is discovered for beating the system and minimizing political and fiscal accountability, it is certain to be exploited for all types of legitimate and illegitimate purposes."[9]

In recent years, with the rise of an international governmental reform movement based on theories of "entrepreneurial" public administration, the government corporation template has come to be valued for more than its usefulness in "beating the system." Conceptions about "third way" institutions that could function between traditional public/private boundaries gained traction in Britain in the 1980s under the influence of Margaret Thatcher and were popularized in the United States by David Osborne and Ted Gaebler in their 1992 book *Reinventing Government*. From this ideological standpoint, the template of the congressionally chartered agency—operating outside the normal regulatory structure of federal administration and able to charge user fees for services—took on new relevance. Proponents argued that government corporations were ideal vehicles by which to deliver social and economic services more flexibly and responsively, while costing the taxpayer less.[10]

The Clinton administration's effort to upgrade the administrative capabilities of the federal government, led by Vice President Albert Gore, was deeply influenced by these ideas. Indeed, Gore's National Performance Review (NPR) was commonly referred to as "Reinventing Government." Two of the NPR's earliest proposals were to semiprivatize the Federal Aviation Administration by creating an Air Traffic Services Corporation and to hive off the business aspects of the General Services Administration into a

Real Property Management Enterprise. Other NPR suggestions for reforming specific federal agencies, while not specifying formal incorporation, called for moving them closer to the template of the government corporation in that they were to be deregulated and encouraged to generate income through commercial activities.[11] Although the National Performance Review's proposals for creating new corporate agencies did not succeed in the 1990s, the ideological climate of the early twenty-first century continues to favor the creation of self-funding institutions that operate outside the regulatory constraints of the executive branch. This sensibility can take surprising forms, as when the conservative Heritage Foundation adopted a trademark New Deal initiative as a role model with a 2007 call "to take the [Air Traffic Control] system out of the federal budget process and make it a self-supporting entity, . . . analogous to the Tennessee Valley Authority (TVA)."[12]

Proliferation and Modification at the Subfederal Level

In marked contrast with the situation at the federal level, the years following the Second World War saw a tremendous expansion of semi-independent, incorporated agencies at the state and local level of American government. For his 1960 doctoral dissertation in political science, Nathaniel S. Preston identified close to eighteen hundred state and local public authorities then in operation. Of this total, approximately 80 percent of the ones for which Preston could determine a founding date had been created after the end of the Second World War.[13] New kinds emerged, but the biggest difference between the authorities of the early postwar period and those of the 1930s was not in how they functioned, but in their source of investment capital. During the 1930s, the federal government, working through the Public Works Administration (PWA) and the Reconstruction Finance Corporation (RFC), was essentially the only source of capital. But in the postwar era authorities were readily able to raise funds in private money markets. Revenue bonds had become a familiar and trusted product for private investors in good part because of the way the Public Works Administration had closely supervised these financial instruments during the 1930s.

Toll roads provided the most dramatic example of the new relationship between authorities and private capital markets. Not that this outcome was predictable in the 1930s. The Pennsylvania Turnpike Commission's attempt, in early 1938, to raise funds with a public offering of revenue bonds fell flat. Investors had little faith that tolls alone would be sufficient to cover the substantial costs of constructing high-speed, limited-access highways, particularly when built to standards that would accommodate heavy trucks as well as cars. Financing had to come from the government. The RFC bought $40.8 million worth of bonds, topping up the PWA's outright grant of $29 million.

Confounding skeptics, the turnpike turned out to be enormously popular and a significant revenue generator. The long lines of motorists when it first opened in the fall of 1940 could be explained by curiosity, but not the continued heavy traffic. With tolls based on $1.50 for the full 160 miles of the original section of the highway, the turnpike's revenues topped a half million dollars in its first three months. During the first year, 2.4 million vehicles used the turnpike: nearly twice the original projection by the planners who had advocated the project as financially feasible.[14] Suddenly it became clear that loans for tolled superhighways were an exceedingly secure investment, assuming prudent cost management and a route for which there was sufficient demand.

The financial success of the Pennsylvania Turnpike spurred other states to emulate the Keystone State. By 1953 six states had authorities that were operating toll highways (Maine, New Jersey, New York, Ohio, Oklahoma, and West Virginia); two had authorities that were beginning construction (Indiana and Massachusetts); and two more had authorized toll-road authorities that were not yet in operation (Florida and Georgia). That same year, ten more states passed legislation to establish such mechanisms or start feasibility studies. The New York Thruway Authority, which built the biggest and most expensive of these projects, the 535-mile express highway spanning the Empire State, had no trouble finding purchasers for its hundreds of millions of dollars' worth of bonds despite their low-interest rates. (The rate on the initial offering was only 1.1 percent!)[15] The surge of tolled superhighways—most financed by authorities—slacked only after Congress passed the Federal-Aid Highway Act of 1956, establishing an interstate system financed principally through gasoline and diesel fuel taxes.[16]

In the postwar era, public authorities were also regularly employed to finance and operate commercial undertakings of a more modest character than modern expressway systems. As in the 1930s, authorities were established to supply goods and services that had been for some time accepted as public utilities (e.g., water, sewers, natural gas, and electricity), although municipalities employed the authority mechanism for new tasks, as well. The most notable of these was the construction and operation of off-street facilities for urban parking. Miller McClintock, director of Harvard University's Bureau for Street Traffic Research, promoted the concept during the 1930s, and it caught on after the war. Major cities such as Pittsburgh, Baltimore, Richmond, San Francisco, Washington, DC, Chicago, and Detroit set up parking authorities in the late 1940s, often in tandem with other efforts to salvage the commercial viability of their urban cores. Many smaller cities—such as Springfield, Massachusetts, discussed in the introduction—followed suit. In only a few years, parking authorities became a ubiquitous feature of urban public administration.[17]

Public Authorities Where There's Nothing to Sell

A large proportion of the new postwar public authorities operated along the same lines as these kinds of bodies had earlier. Although they sold their revenue bonds in private investment markets and sometimes provided novel services like tolled expressways and parking garages, in terms of institutional structure they followed the well-known and widely used template that had crystallized during the New Deal era.

Yet much of what cities and states wanted to build after the war could not readily be made to produce income. The most visible case in the baby boom era was schools. According to a Council of State Governments' report from the early 1950s, the rising birth rate required the construction of hundreds of thousands of new elementary and high school classrooms. Another case was government office buildings, for which there was a "critical need" because of the rapid expansion of the state and local labor force.[18]

States and municipalities faced great challenges trying to provide these kinds of facilities given the fiscal limitations that had earlier impelled them toward public authorities: low debt caps and the difficulty of obtaining voter approval (often by supermarjorities) for incurring debt. Since much of the construction now desired could not generate user fees, the traditional authority model was of little help.

The situation prompted increasingly creative efforts on the part of hard-pressed public officials to produce (or seem to produce) streams of income against which to borrow so that revenue bonds could be issued and building projects proceed. The new round of institutional innovation resulted in techniques by which public authorities could tap into tax-based revenues yet avoid issuing full-faith and credit bonds. These innovations would eventually lead to a new stage in the history of public authorities: the advent of the financing authority, and its junior partner, the moral authority bond. Not only did these new templates spread, they became major features of subfederal public finance.

The creation of the Buffalo Sewer Authority during the Great Depression illustrates how the basic concept behind financing authorities represented an incremental evolution, rather than something wholly new. In chapter 5, we saw how water provision was not a truly divisible good, and therefore not a perfect candidate for traditional revenue-bond financing. A significant part of the requisites for a water system had to do, not with meeting the water needs of individual households and businesses, but with the needs of the fire department. Even if the fire department was charged for its usage, making it into a customer, the problem would not be solved, since safety in the face of fires requires a water system with a large excess capacity that will be seldom or (one hopes) never used. Buffalo was faced with this kind of reality when it had to find a way to pay for an expensive sewer treatment plant to end the city's pollution of the Niagara River. The city was too close to its legal borrowing limit to obtain the necessary funds by issuing its own bonds—even when the federal government offered to lend at low rates and sweeten the deal with grants. The plan to create an authority to take over the city's sewer system was a clever (if disingenuous) solution. As a separate legal entity with no legal limits on borrowing, the authority would be able to accept federal loans to modernize the system, and as a nice byproduct, bring desperately needed construction jobs to the city.

Despite these appealing features of the plan, the city's major property owners opposed it. They objected that the projected income against which the authority's bonds would be floated was to come from user fees levied on everyone with a water connection. This meant that while residents had previously paid with their taxes for sewer service, they were now going to be required to pay more for, as they saw it, the same thing. In addition, the legislation that established the authority turned over to it the city's existing six-hundred-mile system, so opponents charged that they would in effect be paying to use infrastructure they had already purchased with their tax dollars. Expressing outrage that nothing tangible would be forthcoming for Buffalo residents in return for the increased charges, Republican county committee chairman William J. Hickey told the press: "The claim is that it is necessary for the protection of the whole Niagara frontier and towns bordering on Lake Ontario, and that Buffalo should pay the shot."

Buffalo's United Taxpayers League went to court in an attempt to derail the formation of the authority. Raising the issue of the ambiguous distinction between taxes and fees, league president William E. Robertson protested that "the sewer rental feature of the Buffalo sewer authority bill would make the authority, in effect, a separate taxing body."[19] Although the state's highest court ruled against the league's challenge, the situation produced enough unease to become a major topic at the state's 1938 Constitutional Convention, where little support could be found for the way the sewer authority had been organized. Even former governor Al Smith, an enthusiastic proponent of using authority mechanisms to finance public works since his days on the board of the New York Port Authority in the early 1920s, dismissed the Buffalo Sewer Authority as nothing but a subterfuge to avoid triggering the city's debt cap, since it could not possibly produce enough commercial income to truly support itself. To the amusement of the delegates, he wisecracked that "a sewer can never be made a self-liquidating project."[20]

Smith's comment highlights the differences between the Buffalo Sewer Authority and an institutional structure like Cleveland's Muny Light, a city-owned electric utility operation that was actually self-supporting. While Buffalo's sewer authority could commoditize its product, it could not generate enough income to pay for its capital plant and operating expenses—nor was this the expectation of those who set it up. From the start, the sewer authority represented a backdoor strategy by which to finance public infrastructure not possible within existing legal constraints.

In the postwar period, officials developed the strategy further. The first stage was the building authority, based on techniques used in commercial lease financing. In the same way as traditional authorities, building authorities could borrow capital at lower cost than private companies because they could offer tax-free securities, while at the same time remaining free of debt limits or requirements for voter approval. Traditional public authorities used the facilities they financed and constructed to produce goods and services to be sold to the public. For example, an authority would build a bridge and then sell the right to transit this piece of property. The new authorities, by contrast, "leased" or "rented" what they built to the political jurisdictions that had commissioned the structures in the first place. Payment contracts were calculated to cover construction costs, interest, and a reserve fund over a fixed period, after which time title would be conveyed to the commissioning unit (although in some places, to avoid judicial objections, the ultimate transfer of title was not made explicit in the contract). It was the stream of rental payments that constituted the building authority's future income, on the basis of which revenue bonds were floated. This template was a financial and organizational innovation that allowed a new range of public purposes to be pursued.

In an early instance of this technique, the Michigan legislature created the Detroit-Wayne Joint Building Authority in 1949 to construct an administrative complex to be rented to Detroit and Wayne County over a period of thirty years, after which the two governments would take ownership of the property. The fact that two years earlier voters had rejected an $8 million bond issue to build the same facility demonstrated in stark terms how the building authority could function to evade pesky legal barriers to public borrowing.

Taxpayer groups went to court to stop the arrangement, contending that it was "an illegal method of circumventing the law and constitutional provisions," since in reality the authority's bonds were based on a pledge of public credit. Therefore, they argued, the payments promised to the authority should be considered debt, which according to the state constitution, the city and county had no right to assume without voter approval. Ruling against the plaintiffs, the Michigan Supreme Court held to a formal reading of the situation, determining that for legal purposes it was the authority that was to take on debt. With respect to the city and county, if contractual obligations were met from current revenues on a year-to-year basis, these could not, "in a constitutional sense," be considered debts. In yet another demonstration of the way the New Deal had set new public finance patterns in motion, the court drew on its 1937 opinion upholding the maneuver worked out by the Public Works Administration by which Wayne County borrowed federal money to build trash incinerators to be rented to the debt-burdened city of Detroit. In the 1949 decision, the court reiterated verbatim its previous conclusion that "there is no fraud in reaching a desired end by legal means even though some other means to the end would be illegal."[21]

Legal analysts derided the court's reasoning even while they expressed support for the real-world impact of the decision. One commentator, writing in the *Michigan Law Review*, criticized the way the court arrived at its decision, but conceded that the result was probably "laudable," since "debt limits do very often lead to inefficient methods of finance." In this situation, the writer concluded, when the thirty-year contract with the building authority ended, the city and county would end up owning a multimillion-dollar building for little more than what they would have paid to rent the needed space from private landlords over the same period.[22]

It would seem that the justices looked at the situation the same way. Indeed, it is hard to read the text of the decision, with its heartfelt description of the inadequacy of the existing facilities such as the city hall—"built over three-quarters of a century ago" when the city's population was twenty times smaller—and not come away persuaded that the justices were influenced by the outcome they perceived would best serve the public good, rather than simply the letter of the law. This impression is reinforced by the section in which they pointed out that the bond referendum, even though it had failed to garner the necessary two-thirds backing, did secure a majority.[23] (It is worth noting that none of the participants in this controversy ever brought up the fact that if the city and county had been able to build the facility themselves, borrowing on their own, the long-run cost to the public could have been lower than with any of the alternatives under consideration. This missing element in the discussion, and one that continues to be missing from similar discussions to this day, demonstrates the extent to which everyone accepted the archaic framework of public finance in which they operated as immutable.)

In the years that followed, building authorities gained popularity, especially in Pennsylvania, which pioneered the concept during the Great Depression in the face of some of the most draconian debt limits in the country. Governor George Earle, only the second Democrat to be elected to the Keystone State's highest office since the Civil War, was anxious to mount an ambitious public works program to modernize the state's infrastructure as well as to supply jobs. In 1935 his administration came up with the idea of a General State Authority, a legally independent entity that would be able to borrow federal money to construct and then lease to the state a range of facilities that were not commercially self-sustaining: armories, hospitals, teachers colleges, prisons, and office buildings.[24] The idea caught on at a local level, too, with municipalities setting up building authorities for various purposes. After the state, in 1951, authorized subsidies for school districts that rented classroom space from authorities or other nonprofit corporations, local school building authorities became especially popular. By 1960, there were over five hundred building authorities in this one state.[25]

Even President Dwight Eisenhower became a fan of building authorities. Perhaps he became familiar with the concept because of living part-time in the state where they were most plentiful, on his farm bordering the Gettysburg Battlefield. In any case, Eisenhower's initial plan for federal aid to education, outlined to Congress in February 1955, was based on federal loans and grants to state school building authorities. Calling these mechanisms "a tested method of accelerating school construction" in the face of "restrictive debt limits," he urged their wide adoption.[26]

The president's program was not adopted. Democrats, who had just taken control of both houses of Congress, viewed his request for a billion dollars over three years—overwhelmingly in the form of loans, with only $200 million in grants—to be "paltry" given the need. This was despite the fact that Eisenhower envisioned his plan spawning $7 billion in new spending because of the way authority bonds would be able to mobilize private capital. Lister Hill of Alabama, chair of the Senate Committee on

Education and Labor, was scathing in his dismissal of the proposal, calling it a "meager dole," which would only be available after "interminable delay."[27]

The delay to which the senator referred had to do with requiring states to have the requisite institutional mechanics in place before they could apply for federal money. The situation was reminiscent of the difficulty states and localities had participating in Hoover's Emergency Relief and Construction Act (ERCA) of 1932, because few states had the legal framework that allowed for the use of revenue bonds. In the case of Eisenhower's proposal for federal aid for classroom construction, states would have to pass statutes authorizing school building authorities, since they were uncommon at the time. Further complicating the issue, as in the 1930s, was the lack of capacity for quick and effective action at the state level. The *New York Times* story reporting the president's message noted that only fourteen state legislatures were scheduled to convene in 1956, when states would need to act in order to access federal funds if Eisenhower's proposals were enacted. In the 1930s, Harold Ickes and his staff quickly achieved widespread state adoption of a new institutional template; Eisenhower would have needed to match this feat, but there was skepticism about whether he could do so.[28]

Eisenhower's idea for using building authorities as the administrative machinery for a federal-aid-to-education program never caught on. To be fair, any plan for disbursing federal funds to the states for education was probably doomed from the start in this period. In the wake of the 1954 *Brown v. Board* decision, it was hardly likely Congress would approve sending school-aid money to the states without making it conditional on desegregation, and there was even less of a chance that powerful southern Democrats who headed key committees would agree to any funding formula that put their states under pressure to reform racial practices. The president urged that the program "be enacted on its own merits, uncomplicated by provisions dealing with the complex problems of integration," but his plea fell on deaf ears.[29]

Despite the failure of Eisenhower's substantive goal, the institutional strategy he advocated—using building authorities to evade legal barriers to state and local borrowing—turned out to be a winner. By 1960, at least thirty-one states were employing versions of this device to build state office buildings, armories, public schools, university facilities, or some combination thereof. Georgia and Florida were even using building authorities to construct non-tolled highways, which were then rented to the states' departments of transportation. Thus, in the end the template did spread, obviously not as a way of receiving money from Eisenhower's stillborn program, but because it met other needs of states and local governments.[30]

Meanwhile, public officials searching for more ways by which to take action were busy stripping down the building authority into an even more flexible and powerful tool. This was the pure financing authority, a vehicle that functioned simply to obtain low-cost capital in the tax-free municipal bond market for any public purpose involving the construction of new facilities.

Financing authorities proved to be the catalyst for yet another innovation: the so-called moral obligation bond. This financial instrument was essentially a revenue bond secured not only by income from the authority that issued it, but also by some kind of vaguely worded promise that if income was at any point insufficient to make scheduled payments to investors, the general-purpose government that had commissioned the investment would make up the shortfall. Since pledging the credit of a state or municipality without voter approval was illegal in most jurisdictions, such a promise could not be enforced by courts, as the bond covenants clearly stated. Therefore any such pledge was not a legal obligation. To describe the kind of commitment actually being made to investors, the credit rating agency Moody's called it a "moral obligation."[31]

In explanations of how this elaboration of the authority concept began, much has been made of the role of John Mitchell, the nationally prominent bond attorney who advised New York governor Nelson Rockefeller. Mitchell, who would go on to serve as President Nixon's attorney general and later be convicted and serve time in jail for his role in the Watergate cover-up, makes an especially good villain for those who attribute New York State's long-term fiscal problems largely to Rockefeller's enormous borrowing spree in the 1960s, which was facilitated by the moral authority device.[32]

The reality is more prosaic. As with so much of the story of the decades-long efforts to expand state capacity by evading existing statutory and constitutional controls on borrowing rather than changing them, this innovation occurred in an incremental, ad hoc manner, not as some conspiratorial grand plan. For example, the 1932 New York statute creating the State Bridge Authority to build the Rip Van Winkle Bridge over the Hudson specified that should any default occur, bondholders were required to wait until the end of the next legislative session before going to court. The implication was that the state might well come to the aid of the authority should it encounter financial difficulties.

The New York State Dormitory Authority was another agency that offered investors quasi guarantees in order to improve the terms on which it could borrow. The dormitory authority had begun life in the postwar era, building and managing residence halls for state colleges. Soon, however, it dropped its management arm and began operating as a contractor for a variety of public and nonprofit organizations in the state. In the late 1950s, in addition to the usual disclaimer about how authority debt was not a legal obligation of the state, the dormitory authority added to its bond covenants wording that promised that "the Authority would not fail to inform the State of any depletion in its bond reserves, and would ask the state for an appropriation to replenish them."[33]

Thus we see how Mitchell was merely taking the "moral obligation" concept one step further when, in 1960, he drafted the statute for the Housing Finance Agency (HFA). Created as a "public benefit corporation" (the legal term in New York State for a public authority), the HFA was set up to be the financing mechanism for the state's middle-income housing program, known as Mitchell-Lama. The HFA would go on to become a huge multipurpose state bank that by 1972 carried a debt load larger than that of the state itself, but initially Governor Rockefeller's goal for the agency was simply to implement Mitchell-Lama, which voters showed little interest in supporting through bond issues.[34]

The basic concept behind the Housing Finance Agency was to substitute subsidized private capital for direct government outlays. Using these funds, the agency would make mortgage loans at below-market rates to developers who agreed to build rental properties conforming to the program's specifications. To acquire the low-cost capital in the first place, the HFA would issue bonds backed by projected income from the mortgage loans. The only hitch was that investors tended to be nervous about real estate bonds and therefore demanded higher interest rates for them, which would undermine the whole plan. This is where Mitchell's background in the arcane legal specialty of tax-exempt securities came into play. He predicted that investors would be reassured by some kind of explicit statement, even if vague and legally nonbinding, to the effect that the state would stand behind the agency. Based on this belief, he included wording in the Housing Finance Agency's organic legislation implying that in the event that the agency ran into financial troubles, the governor would urge the legislature to appropriate funds sufficient to make all scheduled payments to bondholders. Mitchell's hunch proved correct, and HFA bonds sold briskly at low rates.[35]

The Role of Capital Markets and Courts

It needs to be kept in mind that the success of authority-type institutions that could not generate income streams from customers outside the government itself depended on the willingness of investors and courts to go along with how these entities skirted the spirit if not the letter of the law. For example, participants in the tax-exempt bond market can hardly be imagined to have believed that moral obligation bonds were actually secured by ethical sentiments. As one investment banker put it to a researcher, "If one of the state corporations defaulted on debt, it would resemble an elephant dying on the state house steps—the government would have to do something about it or suffer from the stench." The suffering to which he referred would result from the impact on the government's own credit rating when the investment community perceived it would not stand behind the debts of its agencies, regardless of whether it was actually responsible in a legal sense. Thus the true nature of the obligation was perceived on all sides to be practical, not moral.[36]

Courts, too, went along with the organizational and financial innovations involved in building and financing authorities. Rather than probe whether the bonds of these new kinds of authorities conformed to the intent of their state's constitutional and statutory debt regulations, or inquire into the motives of those who set up the new kinds of authorities and issued their bonds, courts usually took a formal and procedural approach. Like other actors in this story, judges generally appeared sympathetic—and therefore gave the benefit of the doubt—to efforts to overcome the barriers that the existing legal framework placed in the way of badly needed public construction. For example, as described earlier, the Michigan Supreme Court made it obvious in the 1930s and again in the 1940s that it recognized that leasing served the same end as installment buying. The court justified its decision on the basis of a formal reading of the law, refusing to judge intentions, and saying explicitly that it found no illegality in using nominally legal means when the most obvious means to the same end were illegal.

Courts could be quite candid about their rationale for granting governments wide leeway in their efforts to evade legal barriers to borrowing. In 1955, New York State's highest court affirmed the right of the City of Elmira to top up the coffers of the Elmira Parking Authority in the event that financial shortfalls threatened the authority's ability to make scheduled payments to bondholders. In response to plaintiffs' complaints, the court found that even though the constitution forbade political subdivisions of the state from taking responsibility for the debts of public authorities, there were no rules against "the transfer of money or property by State or city to an authority." Thus gifts, even foreseeable ones, were legal. Just in case anyone missed the point, the court articulated its reasoning explicitly: "We should not strain ourselves to find illegality in such programs. The problems of a modern city can never be solved unless arrangements like these . . . are upheld, unless they are patently illegal."[37]

Growing Dependence Nationally on Public Authority Financing

Just as new ideas for evading borrowing barriers diffused throughout the country prior to the 1960s, New York's Housing Finance Agency became a model for other states. Only a decade and a half after the creation of the HFA, thirty states had established one or more similar institutions that floated bonds backed by some kind of a quasi-guarantee of support from general state revenues, in order to provide financing for a wide range of programs.[38] Meanwhile, New York State made such liberal use of the HFA and other financing authorities for ambitious construction projects (including a huge expansion of the state university system) that by the time Rockefeller left the governorship in 1973, the debt of the state's public authorities had ballooned to almost four times that of the Empire State itself.[39] As time went on, these trends only accelerated. In 2004 the New York State comptroller reported that public authority debt had climbed to nine times that of the state.[40]

Certainly the Empire State has been a leader in the use of public authorities as tools for overcoming the fiscal challenges facing state and local governments, but New York's story is not anomalous. As figures 6.1 and 6.2 illustrate, using 2003 data, numerous states carry a heavy load of "nonguaranteed" debt—debt that is typically generated by public authority–type institutions using bonds secured against projected revenues (a good portion of which are to be derived from government payments). As the charts show, in four states this type of debt is higher per capita than in New York, while nine states have higher ratios of nonguaranteed to full-faith and credit debt, and another nine states actually rely entirely on nonguaranteed debt. Reliable time series for detailed data with exactly the categories one would want are not available, but figure I.1, in the introduction, gives a clear if rough sense of the dramatic trend toward borrowing that is nonguaranteed—and therefore performed by public authorities and their ilk, outside of general-purpose government.[41]

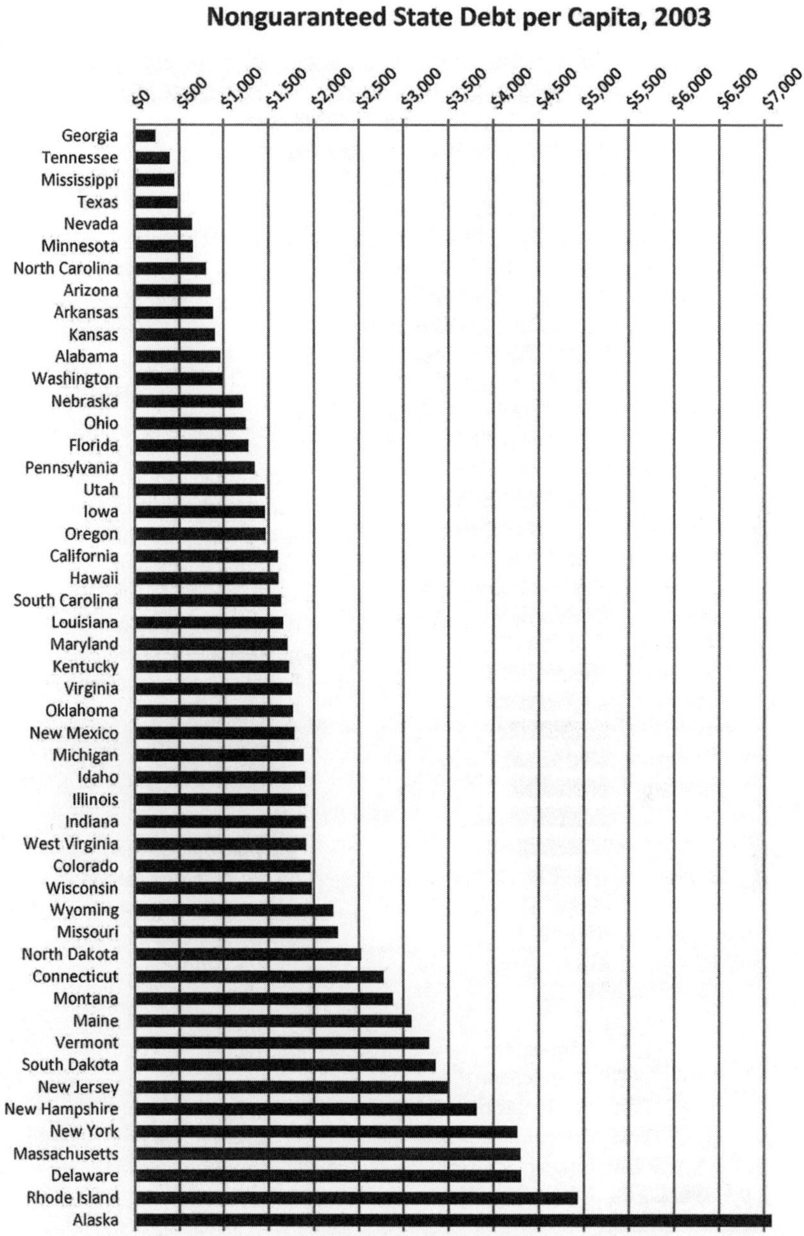

Figure 6.1. States vary widely in their reliance on "nonguaranteed debt," which is backed by projected future streams of revenue and typically issued by public authority–type agencies. In order to make valid comparisons across states of different sizes, this chart displays the extent of revenue borrowing in proportion to population, rather than in absolute terms. Even after taking population into account, the differences are dramatic: from less than $300 per capita in Georgia to more than $7,000 in Alaska.

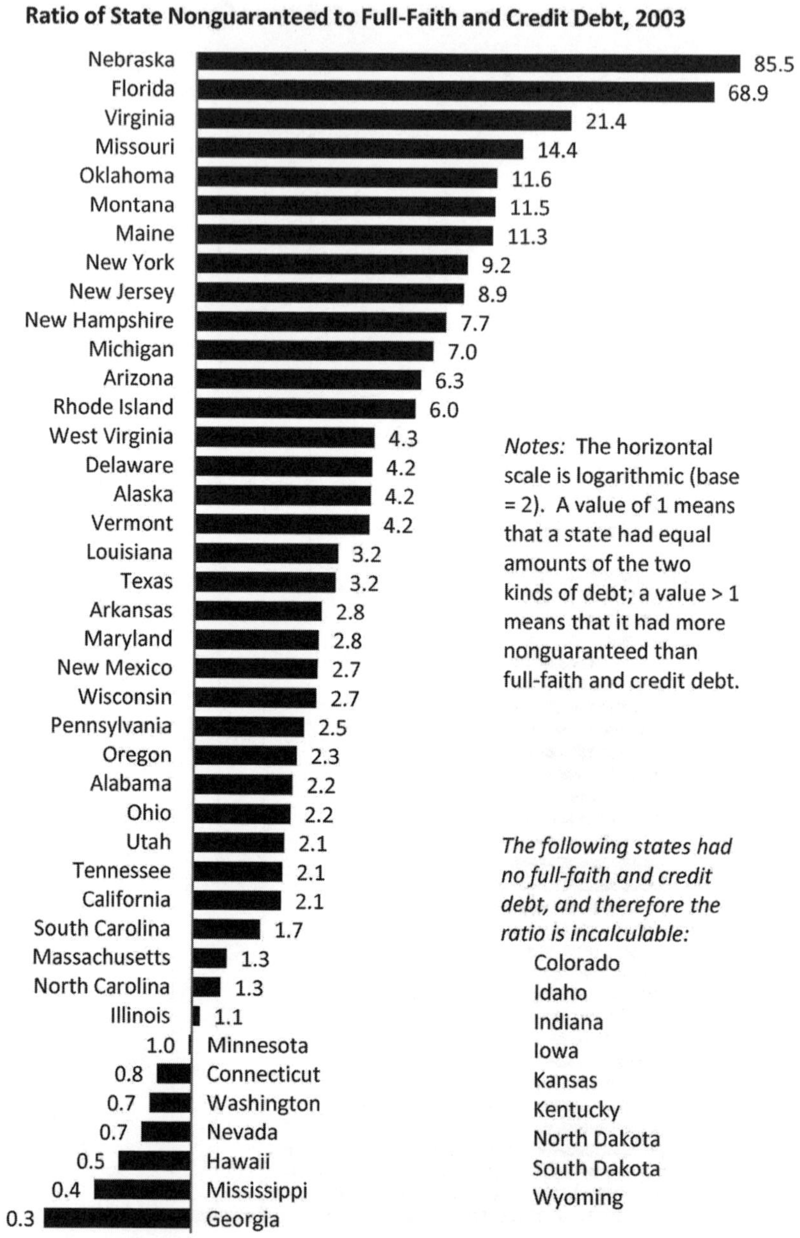

Figure 6.2. This chart shows the reliance of each state on nonguaranteed debt—typically issued by public authorities—in comparison to the traditional "full-faith and credit" debt issued by standard governments. Only seven states rely mostly on traditional debt, while nine rely entirely on nonguaranteed debt.

Underlying Dynamics

Obviously the appeal of authorities was enhanced by the new permutations of the authority concept that allowed these types of structures to be supported at least partially by tax-based general revenues of governments. But this was not the key factor behind their ballooning growth. In the years after the Second World War, the number of traditional authorities also increased rapidly. Thus it becomes clear that the underlying reason for the expansion of these institutions has not been technical innovations (e.g., new kinds of debt instruments), but rather the fact that they seemed uniquely able to cope with what the New York high court in the Elmira Parking Authority case described as "the problems of a modern city."[42]

The problems the court had in mind concerned not only the need for investment capital by which to respond to contemporary expectations for urban infrastructure. Authorities also seemed to offer a solution to the difficulties states and municipalities confronted when faced with new kinds of administrative tasks, especially those involving nonroutine activities. Just as the New Dealers discovered at the federal level in the 1930s, existing executive departments of government can be difficult to harness to new tasks—or sometimes even to entice to pursue their traditional tasks particularly well. Current personnel do not always have the necessary expertise or motivation, and civil service rules make it hard to add staff quickly or compete in terms of salary with the private sector for managerial and technical skill. At the same time, layers of regulations—added over the years to impede graft—tend to impede any action whatsoever.

As we have seen in earlier chapters, these were problems faced by state-builders from McAdoo, Hollis, Buckley, and the municipal socialists, through Hoover, the New Dealers, and most recently the postwar public officials who wanted to expand the range of government action in ways that could not be made to be commercially self-supporting. All tried to address these problems through the use of various kinds of public authorities. Thus, the evolution and popularity of these mechanisms needs to be understood not in isolation, but rather within the larger context of the inadequacy of the administrative apparatus of democratically accountable government in the United States for effectively pursuing goals of economic development, coordinated planning, and for a number of these reformers, greater democracy and social justice.

The epilogue will engage recent debates about how these goals could better be pursued.

EPILOGUE

The Future of Public Authorities

Faced with serious impediments to action, it is hardly surprising that American public officials have been drawn to the public authority strategy. As the stories in this book demonstrate, public authorities were not established and did not take their current form—however unfortunate that form may be—out of distain for the public, or as instruments of class warfare. Indeed, the forces that shaped public authorities had little to do with intentions, which varied greatly, having in common only a desire to get things done in situations where private enterprise was not stepping up to the plate. The dominant forces were legal, institutional, and financial. Many statebuilders, faced with these forces, made the decision to work around, rather than confront, the obstacles they faced. Others confronted the obstacles but lost the political struggles, with the outcome quite different from what they had proposed. Then, once the template for public authorities took hold, the mechanism developed its own powerful constituency of bankers, lawyers, financial consultants, contractors, and construction unions. No wonder New York City mayor Ed Koch confided to a researcher in 1987: "Authorities are the path of least resistance."[1]

Despite the appeal of authorities, the choice to build government capacity using what is essentially a strategy of circumvention comes with real costs. Chief among these is fragmentation of governance power, undermining the ability of elected officials to chart broad policy directions to promote balanced development and greater equality—goals that the private sector is frequently incapable of achieving on its own. As political scientist Alberta M. Sbragia points out, elected officials "often have relatively little control over the capital infrastructure that shapes a city and the opportunities enjoyed by its residents."[2]

To be sure, private parties make the majority of urban development de-

Figure E.1. Western New York, a region that has struggled economically for many years, has a very high number of public authorities. This *Buffalo News* editorial cartoon from 2008, depicting the area drowning in authorities, reflects the widespread public hostility to the many unaccountable agencies that play such a major role in local life.

cisions in the United States, and banks, developers, and industrialists make their investment choices with little or no regard for regional plans or social justice. But when the government-launched sector contains so many independent units pursuing projects aimed at maximizing their own financial viability—in the last analysis, the bondholders must be paid—coherent planning becomes even less possible. And with so many quasi-public initiatives supported by complex financial maneuvers, it is hard for the most sophisticated insiders, much less the general public, to understand the true state of public finances. Thus the possibility of open, democratic decision making about how to allocate available resources becomes elusive. Writing in the *National Municipal Review* in 1953, political scientist Joseph E. McLean summed up the situation vividly when he warned: "General government is in danger of being superseded by a set of authority-type ganglia directed by a small, weak brain."[3] A cartoon expressing similar sentiments, half a century later, is shown in figure E.1.

Given the issues described above and in the introduction, there is ample reason to regret the form public authorities took and to work for gradually replacing them with different kinds of administrative structures. How to do that, in the face of the institutional obstacles confronted by early twentieth-century statebuilders and still in existence today, is not easy to discern. Yet some clues emerge when we consider ideas that were offered in the past, even if not acted upon at the time, and lines of thinking and experimentation taking place in the early twenty-first century.

Alternatives Found in the Stories Told in This Book

Most of the chapters of this book tell stories of particular initiatives that led to the formation of public authorities—or functional equivalents, such as federal corporations—or that influenced their evolution. In each story, the outcome contributed to the development of public authorities as we know them today. But most of the stories also describe alternatives: proposals modified or defeated that came out of a different vision. These roads not taken are a good place to start looking at possibilities for something different in the future.

William McAdoo, Henry Hollis, and Robert Bulkley could all be termed left liberals, in that all were quite ready to use noncapitalist means when the for-profit sector was not meeting needs they wanted met, and all favored a greater degree of equality than America provided. McAdoo's plan for a fleet corporation envisaged a federally owned enterprise with policy set by cabinet members and thus ultimately by the president. It would be an incorporated administrative unit, rather than a standard agency, in order to operate effectively in the business world. Legally distinct from the rest of the executive branch, it would be free to enter into normal business contracts; unencumbered by government purchasing and hiring rules, it would be able to respond quickly to changing market conditions; able to retain funds, rather than wait every year for congressional appropriations, it would be able to make long-range plans. Contrary to McAdoo's proposal, Congress made the agency administratively independent of the administration, thus reducing its value as an instrument of economic planning, as well as its political accountability.

McAdoo's original plan could serve as a model for federal enterprises in the future. To be sure, a more independent agency could be the right choice for functions where policy directions need to be set long-term, by Congress, and be stable and predictable over time, rather than responding to the needs of the moment. But for economic development initiatives, programs to respond to high unemployment, and responses to situations where markets fail to meet national needs, McAdoo's approach would be appropriate, since the best response would vary from year to year and would need to be part of an administration policy based not primarily on technical criteria, but on political choices and philosophies.

McAdoo was forced into compromise by business opposition—from the standpoint of shipping companies, the shortage of vessels looked like a profit opportunity rather than a market failure—and by congressional reluctance to strengthen the executive branch. Quite aside from the narrow self-interest involved in the opposition, McAdoo's model depends on trust that an administration will not use the new powers it is granted for private financial gain or narrow political goals that advance politicians or parties rather than a policy agenda. Reducing corruption and differential access based on campaign contributions would make it more possible to benefit from McAdoo's model.

Some of the reasons McAdoo's original proposal failed offer lessons for the future. McAdoo did not have social movements or an organized constituency behind him. As a technocrat and good-hearted corporate leader, he may not have realized the degree to which this kind of backing was essential. The lack of grassroots pressure was particularly damaging in this instance, since providing goods and services, compared with structuring capital markets or otherwise supporting and subsidizing the for-profit sector, provokes more powerful opposition. Thus, such initiatives require a lot of attention to making arguments and building support. These are issues requiring attention if robust public enterprises are to be part of the federal government's repertoire in the future.

While McAdoo's plan for a federal merchant marine was not far from the approach of moderate European socialists who advocated a mixed economy, Hollis and Bulkley's vision for an agricultural banking system represented a bigger break with the existing economic system. They proposed that the government support a noncommercial financial system to be run by the program's beneficiaries, the farmers themselves. Both mutual help and accountability would have resulted if the experiment had been implemented as Hollis and Bulkley envisaged. Another result would have been an expansion of economic democracy, with ordinary farmers able to negotiate on more equal terms with giant enterprises in the agricultural sector, such as railroads, processors, and wholesalers. In other words, Hollis and Bulkley's approach involved civil society in a way that public authorities certainly do not—nor indeed do many programs organized by general-purpose governments.

The Hollis and Bulkley plan passed Congress relatively unscathed but was implemented in ways that did not allow the more unconventional parts of the model to flourish. It was quickly revised and simultaneously put in limbo by court challenges. Since the model was not really tried, we cannot tell much about its potentials and weaknesses. We do know that it was very appealing at the grass roots, eliciting a massive and quick response. On the minus side, it did not provide enough federal financial and technical support to be viable in anything but good times.

At the local level, Daniel Hoan, the longtime socialist mayor of Milwaukee, advocated "democratic control of collectively owned property."[4] This would have meant full municipal ownership of local public transportation, electricity generation and distribution, and the like. Other municipal socialists and left-wing Progressives of the early twentieth century had the same aspiration, desiring, in Frederic Howe's words, cities "that owned things and did things for people."[5] When public ownership initiatives did succeed, they often resulted in enterprises that were if anything more technologically advanced and cost effective than those run by private firms, as was the case with Detroit's power generation plant and Cleveland's Muny Light. These municipal enterprises provide counterexamples to the common refrain that only by taking such functions out of the control of politicians, and placing them in institutions insulated from the electorate, can goods and services be provided efficiently. To be sure, such outcomes were possible in good part because of the commitment of these socialists and Progressives to honest and effective government, and might not have worked the same way in cities dominated by corrupt political machines. Nonetheless, the work of these politicians represents a vision that was demonstrably practical in the sense of working well if put into practice in good faith.

The fundamental obstacle the municipal socialists and like-minded statebuilders encountered, in short, was not to make such an organizational template work, but to get it instantiated in the first place. As chapter 3 shows, citizens were often very willing to authorize municipal enterprises. The real obstacles were institutional. For some time courts declared that cities had no right to own and operate productive facilities. Even after courts backed off, cities still faced grave difficulties because of their inability to borrow the necessary start-up capital given the low debt limits put in place generations earlier. Needless to say, businessmen also actively opposed local governments expanding into activities they thought should be left to them. Nonetheless, the municipal ownership initiatives represent an alternate template that could be drawn upon in the future. And while the word "socialism" has come to be demonized, the bulk of the rhetoric municipal socialists used was not of a kind to repel Americans and has the merit of putting forward a coherent vision within which it would be possible to define (as happened in Britain) the role and nature of government agencies with more freedom of action than has been the norm in the U.S. public sector.

The corporate agencies of the New Deal are a different story. The federal corporations of the 1930s constitute a rich set of experiments, in terms of the variety of programs the agencies undertook. However, these agencies did not contribute much to the development of alternative institutional templates by which to pursue government activism, because they were so ad hoc and disconnected from any larger vision of what such activism might accomplish. Meanwhile, the work of the Public Works Administration under Harold Ickes was a testament to skill, resourcefulness, and energy. Yet the PWA functioned to channel state and local economic activism into the public authority model as we have come to know it, not to develop alternate visions. One reason was that many New Dealers, including Roosevelt himself, were fiscal conservatives. They were attracted by the prospect of reducing unemployment and building needed infrastructure without fully paying the cost through direct federal outlays. This episode suggests that one key to unlocking the door of the public authority trap we currently find ourselves in is public understanding and support for explicit public spending, when needs are real and plans are sound. At some points, the New Deal was capable of making that argument, but in its work promoting public authorities it undermined support for public-sector spending.

The inherent weakness of New Deal corporation building was noticed by some in the administration, including the president himself. Roosevelt manifested his ambivalence about federal corporations by the way he alternately encouraged and tried to rein them in. With regard to subfederal corporate agencies, Roosevelt also displayed mixed feelings. In the letter FDR sent to the governors of all forty-eight states, urging them to take steps so their states and municipalities could accept federal loans, he listed different options. One was what he called "municipal improvement authorities," defined as bodies without power to tax but with the ability to issue revenue bonds. But the first suggestion on his list, and presumably the one he believed optimal, was for states to change their laws and constitutions so that general-purpose governments could borrow directly to finance public works.[6]

Strengthening General-Purpose Government

Many recent writers on public authorities share with early twentieth-century statebuilders the conviction that the key problem is not public authorities, but general-purpose government itself. Therefore the most critical task is to strengthen the core public sector. Two basic approaches have been suggested.

The first focuses on dismantling the baroque and archaic control regimes over state and local public finance that were put in place in the nineteenth century. These were not a major problem in a largely rural society, but by the twentieth century they turned into straitjackets. Reform would mean allowing states and municipalities to borrow directly, within some kind of regulatory framework for capital spending. With the need for "backdoor financing" using public authority mechanisms, obviated, public finance would become more transparent and accountable. There would also be meaningful cost savings. Donald Axelrod, a public administration scholar who served as assistant budget director for New York State, points out that a salutary byproduct of relaxing legal constraints on borrowing would be the "disbanding of much of the army of bond counsel, financial advisers, and bond underwriters that, at astronomical fees, specialize in ways to bypass constitutions."[7] Although instituting reforms of this kind would be challenging, coming up with evasion strategies has called for enormous amounts of creative thinking, as well. In the words of Jon Magnusson, whose 1957 law review article surveyed the new lease financing maneuvers for which public authorities were being used, "The ingenuity spent in subversion would be better applied in an attack on the root cause of the difficulty: the constitutional restrictions themselves."[8]

The second approach to strengthening the public sector would be to revamp core government's own bureaucratic machinery so that standard line agencies could undertake more tasks commonly delegated to authorities. In general this would involve rethinking the outmoded systems of accountability that are rooted in a very different past. One key change of this kind would be to permit some executive departments to retain funds, since freedom from total dependence on annual appropriations is what allows authorities to do long-range planning. Another would be to allow more scope for management discretion by streamlining various administrative controls, such as those involving personnel and procurement.[9]

The practicality of these kinds of changes is demonstrated by the positive record of commercial-type operations able to retain their own earnings and make their own investment decisions that have operated comfortably within state and local departmental structures, some for many decades. These include such varied enterprises as the Florida Turnpike, housed in the state's Department of Transportation; Cleveland's Muny Light, a division of the city government; and the Norfolk (Virginia) Parking Division, an agency within the city's Department of Finance and Business Services.[10] While the logic of giving considerable flexibility to government units directly involved in commercial-type activities is self-evident, it is also the case that other kinds of public agencies could benefit from greater financial and administrative freedom. This could be done without sacrificing accountability to the policy aims of elected executives and legislatures.[11]

Undoubtedly there are potential pitfalls with these approaches. With regard to debt, there do need to be ways to prevent Rockefellerian excesses in creating new debt—although it should be kept in mind that the onerous existing restrictions failed to stop Rockefeller and his appointees. Similarly, with regard to government procurement and hiring, there clearly are real dangers of corruption and patronage hiring within government departments if no enforceable standards exist. Again, however, these phenomena are widely seen in the public authority world. The point, then, is that the old restrictions, whatever their original value, have become misdirected, not effectively preventing the evils they were intended to prevent, while hamstringing general-purpose government and propelling officials toward increasingly extreme escape strategies.

Allowing states and municipalities to operate revenue-producing infrastructure and float their own bonds for capital projects, while simultaneously revising the regulatory regimes that constrain public agencies from all but the most routine activities, would be a big step forward. Nevertheless, such reforms would primarily affect the provision of goods and services, like bridges and electricity, that can readily be financed by user charges. Left unsolved would be the question of how to build up the public sector as a sphere where human needs can prevail over the logic of the market and the public is encouraged to engage as active citizens, not as passive (and often alienated) consumers of government services. For most of the statebuilders described in earlier pages—even those who prioritized economic growth and balanced development—there were always aspirations to use government to achieve greater social justice and equality. These aspirations were found not just among the municipal socialists, but in a wide spectrum of progressive-minded politicians.

Such a cast of mind is exemplified by William McAdoo. As we saw in chapter 1, he believed that government could and should sometimes participate directly in markets to help guide the economy to higher levels of performance, but that government itself was not a business. As illustrated by the story McAdoo told about the government saving San Francisco from plague-carrying rats, without trying to get reimbursed for the money spent, he wanted government to do what profit-making businesses typically cannot: engage in economic activities that benefit citizens—and often businesses—but confer the benefits widely and indirectly. In the case of a bridge, the main gains go to those who drive across it, and they can be made to pay as they pass toll collectors. By contrast, in San Francisco it was mainly the rats who came in contact with government workers, and they were disinclined to pay user fees. Citizens living near rats would benefit, but not in a way that would allow user charges to be collected. Since plague spreads easily, the benefits really accrued to everyone who lived in or near the city. This is a classic case of what not only a for-profit firm, but even a public authority needing to support itself from user fees, cannot do.

McAdoo's rat vignette points up a fundamental problem that comes with the choice to use public authorities as the key method of building government capacity. These mechanisms, created for services that can be financially self-supporting, have limited ability to deliver services that are hard to shoehorn into a business model. Their decisions have to be based, in the last analysis, on how to please the bondholders by guaranteeing a strong stream of revenue and a surplus of income over expenses. This guiding star does not lead toward social justice, and not necessarily toward healthy regional economic development. Public authorities build state capacity to produce infrastructure that can pay its own way, but not other functions one might hope for from the public sector. McAdoo wanted more: economic activism that fulfilled distinctive purposes of government, such as sustaining shared conditions of existence, protecting against common vulnerabilities to disease and disaster (both natural and human-made), and working to diminish inequality.

This book has documented how American public officials, over the course of the twentieth century, devised strategies to buttress the power of government in the face of seemingly intractable institutional barriers by using the public authority model. Whatever the downsides, this history demonstrates tremendous ingenuity. This same commitment to an activist public sector continues to exist, and some contemporary statebuilders are experimenting with methodologies that move beyond the public authority formula in order to break out of the logic of the market. The experiments are often typically American in their bottom-up quality and reliance on our robust civil society. They seek something very far from any bureaucratic socialism, yet try to put into action parts of the social democratic vision: a concern for taking care of each other (especially the most vulnerable) in the face of the common hazards of life, more economic equality, and more equality in social decision making. One of the most striking examples is a program called Healthy San Francisco, which not only involves direct public participation in the economy, but also delivers services as public goods, rather than commodities.

Healthy San Francisco

Healthy San Francisco (HSF) is a local program to ensure that every citizen receives good health care. It was initiated in 2006 (taking effect between then and 2008) by the City and County of San Francisco.[12] Residents not covered by private or public health insurance, regardless of citizenship or immigration status, generally have the right to enroll. Participants pay a modest sliding-scale monthly fee and equally modest per-service fees; the fees are zero for those at the lowest income levels. A wide range of medical services are provided, including primary and preventive care, specialist visits, laboratory tests, urgent and emergency care, treatment at hospitals, and mental health services. The program is not an insurance plan and does not cover care outside the city or from nonparticipating providers. However, there are nearly thirty clinics (in a city that is only seven miles square), and the program includes the University of California, San Francisco (UCSF) hospital, one of the nation's premiere teaching and research medical centers. Participants choose a clinic as their medical home and have a primary care physician at that clinic. As of 2008, nineteen thousand people were enrolled in the program. A survey in 2009 found that 92 percent of participants would recommend the program to a friend and think other cities should imitate San Francisco.[13]

HSF is administered by the San Francisco Department of Public Health, which is a normal city/county agency. This agency itself provides some services at its own community clinics. However, many services are contracted out, although not to for-profit corporations. For clinic services, HSF contracts with the San Francisco Community Clinic Consortium (SFCCC), a nonprofit umbrella corporation formed in 1982 that links and supports most of the city's community health clinics. (These clinics began developing in the 1950s.) For hospital services, it uses the city/county hospital, the one at UCSF, the local Kaiser-Permanente hospital, and Chinese Hospital.[14]

Some financing is provided by the fees paid by users, but most comes from rerouting public funds that would otherwise cover unreimbursed care for those unable to pay, and most controversially from a mandate, which is in effect a tax, levied on employers who do not provide health insurance.[15] The Golden Gate Restaurant Association went to court to contest the mandate. However, in September 2008 the U.S. Court of Appeals for the Ninth

Circuit decided in favor of the City and County, and in June 2010 the U.S. Supreme Court declined to hear a further appeal.[16]

Since the entire system is run by the municipality, all policies and costs are subject to the normal process of political debate and ultimately to votes by the board of supervisors. Clinic and hospital policies are their own but are overseen by the Department of Public Health. Thus the program is far more democratically accountable than those carried out by public authorities. It also has a specific social-justice goal—to make good health care available to people of all income levels—that can only be advanced by public action, and that requires that revenues from users not be the driving factor in decisions. Unlike a rigid municipal socialist model, however, HSF draws on the values and resources of civil society, in particular on a preexisting network of community clinics, some of them providing free services and most of them rooted in some mixture of social-justice values and a desire to experiment with new ways of providing medical care. This interchange with civil society opens possibilities for flexibility in response to varied conditions, and new approaches to meeting needs, that would be hard to get through a purely governmental organizational structure.

Conclusion

Thus we come full circle. The municipal socialists were heirs of radical traditions that aspired to profoundly redefine the relationship between the economy and politics. Economic decisions, instead of being centralized in the hands of capitalists, would have a democratic component, based on the presumption that the results would respond to the needs of a broader spectrum of people. Politics, in the broad sense of public debate about what kind of society we want to live in, followed by decisions to put a shared vision into effect, would expand. HSF draws on the same traditions, but in comparison with municipal socialists has a higher proportion of the mix drawn from indigenous American radical traditions.

Municipal socialists, inspired by these kinds of ideas, but trying to be effective within the constraints of the American political system, sought a way forward. So did liberals—McAdoo, Hollis, Bulkley, Ickes, and others—holding weaker forms of the same values. The institutional innovations of these statebuilders then got tossed into the evolutionary soup of the American political process, encountering business elites on the one hand, and on the other, statebuilders like Hoover who primarily pursued economic development. The ecological niche was also structured by previous institutional developments, crystallized in legal restrictions. In the end, the innovations evolved toward the class of quasi-public structures known as public authorities that became ubiquitous by the late twentieth century.

Over the course of the twentieth century, American political institutions did develop new forms and capacities. The tragedy of this trajectory is that creative institutional change took place primarily in the quasi-governmental sphere, rather than in the core governments that citizens have at least some control over. If we are to achieve a significant degree of democratic control over the decisions that affect our lives, we will need to reconfigure general-purpose government in major ways.

We also need to develop new and unconventional forms of public economic activism, crafting institutions that are part of democratic political life and yet can operate in ways that standard government bureaucracies cannot. Some of these may be municipal enterprises; some might be experimental hybrids like Healthy San Francisco; some might be publicly launched and supported cooperative structures providing assistance for individuals and small businesses (as Hollis and Bulkley envisaged); some might be independent commissions; and some might be public authorities similar to the ones we have now, only with greater democratic accountability. No single model will suffice.

As Americans, we are good at experiments and variety, and at organizing new methods for achieving our goals. We can surely find ways to fulfill the purposes that motivated public authorities while avoiding the pitfalls of authorities as we know them today, and to embrace broader purposes than public authorities take on. These are our tasks in the coming period.

APPENDIX

FEDERAL CORPORATE AGENCIES

Federal Corporate Agencies

Name	*Purpose*	*Authorization*
	A. Functioning Corporate Agencies When the New Deal Starts (March 1933)	
Panama Railroad Company	To aid in construction and operation of the Panama Canal through operating a variety of commercial enterprises (including a railroad, steamship line, harbor terminals, coaling stations, real estate operations, commissaries, hotels, telephone system, and dairy)	Act of Congress authorizing the acquisition of the privately owned Panama Railroad Company (June 28, 1902)
Federal Land Banks (12)	To provide long-term, first mortgage loans on farm property	Federal Farm Loan Act (July 17, 1916); twelve regional banks chartered by Federal Farm Loan Board (Mar.–Apr. 1917)
United States Shipping Board Emergency Fleet Corporation (Later: United States Shipping Board Merchant Fleet Corporation)	To build up the country's merchant marine, and in event of war, a naval reserve	Act creating United States Shipping Board (Sept. 7, 1916); incorporated by United States Shipping Board in District of Columbia (Apr. 16, 1917)
Federal Intermediate Credit Banks (12)	To provide loans of "intermediate" duration (6 mos. to 3 yrs.) to public and private institutions engaged in farm finance	Farm Credit Act (June 19, 1923)
Inland Waterways Corporation	To operate, on a commercial basis, the barge lines on the Mississippi River and its tributaries that the federal government had managed during the war	Act creating Inland Waterways Corporation (June 3, 1924)
Reconstruction Finance Corporation (RFC)	To provide emergency financing facilities for financial institutions in order to aid agriculture, commerce, and industry	Act creating Reconstruction Finance Corporation, (Jan. 22, 1932)

Regional Agriculture Credit Corporations (12)	To provide emergency short-term loans to farmers	Emergency Relief and Reconstruction Act (July 21, 1932); RFC authorized to charter in the twelve federal land-bank districts
Federal Home Loan Banks (12)	To provide a central credit reserve system for home financing institutions	Federal Home Loan Bank Act (July 22, 1932); Federal Home Loan Bank Board chartered twelve regional banks
	B. New Deal Corporate Agencies	
Tennessee Valley Authority (TVA)	To improve navigation and provide flood control on the Tennessee River, to provide reforestation and economic development of the Tennessee Valley, and to generate and distribute electrical energy	Tennessee Valley Authority Act of 1933 (May 18, 1933)
Home Owners Loan Corporation (HOLC)	To refinance distressed urban home loans with long-term mortgages at low rates	Home Owners' Loan Act (June 14, 1933)
Federal Deposit Insurance Corporation (FDIC)	To insure accounts in banks up to $5,000	Banking Act of 1933 (June 16, 1933)
Banks for Cooperatives (12)	To make loans to farmers' cooperative associations	Farm Credit Act of 1933 (June 16, 1933)
Production Credit Corporations (12)	To aid in organizing farm credit cooperatives	Farm Credit Act of 1933 (June 16, 1933)
Federal Surplus Relief Corporation (Later: Federal Surplus Commodities Corporation)	To remove surplus agricultural commodities from the market by distributing them to state relief agencies	Administrator of the Federal Emergency Relief Administration; incorporated in Delaware (Oct. 4, 1933)
Commodity Credit Corporation	To make loans on farm commodities subject to production control through the Agricultural Adjustment Act	Executive Order 6340 (Oct. 16, 1933); incorporated in Delaware (Oct. 17, 1933)

(*Continued*)

Name	*Purpose*	*Authorization*
Federal Subsistence Homesteads Corporation	To carry out subsistence homesteads program mandated by National Industrial Recovery Act	Executive Order 6209 (July 21, 1933); incorporated in Delaware (Nov. 21, 1933)
Public Works Emergency Housing Corporation	To function as an operational arm of the Public Works Administration Housing Division	Incorporated in Delaware (Oct. 28, 1933) and subsequently designated a federal agency by Executive Order 6470 (Nov. 29, 1933)
Public Works Emergency Leasing Corporation	To assist the PWA in its business operations, particularly with regard to projects involving leasing	Administrator of the Federal Emergency Administration of Public Works, incorporated in Delaware (Jan. 2, 1934)
Electric Home and Farm Authority	To finance consumer purchases of electrical appliances	Executive Order 6514 (Dec. 19, 1933); incorporated in Delaware (Jan. 13, 1934)
Tennessee Valley Associated Cooperatives, Inc.	To finance cooperatives in the Tennessee Valley	Board of Directors of Tennessee Valley Authority; incorporated in Tennessee (Jan. 23, 1934)
Federal Farm Mortgage Corporation	To provide mortgage credit to farmers	Federal Farm Mortgage Corporation Act (Jan. 31, 1934)
Export-Import Bank of Washington [DC]	To promote trade by providing financing for exports and imports (especially, at the beginning, with the Soviet Union)	Executive Order 6581 (Feb. 2, 1934); incorporated in District of Columbia (Feb. 12, 1934)
Second Export-Import Bank of Washington [DC]	To promote trade by providing financing for exports and imports (especially with Cuba)	Executive Order 6638 (Mar. 9, 1934); incorporated in District of Columbia (Mar. 12, 1934)
Virgin Islands Company	To help effect economic rehabilitation of the Virgin Islands	Ordinance of the Colonial Council of the Municipalities of St. John and St. Thomas (Apr. 16, 1934)
Federal Savings and Loan Insurance Corporation (FSLIC)	To insure accounts in home financing institutions up to $5,000	National Housing Act (June 27, 1934)

Federal National Mortgage Association (Fannie Mae)	To provide a secondary market for mortgages insured by Federal Housing Administration	National Housing Act (June 27, 1934)
Federal Prison Industries, Inc.	To operate shops and factories in federal penal institutions producing products to be sold to other government agencies, and thereby provide employment and vocational rehabilitation for prisoners	Act of Congress directing the president to set up a body corporate (June 23, 1934); Executive Order 6917 (Dec. 11, 1934)
RFC Mortgage Company	To provide mortgage loans on income-producing real property	Act of Congress continuing Reconstruction Finance Corporation (Jan. 31, 1935); incorporated in Maryland (Mar. 14, 1935)
Disaster Loan Corporation	To provide loans in the event of floods or other catastrophes	Act of Congress creating Disaster Loan Corporation (Feb. 11, 1937)
U.S. Public Housing Authority (Later: Federal Public Housing Authority)	To provide financial and technical assistance to local bodies providing low-rent housing	United States Housing Act (Sept. 1, 1937)
Federal Crop Insurance Corporation	To provide crop insurance	Federal Crop Insurance Act (Feb. 16, 1938)
	C. Second World War Corporate Agencies	
Metals Reserve Company	To produce, acquire, or sell strategic materials as defined by the president	Amendments to Reconstruction Finance Corporation Act (June 25, 1940); chartered by RFC (June 28, 1940)
Rubber Reserve Co.	To secure rubber from abroad and develop synthetic rubber in the United States	Amendments to Reconstruction Finance Corporation Act (June 25, 1940); chartered by RFC (June 28, 1940)
Defense Plant Corporation	To erect, lease, or finance plants engaged in war production	Amendments to Reconstruction Finance Corporation Act (June 25, 1940); chartered by RFC (Aug. 22, 1940)

(*Continued*)

Name	*Purpose*	*Authorization*
Defense Supplies Corporation	To produce, acquire, or sell strategic materials and supplies, including land, arms, ammunition, railroad equipment, and aircraft	Amendments to Reconstruction Finance Corporation Act (June 25, 1940); chartered by RFC (Aug. 29, 1940)
Defense Homes Corporation	To build and operate rental housing in the vicinity of war plants	Letter from President Roosevelt (Oct. 18, 1940) allocating money from emergency funds established by military appropriation acts; incorporated by RFC in Maryland (Oct. 23, 1940)
War Damage Corporation	To provide for insurance against loss or damage to real and personal property resulting from enemy attack	Amendments to Reconstruction Finance Corporation Act (June 25, 1940); chartered by RFC (Dec. 13, 1941)
United States Commercial Company	To engage in preemptive buying in world markets to prevent the Axis from obtaining strategic raw materials	Amendments to Reconstruction Finance Corporation Act (June 25, 1940); chartered by RFC (Mar. 26, 1942)
Institute of Inter-American Affairs	To carry out programs in the Western Hemisphere related to health, sanitation, food production, and education	Appropriation Act (Dec. 17, 1941); incorporated in Delaware by Coordinator of Inter-American Affairs (Mar. 31, 1942)
Smaller War Plants Corporation	To mobilize the capacity of small business in war production	Chartered by Congress (June 11, 1942)
Cargoes, Inc.	To design and construct experimental cargo vessels and aircraft	Privately organized company acquired by Lend-Lease Administration, based on presidential authorization (June 17, 1942)
Inter-American Navigation Corporation	To construct, acquire, and operate wooden vessels to supplement ocean shipping in the Western Hemisphere, primarily in the Gulf and Caribbean	Appropriation Act (Dec. 17, 1941); incorporated in Delaware by coordinator of Inter-American Affairs (July 14, 1942)

Prencinradio, Inc.	To further the purposes of the Inter-American program through the use of media	Appropriation Act (Dec. 17, 1941); incorporated in Delaware by coordinator of Inter-American Affairs (July 20, 1942)
Rubber Development Corporation	To develop and acquire natural rubber, principally from Latin America	Amendments to Reconstruction Finance Corporation Act (June 11, 1942); RFC acquired and renamed the privately owned Pacific Development Company, Inc. (Feb. 16, 1943)
Institute of Inter-American Transportation	To improve transportation in the Western Hemisphere, particularly rehabilitation of Mexican National Railways	Appropriation Act (July 25, 1942); incorporated in Delaware by coordinator of Inter-American Affairs (June 26, 1943)
Petroleum Reserves Corporation	To buy and sell crude petroleum from sources outside the United States	Amendments to Reconstruction Finance Corporation Act (June 25, 1940); chartered by RFC (June 30, 1943)
Inter-American Educational Foundation, Inc.	To promote programs to improve the educational systems of the Western Hemisphere	Appropriation Act (July 12, 1943); incorporated in Delaware by coordinator of Inter-American Affairs (Sept. 25, 1943)

Note: This chart is based primarily on the 1944 report issued by the Joint Committee on Reduction of Nonessential Federal Expenditures (known as the Byrd Report), Senate Doc. 227, 78th Cong., 2nd sess. Supplementary information from General Accounting Office, *Reference Manual of Government Corporations*, Senate Doc. 86, 79th Cong., 1st sess.; Ruth G. Weintraub, *Government Corporations and State Law* (New York: Columbia University Press, 1939), 180–94; John McDiarmid, *Government Corporations and Federal Funds* (Chicago: University of Chicago Press, 1938), 34–50; Congressional Record, Senate, 74th Cong., 1st sess. (Feb. 6, 1935), 1546–61; Carl H. Moore, *The Federal Reserve System: A History of the First 75 Years* (Jefferson, NC: McFarland, 1990), 21, 29; and National Archives, *Guide to Records of the Reconstruction Finance Corporation*, online.

The Federal Reserve is not included in this chart, since it is not technically a public corporation, but instead an integrated system of twelve federally chartered Federal Reserve Banks, which are tax-exempt corporations owned by their member banks and managed at the national level by the Federal Reserve Board. The members of the board are appointed by the president and confirmed by Congress for fixed terms. This structure influenced the design of later corporate agencies. The purpose of the Federal Reserve was to manage the nation's money supply through market and regulatory interventions into the commercial banking system. It was authorized by the Federal Reserve Act (Dec. 23, 1913); the twelve regional Federal Reserve Banks were chartered by the Federal Reserve Board in Aug.–Nov. 1914.

NOTES

INTRODUCTION

1. Donald Axelrod, *Shadow Government: The Hidden World of Public Authorities—And How They Control Over $1 Trillion of Your Money* (New York: John Wiley, 1992).
2. Tennessee Valley Authority, *Report to SEC, Fiscal Year 2011*, 11, http://files.shareholder.com/downloads/TVC/1868315477x0xS1376986-11-74/1376986/filing.pdf (accessed May 14, 2012).
3. New Jersey Sports and Exposition Authority, "Financial Statements as of and for the Years Ended December 31, 2007 and 2006," 4–5, 7, http://www.njsea.com/Offers/pdf/NJSEAFS12_07_06.pdf (accessed August 31, 2009).
4. Peter Hendee Brown, *America's Waterfront Revival: Port Authorities and Urban Redevelopment* (Philadelphia: University of Pennsylvania Press, 2009), chap. 2; and Hillsborough County Port District, Florida, "Comprehensive Annual Financial Report of the Tampa Port Authority, Fiscal Year Ended September 30, 2008," iv, http://www.tampaport.com/content/download/6639/28840/file/FY2008%20CAFR%20PUBLISHED.pdf (accessed September 28, 2009).
5. Springfield Parking Authority website, http://www.parkspa.com/aboutus.shtml (accessed January 31, 2010).
6. Infrastructure Management Group, *Assessment Report on the City of Springfield Parking System* (August 2005), 9, 12, 14, 18, 43, http://www.mass.gov/Asfcb/docs/reports/parking_study.pdf (accessed January 31, 2010).
7. Robert A. Caro, *The Power Broker: Robert Moses and the Fall of New York* (New York: Alfred A. Knopf, 1974); and Robert A. Caro, "The City-Shaper," *New Yorker*, January 5, 1998, 40.
8. A 2009 report by the Congressional Reference Service lists seventeen currently existing government corporations but states that there can be no definitive list because "the U.S. Code does not provide a single definition of the term 'government corporation.' " Thus, each compiler makes her/his own determination. In a 1988 report the General Accounting Office counted forty-four government corporations. Kevin R. Kosar, *Federal Government Corporations: An Overview* (Washington, DC: Congressional Research Service, 2009), 2, 4n21. See also A. Michael Froomkin, "Reinventing the Government Corporation," *University of Illinois Law Review* 1995 (1995): 543–634.

   The twelve Federal Reserve Banks are not technically government corporations.

They are federally chartered, tax-exempt incorporated institutions owned by their member banks, not the government, although they are coordinated at the national level by the Federal Reserve Board whose members are appointed by the president and confirmed by Congress for fixed terms. Congress established the Federal Reserve system in 1913 to manage the nation's money supply through market and regulatory interventions into the commercial banking system, and its format influenced the design of many later federal programs.

9. United States Government, *Budget of the U.S. Government, Fiscal Year 2010: Analytical Perspectives*, table 7–14, p. 86. This figure is for six government-created corporate agencies (or integrated systems of agencies), three that relate to housing (Fannie Mae, Freddie Mac, Federal Home Loan Banks) and three that relate to agriculture (Agricultural Credit Bank, Farm Credit Banks, Federal Agricultural Mortgage Corporation).
10. Jordan A. Schwarz, *The New Dealers: Power Politics in the Age of Roosevelt* ([1993] New York: Vintage Books, 1994), xi.
11. For estimates of total number, see Nicholas Henry, *Public Administration and Public Affairs* (Upper Saddle River, NJ: Prentice-Hall, 1999), 373. For definitional issues, see Annmarie Hauck Walsh, *The Public's Business: The Politics and Practices of Government Corporations* ([1978] Cambridge, MA: MIT Press, 1980), 5–6, 353–72, 373n1; and Jerry Mitchell, "The Policy Activities of Public Authorities," *Policy Studies Journal* 18 (Summer 1990): 928–42. The *U.S. Census, Census of Governments* is not a definitive source, as it lumps together special districts with public authorities. While the two share certain characteristics, such as structural independence from elected officials (plus a common history), most scholars differentiate between them—the basic distinction being that special districts are governed by elected boards and have the power to tax, whereas public authorities are governed by appointed boards and have no taxing power. For efforts to identify all public authorities in New York, see Office of the State Comptroller, *Public Authorities in New York State: Accelerating Momentum to Achieve Reform* (Albany, NY: Office of Budget and Policy Analysis, February 2005), 7.
12. Unpublished Census Bureau data for 1949 cited in J. Richard Aronson and John L. Hilley, *Financing State and Local Governments* (Washington, DC: Brookings Institution, 1986), 251. U.S. Department of Commerce, Census Office, *2002 Census of Governments*, vol. 4, no. 5: *Government Finances* (Washington, DC: GPO, 2005), table 13, p.15. After 2002, the Census Bureau no longer distinguished between debt that was "guaranteed" and "nonguaranteed," so no later figures are available. Dollar value adjustments were done based on Bureau of Economic Analysis, U.S. Department of Commerce, *National Income and Product Accounts Tables*, table 1.1.4, Price Indexes for Gross Domestic Product (options selected: annual series and all years), available at http://www.bea.gov/national/nipaweb/TableView.asp?SelectedTable=4&ViewSeries=NO&Java=no&Request3Place=N&3Place=N&FromView=YES&Freq=Year&FirstYear=2008&LastYear=2010&3Place=N&AllYearsChk=YES&Update=Update&JavaBox=no#Mid (accessed March 5, 2011).
13. Joanna Cagan and Neil DeMause, *Field of Schemes: How the Great Stadium Swindle Turns Public Money into Private Profit* (Monroe, ME: Common Courage Press, 1998), 155–58, esp. 157; Ziona Austrian and Mark S. Rosentraub, "Cleveland's Gateway to the Future," in *Sports, Jobs, and Taxes: The Economic Impact of Sports Teams and Stadiums*, ed. Roger G. Noll and Andrew S. Zimbalist (Washington, DC: Brookings Institution, 1997), 355–84; and *Cleveland Plain Dealer*, June 2, 1995, 4B.

14. Henry, *Public Administration and Public Affairs*, 396; Jameson W. Doig, "'If I See a Murderous Fellow Sharpening a Knife Cleverly . . .': The Wilsonian Dichotomy and the Public Authority Tradition," *Public Administration Review* 43 (July–August 1983): 295, 297; and Harold Hestnes, "Public Authorities: Should the State Take Away Their Power?" *Boston Globe*, November 7, 1986, 28, quoted in Jerry Mitchell, *The American Experiment with Government Corporations* (Armonk, NY: M. E. Sharpe, 1999), 65.
15. Walsh, *The Public's Business*, 3.
16. Alberta M. Sbragia, *Debt Wish: Entrepreneurial Cities, U.S. Federalism, and Economic Development* (Pittsburgh, PA: University of Pittsburgh Press, 1996), 14–15.
17. For example, James T. Bennett and Thomas J. DiLorenzo, *Underground Government: The Off-Budget Public Sector* (Washington, DC: Cato Institute, 1983); Axelrod, *Shadow Government*; Thomas H. Stanton, *A State of Risk: Will Government-Sponsored Enterprises Be the Next Financial Crisis?* (New York: HarperBusiness, 1991); Bert Ely, *The Farm Credit System: Reckless Past, Doubtful Future* (Alexandria, VA: Ely, 1999); and Peter J. Wallison, ed., *Serving Two Masters, But Out of Control: Fannie Mae and Freddie Mac* (Washington, DC: AEI Press, 2001).
18. Emmette S. Redford and Charles B. Hagan, *American Government and the Economy* (New York: Macmillan, 1968), 623.
19. Richard Hofstadter, *The Age of Reform: From Bryan to F.D.R.* (New York: Knopf, 1955).
20. Martin J. Sklar, "Woodrow Wilson and the Political Economy of Modern United States Liberalism," *Studies on the Left* 1 (Fall 1960): 41. See also Samuel Haber, *Efficiency and Uplift: Scientific Management and The Progressive Era, 1890–1920* (Chicago: University of Chicago Press, 1964); Gabriel Kolko, *The Triumph of Conservatism: A Reinterpretation of American History* (New York: Free Press, 1963); and James Weinstein, *The Corporate Ideal in the Liberal State, 1900–1918* (Boston: Beacon Press, 1968).
21. Jack H. Knott and Gary J. Miller, *Reforming Bureaucracy: The Politics of Institutional Choice* (Englewood Cliffs, NJ: Prentice-Hall, 1987), 3.
22. Walsh, *The Public's Business*, 25; and Doig, "'If I See a Murderous Fellow Sharpening a Knife Cleverly . . . ,'" 295. The rise of the Right in American politics in the 1970s and 1980s prompted a reappraisal of liberalism, which is still under way. See, for example: Richard L. McCormick, "The Discovery That Business Corrupts Politics: A Reappraisal of the Origins of Progressivism," *American Historical Review* 86 (April 1981): 247–74; Michael Frisch, "Urban Theorists, Urban Reform, and American Political Culture in the Progressive Period," *Political Science Quarterly* 97 (Summer 1982): 295–315; Alan Dawley, *Struggles for Justice: Social Responsibility and the Liberal State* (Cambridge, MA: Belknap Press of Harvard University Press, 1991); Gary Gerstle, "The Protean Character of American Liberalism," *American Historical Review* 99 (October 1994): 1043–73; Judith Sealander, *Grand Plans: Business Progressivism and Social Change in Ohio's Miami Valley, 1890–1929* (Lexington: University Press of Kentucky, 1988); and Alan Brinkley, "Liberalism's Third Crisis," *American Prospect* 21 (Spring 1995): 28–34.
23. Roosevelt's letter quoted in Robert G. Smith, *Ad Hoc Governments: Special Purpose Transportation Authorities in Britain and the United States* (Beverly Hills, CA: Sage, 1974), 107–8.
24. E. H. Foley, "Legal Problems Affecting the Non-Federal Phases of the Public Works Program," *American Bar Association, Section of Municipal Law*, August 1934, 30.

CHAPTER 1

1. Quoted in Jordan A. Schwarz, *The New Dealers: Power Politics in the Age of Roosevelt* ([1993] New York: Vintage, 1994), 4.
2. Quoted in John J. Broesamle, *William Gibbs McAdoo: A Passion for Change, 1863–1917* (Port Washington, NY: Kennikat Press, 1973), 14.
3. Otis L. Graham, Jr., "William Gibbs McAdoo," *Dictionary of American Biography*, Supplement 3 (New York: Charles Scribner's Sons, 1973), 479–80. Quote from Broesamle, *William Gibbs McAdoo*, 12.
4. Broesamle, *William Gibbs McAdoo*, 16–31; and William G. McAdoo, *Crowded Years: The Reminiscences of William G. McAdoo* (Boston: Houghton Mifflin, 1931), 71–108. For a discussion that places this episode within the context of New York transit politics see Clifton Hood, *722 Miles: The Building of the Subways and How They Transformed New York* (New York: Simon and Schuster, 1993), 145–50.
5. Broesamle, *William Gibbs McAdoo*, 239n12 and 31–37.
6. Ibid., 30. For "welfare capitalist" thought in this era, see Daniel Nelson, *Managers and Workers: Origins of the New Factory System in the United States, 1880–1920* (Madison: University of Wisconsin Press, 1975), chap. 6.
7. McAdoo, *Crowded Years*, 106.
8. The teacher's equal pay movement achieved success in 1911. Mary Synon, *McAdoo: The Man and His Times* (New York: Bobbs-Merrill, 1924), 38; Grace Strachan, president of the Interborough Association of Women Teachers, to McAdoo, July 16, 1909, McAdoo Papers, Library of Congress [hereafter McAdoo Papers], box 91; "Mayor Now Favors Equal Pay Measure," *New York Times*, December 18, 1909; and Robert E. Doherty, "Tempest on the Hudson: The Struggle for 'Equal Work for Equal Pay' in the New York City Public Schools, 1907–1911," *History of Education Quarterly* 19 (Winter 1979): 413–34.

   McAdoo's egalitarian commitments were less advanced when it came to employment rights for African-Americans. Concerted efforts to physically separate black and white clerks working for the federal government had actually started during the Republican administrations of Roosevelt and Taft, in line with trends in the larger society in the early twentieth century, but these instances had been sporadic and informal. The Treasury and the Post Office were the two departments with significant numbers of black employees at this time, and during the Wilson administration both introduced formal segregation policies. Unlike the Jim Crow enthusiast Albert S. Burleson, Wilson's postmaster general, McAdoo is not known to have personally ordered separation of the races in his department. The record is murky, but what is clear is that McAdoo at least allowed high-level subordinates to make their own decisions on this matter. When his rabidly racist assistant secretary, John Skelton Williams, issued written orders in the summer of 1913 that restrooms in the Treasury building be differentiated by race, McAdoo did not override him. On the other hand, when Charles Sumner Hamlin, a committed racial liberal from Massachusetts, replaced Williams as assistant secretary and issued orders in the spring of 1914 that Treasury's newly completed building for the Bureau of Printing and Engraving would not operate with separate restrooms for blacks and whites, McAdoo went along with this policy, also. Broesamle, *William Gibbs McAdoo*, 158–66; August Meier and Elliott Rudwick, "The Rise of Segregation in the Federal Bureaucracy, 1900–1930," *Phylon* 28 (1967): 178–84; and Nicholas Patler, *Jim Crow and the Wilson Administration* (Boulder: University Press of Colorado, 2004), chap. 1.
9. William G. McAdoo, "The Relations between Public Service Corporations and the

Public," Lecture delivered before the Graduate School of Business Administration, Harvard University, April 6, 1910, McAdoo Papers, box 563, quotes from 7, 37.

10. W. G. McAdoo, "A Naval Auxiliary Merchant Marine," Speech to Indianapolis Chamber of Commerce, October 13, 1915, McAdoo Papers, box 563, 22.
11. Burton I. Kaufman, *Efficiency and Expansion: Foreign Trade Organization in the Wilson Administration* (Westport, CT: Greenwood Press, 1974), 40.
12. René De La Pedraja, *The Rise and Decline of U.S. Merchant Shipping in the Twentieth Century* (New York: Twayne, 1992), 47.
13. Cited in Broesamle, *William Gibbs McAdoo*, 212.
14. Cited in William G. McAdoo, "Address to the Chamber of Commerce of the United States," Washington, DC, February 4, 1915, Senate Doc. 950, 63rd Cong., 3rd sess. (1915), 10.
15. Alfred D. Chandler, Jr., *The Visible Hand: The Managerial Revolution in American Business* (Cambridge, MA: Harvard University Press, 1977), 189–92; Bernard Mergen, "The Government as Manager: Emergency Fleet Shipbuilding, 1917–1919," in *Business and Its Environment: Essays for Thomas C. Cochran*, ed. Harold Issadore Sharlin (Westport, CT: Greenwood Press, 1983), 50–51; Samuel A. Lawrence, *United States Merchant Shipping: Politics and Policies* (Washington, DC: Brookings Institution, 1966), 35; and Richard Sicotte, "Economic Crisis and Political Response: The Political Economy of the Shipping Act of 1916," *Journal of Economic History* 59 (December 1999): 861–84.
16. Arthur S. Link, *Wilson: The Struggle for Neutrality, 1914–1915* (Princeton, NJ: Princeton University Press, 1960), 87, 76; Jeffrey J. Safford, *Wilsonian Maritime Diplomacy, 1913–1921* (New Brunswick, NJ: Rutgers University Press, 1978), 37; and Lawrence C. Allin, "Ill-Timed Initiative: The Ship Purchase Bill of 1915," *American Neptune* 23 (July 1973): 181–82.
17. McAdoo, *Crowded Years*, 296.
18. Quoted in Link, *Wilson: Struggle for Neutrality*, 87.
19. The literature on Wilson's conception of the relationship between American economic prosperity and world progress is reviewed in Safford, *Wilsonian Maritime Diplomacy*, 19, quote from 21.
20. Quoted in Broesamle, *William Gibbs McAdoo*, 200.
21. McAdoo, *Crowded Years*, 296. Quotes from David M. Kennedy, *Over Here: The First World War and American Society* (New York: Oxford University Press, 1980), 302, 303.
22. H.R. 18666, submitted September 4, 1914, copy in McAdoo Papers, box 554. Quote from statement of purpose at the beginning. This bill was a slightly revised version of the original H.R. 18518, considered in hearings at the end of August. Link, *Wilson: Struggle for Neutrality*, 87.
23. Cited in Broesamle, *William Gibbs McAdoo*, 222.
24. William H. Becker, *The Dynamics of Business-Government Relations: Industry and Exports, 1893–1921* (Chicago: University of Chicago Press, 1982), 147.
25. McAdoo, *Crowded Years*, 305.
26. Cited in Link, *Wilson: Struggle for Neutrality*, 147.
27. Philadelphia Bd. of Trade to Rep. George W. Edmonds, August 28, 1914, in U.S. Congress, House, Committee on Merchant Marine and Fisheries, *Hearings on H.R. 18518*, 63rd Cong., 2nd sess. (1914), 34 [hereafter *1914 Shipping Bill Hearings*].
28. Ibid., 18.
29. Ibid., 28.

30. U.S. Congress, House, Committee on Merchant Marine and Fisheries, *Hearings on H.R. 10500*, 64th Cong., 1st sess. (1916), 277 [hereafter *1916 Shipping Bill Hearings*].
31. Link, *Wilson: Struggle for Neutrality*, 89–90.
32. *1914 Shipping Bill Hearings*, 25.
33. McAdoo, "Address to the Chamber of Commerce," 11.
34. Ibid., 15–16. As it turned out, the bureau, which was under McAdoo's supervision in the Treasury, made a profit of about $17 million. McAdoo, *Crowded Years*, 304; and Link, *Wilson: Struggle for Neutrality*, 83n31.
35. *1916 Shipping Bill Hearings*, 266; *1914 Shipping Bill Hearings*, quote from 17.
36. Arthur S. Link et al., eds., *The Papers of Woodrow Wilson*, vol. 31 (Princeton, NJ: Princeton University Press, 1979), 418.
37. *1914 Shipping Bill Hearings*, 29.
38. McAdoo, "A Naval Auxiliary Merchant Marine," quotes from 11; and Broesamle, *William Gibbs McAdoo*, 223.
39. McAdoo, "A Naval Auxiliary Merchant Marine," 10.
40. *1916 Shipping Bill Hearings*, 269.
41. Ibid., 269–70; Harold Archer Van Dorn, *Government Owned Corporations* (New York: Alfred A. Knopf, 1926), 233–42, quotes from 238, 239–40; and John McDiarmid, *Government Corporations and Federal Funds* (Chicago: University of Chicago Press, 1938), 74–83.
42. U.S. Congress, House, Committee on the Territories, "Construction of the Alaskan Railroad," 66th Cong., 1st sess., Report No. 231 (August 18, 1919), 2–4, quotes from 2 and 3; Edwin M. Fitch, *The Alaska Railroad* (New York: Praeger, 1967), chap. 2; and Arthur Stanley Link, *Wilson: The New Freedom* (Princeton, NJ: Princeton University Press, 1956), 127.
43. Neil B. Freeman, *The Politics of Power: Ontario Hydro and Its Government, 1906–1995* (Toronto: University of Toronto Press, 1996), 10–12; and Thomas K. McCraw, *TVA and the Power Fight, 1933–1939* (Philadelphia: J. B. Lippincott, 1971), 26–30, quote from 26.
44. John Thurston, *Government Proprietary Corporations in the English-Speaking Countries* (Cambridge, MA: Harvard University Press, 1937), 18–21.
45. The three park districts were the South Park Commission, the West Park Commission, and the Lincoln Park Board. Paul Studenski, *The Government of Metropolitan Areas in the United States* (New York: National Municipal League, 1930), 260. Michael Patrick McCarthy makes the point that Chicago in the Progressive Era was essentially "a confederation of eight separate jurisdictions: the City, three Park Boards, the Board of Education, Public Library Board, the Sanitation District and Cook County." McCarthy, "Businessmen and Professionals in Municipal Reform: The Chicago Experience, 1887–1920" (PhD diss., Northwestern University, 1970), 44; *Massachusetts Statutes of 1894*, chap. 548, sections 23 and 37; and Charles W. Cheape, *Moving the Masses: Urban Public Transit in New York, Boston, and Philadelphia, 1880–1912* (Cambridge, MA: Harvard University Press, 1980), 142. Judith Sealander provides a fascinating account of the political struggle surrounding the creation of the Conservancy District, which included a vociferous opposition movement that labeled this administrative mechanism as "undemocratic as the Stamp Act," in *Grand Plans: Business Progressivism and Social Change in Ohio's Miami Valley, 1890–1929* (Lexington: University Press of Kentucky, 1988), chap. 3, quote in text

from 54, quote in this note from 71. William J. Quirk and Leon E. Wein, "A Short Constitutional History of Entities Commonly Known as Authorities," *Cornell Law Review* 56 (April 1971): 562n253. In the case of the bonds issued by New York's river districts, there was no guarantee that they were backed by the credit of the state. Joel A. Tarr, "The Evolution of the Urban Infrastructure in the Nineteenth and Twentieth Centuries," in *Perspectives on Urban Infrastructure* , ed. Royce Hanson (Washington, DC: National Academy Press, 1984), 28.

46. Richard M. Abrams, "Business and Government," in *Encyclopedia of American Political History*, vol. 1, ed. Jack P. Greene (New York: Charles Scribner's Sons, 1984), quote from 128; Oliver Field, "Government Corporations: A Proposal," *Harvard Law Review* 48 (March 1935): 775–76; and Richard E. Ellis, *The Union at Risk: Jacksonian Democracy, States' Rights, and the Nullification Crisis* (New York: Oxford University Press, 1987), 19–20.
47. Richard R. John, "Affairs of Office: The Executive Departments, the Election of 1828, and the Making of the Democratic Party," in *The Democratic Experiment*, ed. Meg Jacobs, William J. Novak, and Julian E. Zelizer (Princeton, NJ: Princeton University Press, 2003); Ellis, *The Union at Risk*, 22, 33–40, Jackson quoted, 19; and Bray Hammond, *Banks and Politics in America: From the Revolution to the Civil War* (Princeton, NJ: Princeton University Press, 1957), chap. 14.
48. Heather Cox Richardson, *The Greatest Nation of the Earth: Republican Economic Policies during the Civil War* (Cambridge, MA: Harvard University Press: 1997), chap. 6; Robert William Fogel, *The Union Pacific Railroad: A Case in Premature Enterprise* (Baltimore: Johns Hopkins Press, 1960), 26–28, quotes from 27, 50. 12 Stat. 489 (1862), sec. 1 and 13 Stat. 356 (1864), sec. 13; and Wallace D. Farnham, "'The Weakened Spring of Government': A Study in Nineteenth-Century American History," *American Historical Review* 68 (April 1963): 662–80.
49. Melvin I. Urofsky, "Josephus Daniels and the Armor Trust," *North Carolina Historical Review* 45 (July 1968): 237–63, quote from 241; and Josephus Daniels, *The Wilson Era: Years of Peace, 1910–1917* (Chapel Hill: University of North Carolina Press, 1944), 358–63.
50. Albert S. Abel, "The Public Corporation in the United States," in *Government Enterprise: A Comparative Study*, ed. W. G. Friedmann and J. F. Garner (New York: Columbia University Press, 1970), 182; Harvey Franklin Pinney, "Federal Government Corporations as Instrumentalities of Government and of Administration" (PhD diss., New York University, 1937), 252–65; and John A. McIntire, "Government Corporations as Administrative Agencies: An Approach," *George Washington Law Review* 4 (January 1936): 179–82.
51. Link, *Wilson: New Freedom*, 202–13, McAdoo quote at 211; and 38 Stat. 251 secs. 2 and 4. The ambiguous status of the Federal Reserve would be exploited by Representative Wright Patman (D-TX), who fought doggedly against it throughout his almost five decades in Congress. In the 1930s, Patman encouraged the District of Columbia to attempt to collect property taxes on the Fed's imposing new office building in order to embarrass the institution, which he saw as too insulated from public input, although always happy to assert its governmental identity when advantageous. William Greider, *Secrets of the Temple: How the Federal Reserve Runs the Country* (New York: Touchstone, 1987), 48–50.
52. A copy of this bill, H.R. 10500, can be found in McAdoo Papers, box 554.
53. Dale N. Shook, *William G. McAdoo and the Development of National Economic Policy,*

1913–1918 (New York: Garland, 1987), 128–29; Safford, *Wilsonian Maritime Diplomacy*, 51–62; Link, *Wilson: Struggle for Neutrality*, 90; and Kaufman, *Efficiency and Expansion*, 98.

54. Link, *Wilson: Struggle for Neutrality*, 143–45, quotes from 145.
55. Franklin L. Burdette, *Filibustering in the Senate* (Princeton, NJ: Princeton University Press, 1940), 103–6, quotes from 106; Safford, *Wilsonian Maritime Diplomacy*, 62–65; McAdoo, *Crowded Years*, 307–9; and Link, *Wilson: Struggle for Neutrality*, 143–60, quotes from 145. The House passed the bill on February 16, 1915, by a vote of 214 to 122, with 7 abstentions. Congressional Record, 63rd Cong., 3rd sess., 3923.
56. Safford, *Wilsonian Maritime Diplomacy*, 71–73, 84–86; and Broesamle, *William Gibbs McAdoo*, 230.
57. W. G. McAdoo, "The Progress and Prosperity of the United States under the Present Democratic Administration," speech to Raleigh, North Carolina, Chamber of Commerce, May 31, 1916, in McAdoo Papers, box 563.
58. McAdoo, *Crowded Years*, 312.
59. *1916 Shipping Bill Hearings*, 269; and Becker, *Dynamics of Business-Government Relations*, 148.
60. Quoted in Safford, *Wilsonian Maritime Diplomacy*, 89. Kennedy, *Over Here*, 308.
61. Safford, *Wilsonian Maritime Diplomacy*, 92.
62. Broesamle, *William Gibbs McAdoo*, 229.
63. Safford, *Wilsonian Maritime Diplomacy*, quote from 82; and 39 Stat. 728.
64. Leonard D. White, *Introduction to the Study of Public Administration*, 4th ed. (New York: Macmillan, 1958), chap. 9; and Becker, *Dynamics of Business-Government Relations*, 148–49.
65. Van Dorn, *Government Owned Corporations*, 47.
66. Darrell Hevenor Smith and Paul V. Betters, *The United States Shipping Board: Its History, Activities and Organization* (Washington, DC: Brookings Institution, 1931), 37; and Kennedy, *Over Here*, 339.
67. De La Pedraja, *The Rise and Decline of U.S. Merchant Shipping*, 59.
68. Mergen, "The Government as Manager," 51, 73, and passim; Miles Colean, *Housing for Defense* (New York: Twentieth Century Fund, 1940), 155; and Van Dorn, *Government Owned Corporations*, 57–59.
69. Van Dorn, *Government Owned Corporations*, passim.
70. Ibid., 72.
71. Smith and Betters, *The United States Shipping Board*, 1; and Pinney, "Federal Government Corporations," 266–73.
72. McAdoo to Wilson, September 4, 1916, in "Presidential Papers Microfilm: Woodrow Wilson Papers," Library of Congress, Series 2, reel 82.
73. This long struggle is recounted in Barry Dean Karl, *Executive Reorganization and Reform in the New Deal: The Genesis of Administrative Management, 1900–1939* (Cambridge, MA: Harvard University Press, 1963).
74. Stephen Skowronek, *Building a New American State: The Expansion of National Administrative Capacities, 1877–1920* (Cambridge: Cambridge University Press, 1982), 204.

CHAPTER 2

1. Federal Farm Loan Act, 39 Stat. 360.
2. Clara Eliot, *The Farmer's Campaign for Credit* (New York: D. Appleton, 1927), 1–29.

3. Party platforms for Democrats, Republicans, Progressives, and Socialists in *History of American Presidential Elections, 1789–1968*, vol. 3, ed. Arthur M. Schlesinger, Jr., and Fred L. Israel (New York: Chelsea House, 1971), 2167–203. The Socialists' 1912 platform deplored the high prices farmers had to pay for machinery, transportation, and crop storage, and placed the blame on "capitalist concentration." The cost of borrowing money was not included in this list of grievances, perhaps reflecting the fact that better access to credit was not at this time a grassroots issue in the countryside. Schlesinger and Israel, *History of American Presidential Elections*, 2198.
4. "An Inaugural Address," *The Papers of Woodrow Wilson*, vol. 27, ed. Arthur S. Link (Princeton, NJ: Princeton University Press, 1978), 150.
5. Congressional Record, 64th Cong., 1st sess., 3543.
6. Murray R. Benedict, *Farm Policies of the United States, 1790–1950* (New York: Twentieth Century Fund, 1953), 139.
7. Stuart William Shulman, "The Origin of the Federal Farm Loan Act: Agenda Setting in the Progressive Era Print Press" (PhD diss., University of Oregon, 1999), 53.
8. W. Gifford Hoag, *The Farm Credit System: A History of Financial Self-Help* (Danville, IL: Interstate Printers and Publishers, 1976), 34; and Eliot, *Farmer's Campaign*, 56.
9. Figures from a Department of Agriculture study cited in S. Rep. No. 144, 64th Cong., 1st sess. (1916) at 7–8.
10. W. Elliot Brownlee, *Dynamics of Ascent: A History of the American Economy* (New York: Alfred A. Knopf, 1974), 230.
11. Theodore Saloutos and John D. Hicks, *Agricultural Discontent in the Middle West* (Madison: University of Wisconsin Press, 1951), 22–23; and E. W. Kemmerer, "Agricultural Credit in the United States," *American Economic Review* 2 (December 1912): 859n6.
12. David B. Danbom, *The Resisted Revolution: Urban America and the Industrialization of Agriculture, 1900–1930* (Ames: Iowa State University Press, 1979), chap. 2; and Shulman, "The Origin of the Federal Farm Loan Act," 110–11, 138–39.
13. Meg Jacobs, *Pocketbook Politics: Economic Citizenship in Twentieth-Century America* (Princeton, NJ: Princeton University Press, 2005), 42, and chap. 1 passim.
14. Alan L. Olmstead and Paul W. Rhode, "The Transformation of Northern Agriculture, 1910–1990," in *The Cambridge Economic History of the United States*, ed. Stanley L. Engerman and Robert E. Gallman (Cambridge: Cambridge University Press, 2000), 2:697, 701.
15. Mrs. Edith Ellicott Smith, "The Farmer's Share in the High Cost of Living," *Annals of the American Academy of Political and Social Science* 48 (July 1913): 255.
16. "The Soaring Cost of Life in America: Secretary Wilson and Eminent Economists Discuss the Problem of the Day and Some Ways to Solve It," *New York Times*, January 2, 1910.
17. Danbom, *The Resisted Revolution*, 42, 43.
18. *Report of the Commission on Country Life* ([1911] New York: Arno Press, 1975), 20, 135. Originally published as Senate Doc. 705, 60th Cong., 2nd sess.
19. J. Hermes, "The Land Mortgage Associations (Landschaften)," in *Articles on German Banking, Publications of the National Monetary Commission*, vol. 11 (Washington, DC: GPO, 1911), 287–324, quote at 291 (previously published as Senate Doc. 508, 61st Cong., 2nd sess. [1910]); Myron T. Herrick and R. Ingalls, "How to Finance the Farmer," Senate Doc. 396, 64th Cong., 1st sess. (1916), 8–9, 32–43; and "Letter from President William H. Taft to the Governors of the States," in U.S. Department

of State, *Preliminary Report on Land and Agricultural Credit in Europe* (Washington, DC: GPO, 1912), 3.

20. Wayne Flynt, *Duncan Upshaw Fletcher: Dixie's Reluctant Progressive* (Tallahassee: Florida State University Press, 1971), 4–5, 77–84; "Southerners to Hear Taft," *New York Times*, February 13, 1911; "Agricultural Cooperation and Rural Credit in Europe," Senate Doc. 261, 63rd Cong., 2nd sess. (1914), 7 and 8; George E. Putnam, "The Land Credit Problem," *Bulletin of the University of Kansas Humanistic Studies* 2 (December 1916): 40–41; and "Agricultural Investigation," *Los Angeles Times*, June 1, 1913.
21. "Agricultural Cooperation and Rural Credit in Europe," 9–10.
22. Ellen Furlough and Carl Strikwerda, "Economics, Consumer Culture, and Gender: An Introduction to the Politics of Consumer Cooperation," in *Consumers against Capitalism? Consumer Cooperation in Europe, North America and Japan*, ed. Furlough and Strikwerda (Lanham, MD: Rowan and Littlefield, 1999), 1–65; Daniel T. Rodgers, *Atlantic Crossings: Social Politics in a Progressive Age* (Cambridge, MA: Harvard University Press, 1998), 330; and James Livingston, *Origins of the Federal Reserve System: Money Class, and Corporate Capitalism*, 1890–1913 (Ithaca, NY: Cornell University Press, 1986), 218n4.
23. "Agricultural Cooperation and Rural Credit in Europe," 21, 22.
24. B. F. Harris, "What I Am Trying to Do," *World's Work* 26, no. 4 (August 1913): 436.
25. B. F. Harris, *The Problems of Rural Life from the Banker's Standpoint* (Chicago: Union Stock Yard and Transit, 1912), 4, 5.
26. Douglas Steeples and David O. Whitten, *Democracy in Desperation: The Depression of 1893* (Westport, CT: Greenwood Press, 1998), chap. 3; Arthur S. Link, *Wilson: The New Freedom* (Princeton, NJ: Princeton University Press, 1956), 203–23; James Livingston, *Origins of the Federal Reserve System: Money, Class, and Corporate Capitalism, 1890–1913* (Ithaca, NY: Cornell University Press, 1986), chap. 8; and Elizabeth Sanders, *Roots of Reform: Farmers, Workers, and the American State, 1877–1917* (Chicago: University of Chicago Press, 1999), 236–59.
27. John Milton Cooper, Jr., *Pivotal Decades: The United States, 1900–1920* (New York: W. W. Norton, 1990), 196.
28. Livingston, *Origins of the Federal Reserve System*, 217.
29. *Sun* quoted in Link, *Wilson: The New Freedom*, 216; Federal Reserve Act, 38 Stat. 251 (1913), sec. 13, sec. 24; Henry Parker Willis, *The Federal Reserve System: Legislation, Organization and Operation* (New York: Ronald Press, 1923), 223, 247–57; and Richard Abrams, "Woodrow Wilson and the Southern Congressmen, 1913–1916," *Journal of Southern History* 22 (November 1956): 421.
30. "An Annual Message to Congress" (December 2, 1913), *The Papers of Woodrow Wilson*, ed. Arthur S. Link et al. (Princeton, NJ: Princeton University Press, 1979), 29:5.
31. Quoted in Link, *Wilson: The New Freedom*, 262.
32. S. 4246, 63rd Cong., 2nd sess. (January 29, 1914), quote from sec. 18, in *Bills Introduced in the United States Senate and the House of Representatives during the Sixty-Third Congress Relative to Rural Credits* (Washington, DC: GPO, 1915). The first income tax law, made possible by the ratification of the Sixteenth Amendment in February 1913, was technically the second section of the Underwood-Simmons Tariff Act, passed in October 1913. Sidney Ratner, *American Taxation: Its History as a Social Force in Democracy* (New York: W. W. Norton, 1942), 333–34.
33. "Farm-Land Banks," *Wall Street Journal*, February 25, 1914.
34. Robert J. Bulkley, "Extension of Remarks," Congressional Record, 63rd Cong. 3rd

sess., v. 52, pt. 6 (appendix) and Herrick and Ingalls, *How to Finance the Farmer*, 19–23, quote at 14.

35. Subcommittees of the Committees on Banking and Currency of the Senate and the House, "Joint Hearings on Rural Credits," 63rd Cong., 2nd sess., 1914, 42 (hereafter, "Joint Hearings").
36. Grange officer quoted in ibid. at 263.
37. "Fight over Rural Credits," *New York Times*, January 31, 1914.
38. "Joint Hearings," 257.
39. Ibid., 264.
40. Ibid., 693.
41. Ibid., 694.
42. H.R. 4811, 63rd Cong., 1st sess. (May 6, 1913), H.R. 11897, 63rd Cong., 2nd sess., (January 19, 1914), H.R. 21590, 63rd Cong., 3rd sess. (March 2, 1915), *Bills Introduced*; Ruth Velma Corbin, "Federal Rural Credits, 1916–1936" (MA thesis, University of Wisconsin, 1936), 23; and Benedict, *Farm Policies*, 146–47.
43. Elizabeth Sanders, "Farmers and the State in the Progressive Era," in *Changes in the State: Causes and Consequences*, ed. Edward S. Greenberg and Thomas F. Mayer (Newbury Park, CA: Sage Publications, 1990), 203.
44. Robert E. Putnam, "The Federal Farm Loan System," *American Economic Review* 9 (March 1919): 57.
45. Johnson's dream of establishing a municipally owned electrical power system for Cleveland was ultimately brought to fruition in 1914 by another of his protégées, Newton D. Baker, who like Bulkley, would go on to a national political career. William Donald Jenkins, "Robert Bulkley, Progressive Profile" (PhD diss., Case Western Reserve University, 1969), 16–17; and Hoyt Landon Warner, *Progressivism in Ohio, 1897–1917* (Columbus: Ohio State University Press, 1964), 61–62. After serving two terms as mayor of Cleveland, Baker became secretary of war in the second Wilson administration. *Encyclopedia of Cleveland History* , s.v. "Baker, Newton Diehl," http://ech.cwru.edu/ech-cgi/article.pl?id=BDN (accessed August 7, 2005).
46. Bulkley to Newton D. Baker (January 13, 1913), Robert Johns Bulkley Papers, Western Reserve History Society, container 4, folder 3 (hereafter Bulkley Papers); Ronnie J. Phillips and David Mushinski, "The Role Of Morris Plan Lending Institutions in Expanding Consumer Micro-Credit in the United States," Colorado State University Department of Economics Working Paper, March 8, 2001, http://ssrn.com/abstract=287569 (accessed July 14, 2005), 4–10; James Grant, *Money of the Mind: Borrowing and Lending in America from the Civil War to Michael Milken* (New York: Farrar, Straus and Giroux, 1992), 94, quote from 95; and Louis N. Robinson, "The Morris Plan," *American Economic Review* 21 (June 1931): 222.
47. "Election Results, Congress and the Presidency, 1860–1992," *Congressional Quarterly's Guide to U.S. Elections*, 3rd ed. (Washington, DC: Congressional Quarterly, 1994), 1344.
48. Bulkley to Newton D. Baker (May 28, 1910), Bulkley Papers, container 1, folder 2; and Jenkins, "Robert Bulkley," 78–79.
49. "Two New England Solons and Their Wives Who Can Boast Distinguished Ancestry," *Washington Post*, May 4, 1913; "Hollis, Henry French," *The National Cyclopaedia of American Biography*, vol. 15 (New York: James T. White, 1916), 272–73; and "Would Limit Harvard Men's Pocket Money," *Boston Advertiser*, March 24, 1914, in Henry French Hollis bibliographical folder, Harvard University Archives (hereafter cited as Hollis Papers).

50. "Senator Hollis' Forecast on Suffrage Is Attacked," *Christian Science Monitor*, April 15, 1913; "New Hampshire Still Trying to Elect Senator," *Christian Science Monitor*, January 16, 1913; "Manager for Bass Gives His Ballot to a Democrat," *Christian Science Monitor*, January 24, 1913; "Elect H. F. Hollis to Senate," *New York Times*, March 14, 1913; and "New Hampshire Democrats Elect Hollis on 40th Ballot," *Christian Science Monitor*, March 13, 1913.
51. Fred C. Kelly, "Statesmen, Real and Near," *Boston Morning Herald*, April 2, 1913, Hollis Papers.
52. "Parties Put to Test: Senator Hollis Sees Disappearance of at Least One," *Washington Post*, April 30, 1913.
53. "H. F. Hollis Predicts Federal Control," *Christian Science Monitor*, April 16, 1915.
54. "Career of New Senator," *Concord (New Hampshire) Monitor*, March 13, 1913, Hollis Papers; and "Joint Hearings," 455.
55. Arthur S. Link, *Woodrow Wilson and the Progressive Era, 1910–1917* (New York: Harper and Brothers, 1954), 18–20, 54–55, 80.
56. "Reject Class Legislation," *Christian Science Monitor*, May 8, 1913.
57. S. 5542 & H.R. 16478, 63rd Cong., 3rd sess. (May 12, 1914), *Bills Introduced*.
58. Robert J. Bulkley, "The Federal Farm-Loan Act," *Journal of Political Economy* 25 (February 1917): 139.
59. W. Stull Holt, *The Federal Farm Loan Bureau* (Baltimore: Johns Hopkins Press, 1924), 14.
60. Alaska Rail Road Act, 38 Stat. 305 (1914); Edwin M. Fitch, *The Alaska Railroad* (New York: Frederick A. Praeger, 1967), chap. 2; and Melvin I. Urofsky, "Josephus Daniels and the Armor Trust," *North Carolina Historical Review* 45 (July 1968): 237–63.
61. Florence E. Parker, *Consumers Cooperative Societies in the United States in 1920* (Washington, DC: U.S. Bureau of Labor Statistics, Bulletin No. 313, 1923), esp. 2, 6, 15–21; and Joseph G. Knapp, *The Rise of American Cooperative Enterprise: 1620–1920* (Danville, IL: Interstate Printers and Publishers, 1969), chap. 21.
62. Robert J. Bulkley, "The Federal Farm-Loan Act," *Journal of Political Economy* 25 (February 1917): 141.
63. Wilson quote from David Sarashon, *The Party of Reform: Democrats in the Progressive Era* (Jackson: University Press of Mississippi, 1989), 186; Link, *Wilson: The New Freedom*, 261–64; and "Rural Credit Plan Shelved," *New York Times*, May 13, 1914.
64. Federal Farm Loan Act, 39 Stat. 360 (July 17, 1916); Arthur S. Link, *Wilson: Confusions and Crises, 1915–1916* (Princeton, NJ: Princeton University Press, 1964), 345–50; and Lewis L. Gould, *Reform and Regulation: American Politics from Roosevelt to Wilson*, 3rd ed. (Prospect Heights, IL: Waveland Press, 1996), 187.
65. Murray A. Benedict, *Can We Solve the Farm Problem? An Analysis of Federal Aid to Agriculture* (New York: Twentieth Century Fund, 1955), 134.
66. Earl Sylvester Sparks, *History and Theory of Agricultural Credit in the United States* (New York: Thomas Y. Crowell, 1932), 158.
67. Ibid., 131–32.
68. W. Stull Holt, *The Federal Farm Loan Bureau*, 32.
69. Sparks, *History and Theory of Agricultural Credit*, 133, 126–28.
70. David E. Hamilton, *From New Day to New Deal: American Farm Policy from Hoover to Roosevelt, 1928–1933* (Chapel Hill: University of North Carolina Press, 1991), 18.
71. George E. Putnam, "The Federal Farm Loan Act," *American Economic Review* 6, no. 4 (December 1916): 784.
72. Hoag, *The Farm Credit System*, 84.

73. C. W. Thompson, "The Federal Farm Loan Act," *American Economic Review* 7, no. 1, Supplement (March 1917): 130. Thompson was an economist with the Department of Agriculture.
74. Holt, *The Federal Farm Loan Bureau*, 28–29nn26–27.
75. "Colored Farmers Tell How They Got Relief," *Borrower's Bulletin* (Washington, DC: Federal Farm Loan Bureau, U.S. Treasury Department) 1, no. 3 (January 1918): 6.
76. Harold Archer Van Dorn, *Government Owned Corporations* (New York: Knopf, 1926), 38.
77. Benedict, *Farm Policies of the United States*, 147; George E. Putnam, "Recent Developments in the Federal Farm Loan System," *American Economic Review* 11, no. 3 (September 1921): 432–33; and Hamilton, *From New Day to New Deal*, 152.
78. Federal Farm Loan Act, 39 Stat. 360 (1916), sec. 12, sec. 20.
79. Holt, *The Federal Farm Loan Bureau*, 32.
80. Ratner, *American Taxation*, 370–72.
81. Peter Fearon, *War, Prosperity and Depression: The U.S. Economy, 1917–45* (Lawrence: University Press of Kansas, 1987), 15–18, chap. 2.
82. Sparks, *History and Theory of Agricultural Credit*, 123–24; and Holt, *The Federal Farm Loan Bureau*, 45–46.
83. Putnam, "Recent Developments in the Federal Farm Loan System," 432.
84. Smith v. Kansas City Title and Trust Company, 255 U.S. 180 (1921), at 181 and 184 and Farm Mortgage Bankers Association of America, *Directory of Officers and Members*, January 1922, 50, http://books.google.com/books/download/Reports_and_publications.pdf?id=yZvPAAAAMAAJ&hl=en&capid=AFLRE73ygI6p9wFPlXHyaI0xlgmVcx04TTjggEC2pLWUWfHytVAFF6LG07mjs6kG3u4wlLpPH318KEp8efgjzcn-KDa9qBapKQ&continue=http://books.google.com/books/download/Reports_and_publications.pdf%3Fid%3DyZvPAAAAMAAJ%260utput%3Dpdf%26hl%3Den (accessed July 21, 2011).
85. Federal Farm Loan Act, 39 Stat. 360, sec. 1.
86. McCulloch v. Maryland, 17 U.S. 316 (1819).
87. Following his efforts on behalf of the private banking interests that wanted to invalidate the land banks, Bullitt spent the next year as special counsel to the Emergency Fleet Corporation, the other early template for authority-like federal agencies. "William Bullitt, Ex-U.S. Aide, Dead," *New York Times*, October 4, 1957.
88. Betty Glad, "Hughes, Charles Evans," *American National Biography* Online, February 2000, http://www.anb.org/articles/11/11-00439.html (accessed November 1, 2006).
89. Michael C. Tolley. "Willoughby, Westel Woodbury," *American National Biography Online*, February 2000, http://www.anb.org/articles/14/14-00708.html (accessed October 27, 2006).
90. Smith v. Kansas City, 255 U.S. at 192–93 (1921).
91. Hammer v. Dagenhart, 247 U.S. 251 (1918).
92. Ibid. at 272.
93. Ibid. at 276.
94. Ibid. at 275.
95. Smith v. Kansas City Title and Trust Company, 255 U.S.180 (1921), at 211.
96. Ibid. at 210.
97. U.S. Bureau of the Census, *Historical Statistics of the United States, Colonial Times to 1970*, Part 1 (Washington, DC: GPO, 1975), table K-1, p. 457. By 1990 the share of the American population living on farms had dropped below 2 percent. Susan B.

Carter et al., eds., *Historical Statistics of the United States, Millennial Edition* (New York: Cambridge University Press, 2006), 4:40, table Da 1–13. No later figures are available, because after this the Department of Agriculture, which had taken over this aspect of data collection from the Census Bureau, stopped determining farm residence, given that living on farms was no longer a reliable indication that individuals were engaged in farming as a livelihood.

98. More specifically, the ruling offered an arbitrary formula for writing legislation for federal agencies set up to intervene in capital markets. In later years, legislative drafters working for Republican and Democratic administrations alike regularly inserted a section stating that the entity being established could be used as a depository of public money and a financial agent of the government. John Thurston, *Government Proprietary Corporation in the English-Speaking Countries* (Cambridge, MA: Harvard University Press, 1937), 28.

CHAPTER 3

1. Daniel W. Hoan, *The Failure of Regulation* (Chicago: Socialist Party of the United States, 1914), 6, 88; and Douglas E. Booth, "Municipal Socialism and City Government Reform: The Milwaukee Experience, 1910–1940," *Journal of Urban History* 12 (November 1985): 60.
2. For numbers of officeholders, see James Weinstein, *The Decline of Socialism in America, 1912–1925* ([1967] New York: Vintage, 1969), 93, 103–118. The argument summarized here can be found in Ira Kipnis, *The American Socialist Movement, 1897–1912* ([1952] Westport, CT: Greenwood Press, 1968), 345–48; Michael Bassett, "Municipal Reform and the Socialist Party, 1910–1914," *Australian Journal of Politics and History* 19 (August 1973): 179–87; Bruce M. Stave, "Introduction," *Socialism and the Cities*, ed. Bruce M. Stave (Port Washington, NY: Kennikat Press, 1975), 3–12; and Donald T. Critchlow "Introduction," *Socialism in the Heartland: The Midwestern Experience, 1900–1925*, ed. Donald T. Critchlow (Notre Dame, IN: University of Notre Dame Press, 1986), 1–17. The historiographical consensus echoes the post-election editorial analyses in American newspapers and magazines of the time according to Richard W. Judd, *Socialist Cities: Municipal Politics and the Grass Roots of American Socialism* (Albany: State University of New York Press, 1989), 192–93n34. Bridgeport socialists captured the mayoralty and a majority of the seats up for election on the Common Council in 1933. See Cecelia Bucki, *Bridgeport's Socialist New Deal, 1915–36* (Urbana: University of Illinois Press, 2001).
3. Frederic C. Howe, *The Confessions of a Reformer* (New York: Scribner's Sons, 1925), 5.
4. Richard Oestreicher, "Urban Working-Class Political Behavior and Theories of American Electoral Politics, 1870–1940," *Journal of American History* 74 (March 1988): 1257–86; and Alexander Keyssar, *The Right to Vote: The Contested History of Democracy in the United States* (New York: Basic, 2000), 170–71.
5. Daniel T. Rodgers, *Atlantic Crossings: Social Politics in a Progressive Age* (Cambridge, MA: Belknap, 1998), 112–59, quote at 129; and "Populist Party Platform," in *Great Issues in American History*, ed. Richard Hofstadter and Beatrice K. Hofstadter ([1958] New York: Vintage, 1982), 142.
6. Selig Perlman, "Upheaval and Reorganization," in *History of Labour in the United States*, ed. John Commons et al. (New York: A. M. Kelley, 1966), 2:245–48; Ernest S. Griffith, *A History of American City Government: The Conspicuous Failure, 1870–1900* (New York: Praeger, 1974), 117–20; "The Nationals, Their Origin and Their Aims,"

Atlantic Monthly 42 (November 1878), 521–30, quote at 529; Philip J. Ethington, *The Public City: The Political Construction of Urban Life in San Francisco, 1850–1900* (Cambridge: Cambridge University Press, 1994), 338; Philip S. Foner, *History of the Labor Movement in the United States* (7 vols., New York: International Publishers, 1947–1987), 2:121; and David Scobey, "Boycotting the Politics Factory: Labor Radicalism and the New York City Mayoral Election of 1884," *Radical History Review* 28–30 (1984): 282–83. The date in the title is a misprint; it should be 1866.

7. Rodgers, *Atlantic Crossings*, 147; Melvin G. Holli, *Reform in Detroit: Hazen S. Pingree and Urban Politics* (New York: Oxford University Press, 1969), 52; Roger Sale, *Seattle: Past to Present* (Seattle: University of Washington Press, 1976), 73; Jay L. Brigham, *Empowering the West: Electrical Politics before FDR* (Lawrence: University Press of Kansas, 1998), 102; and Paul Barrett, *The Automobile and Urban Transit: The Formation of Public Policy in Chicago, 1900–1930* (Philadelphia: Temple University Press, 1983), 31, 228n79.
8. Shelton Stromquist, "The Crucible of Class: Cleveland Politics and the Origins of Municipal Reform in the Progressive Era," *Journal of Urban History* 23 (January 1997): 200, quote at 197; and Kenneth Finegold, *Experts and Politicians: Reform Challenges to Machine Politics in New York, Cleveland, and Chicago* (Princeton, NJ: Princeton University Press, 1995), 78.
9. Ernest S. Griffith, *A History of American City Government: The Progressive Years and Their Aftermath, 1900–1920* (New York: Praeger, 1974), 147.
10. Thomas F. Campbell, "Municipal Ownership," in *The Encyclopedia of Cleveland History*, ed. David D. Van Tassel (Bloomington: Indiana University Press, 1996), 717.
11. Griffith, *A History of American City Government*, 250; and Holli, *Reform in Detroit*, 42, 74–124.
12. Finegold, *Experts and Politicians*, 138–50; and John D. Buenker, "Edward F. Dunne: The Limits of Municipal Reform," in *The Mayors: The Chicago Political Tradition*, ed. Paul M. Green and Melvin G. Holli (Carbondale: Southern Illinois University Press, 1987), 33–49.
13. Eric H. Monkkonen, *America Becomes Urban: The Development of U.S. Cities and Towns, 1780–1980* (Berkeley: University of California Press, 1988), 214.
14. Martin V. Melosi, *The Sanitary City: Urban Infrastructure in America from Colonial Times to the Present* (Baltimore: Johns Hopkins University Press, 2000), 120.
15. Lent D. Upson, *Practice of Municipal Administration* (New York: Century, 1926), 505.
16. Joel A. Tarr, "The Evolution of the Urban Infrastructure in the Nineteenth and Twentieth Centuries," in *Perspectives on Urban Infrastructure*, ed. Royce Hanson (Washington, DC: National Academy Press, 1984), 28.
17. Ann Durkin Keating, "Public Private Partnerships in Public Works," *Essays in Public Works History* 16 (December 1989): 100–102; Edward C. Kirkland, *Industry Comes of Age: Business, Labor, and Public Policy, 1860–1897* (New York: Holt, Rinehart and Winston, 1961), 243; and Stanley K. Schultz and Clay McShane, "To Engineer the Metropolis: Sewers, Sanitation, and City Planning in Late-Nineteenth-Century America," *Journal of American History* 65 (September 1978): 395.
18. Brigham, *Empowering the West*, 96–142; David W. Wilma et al., *Power for the People: A History of Seattle City Light* (Seattle: University of Washington Press, 2010), chap. 3; and Nelson Van Valen, "A Neglected Aspect of the Owens River Aqueduct Story: The Inception of the Los Angeles Municipal Electric System," *Southern California Quarterly* 59 (1977): 85–109.

19. Carl C. Plehn, *Government Finance in the United States* (Chicago: A. C. McClurg, 1915), 87–88, quote at 85.
20. Rodgers, *Atlantic Crossings*, 155, 143; and Morton Keller, "Social and Economic Regulation in the Progressive Era," in *Progressivism and the New Democracy*, ed. Sidney M. Milkis and Jerome M. Mileur (Amherst: University of Massachusetts Press, 1999), 133.
21. Frederic C. Howe, *The City: The Hope of Democracy* (New York: Charles Scribner's Sons, 1905), chap. 9, quote at 138.
22. Ibid., chap. 10; Morton Keller, *Affairs of State: Public Life in Late Nineteenth Century America* (Cambridge, MA: Belknap, 1977), 332–35; and Hendrik Hartog, *Public Property and Private Power: The Corporation of the City of New York in American Law, 1730–1870* (Chapel Hill: University of North Carolina Press, 1983), 220–25, Dillon quoted at 2.
23. Hartog, *Public Property and Private Power*, 224.
24. William J. Novak, "The Legal Origins of the Modern American State," *American Bar Foundation Working Paper #9925* (1999): 22.
25. Holton v. City of Camilla, 134 Ga. 560 (1910).
26. The following discussion relies on Chad Gaffield, "Big Business, the Working Class, and Socialism in Schenectady, 1911–1916," *Labor History* 19 (Summer 1978): 350–72; Kenneth E. Hendrickson, Jr., "George R. Lunn and the Socialist Era in Schenectady, New York, 1909–1916," *New York History* 47 (January 1966): 22–40; Kenneth E. Hendrickson, Jr., "Tribune of the People: George R. Lunn and the Rise and Fall of Christian Socialism in Schenectady," in *Socialism and the Cities*, ed. Stave, 72–98; Sandra Opdycke, "Building the Cooperative Commonwealth in Schenectady, New York: Municipal Socialism in a Small Industrial City, 1912–1913" (MA thesis, Columbia University, 1990); and Joseph A. Spencer, "George R. Lunn and the First Socialist Administration in Schenectady, New York, 1910–1913" (MA thesis, City College, 1974), esp. 102–7.
27. C. A. Mullen, "Schenectady's Fight against Its Ice Combine," *Coming Nation*, August 17, 1912, 7; and George Lunn, "Inaugural Message," Minutes of the Common Council, January 8, 1912, City of Schenectady (Schenectady County Historical Society, Schenectady, NY).
28. "Injunction Stops Sale of Ice by City—Lunn and His Associates Have New Scheme," *Schenectady Gazette*, July 4, 1912, 1.
29. Mullen, "Schenectady's Fight against Its Ice Combine," 7. Lunn's administration also initiated a municipal grocery store and a coal business. The grocery store, like the ice operation, evolved into a cooperative enterprise after a court injunction. Evidence regarding the coal venture is sketchy. It may well have been successful in commercial terms and in any case put competitive pressure on private firms to hold down their rates during the two winters the Lunn administration was in office. Joseph A. Spencer interprets these activities as evidence that the Schenectady socialists were attempting "to go beyond mere reformism." Spencer, "George R. Lunn and the First Socialist Administration in Schenectady," 107–13, quote at 113.

    In Milwaukee, Daniel Hoan also continually pushed to expand the range of municipal services, although as a lawyer, he took more care to operate within the law. After the success of the city's food markets during the First World War, Hoan tried to establish public markets on an ongoing basis. He was able to get authorization from the state legislature in 1923, but the nonsocialist majority on the Common Council defeated his initiative by failing to appropriate funding. Blocked from establishing government-owned enterprises, Hoan turned to supporting cooperatively organized economic activities, as had his predecessors in Schenectady. The most ambitious was the Garden Homes development, an effort to create affordable housing in attractive neighborhoods on a noncommercial basis. The Garden Homes initiative resulted in the building of over one hundred houses in the early 1920s. Floyd John Stachowski, "The Political Career of Daniel Webster Hoan" (PhD diss., Northwestern University, 1966), 73, 113, 117–37; and Gail Radford, *Modern Housing for America: Policy Struggles in the New Deal Era* (Chicago: University of Chicago Press, 1996), 50–51.

30. Alice M. Holden, "Current Municipal Affairs," *American Political Science Review*, 7 (November 1913): 666–67; and Alice M. Holden, "Municipal Ice Plants," *American Political Science Review* 9 (August 1915): 565.
31. Kansas City v. Orear, 277 Mo. 303, 307 (1919).
32. Ibid., Mo. 303, 331 (1919).
33. Ibid., Mo. 303, 319–20 (1919), emphasis added; and Laurence S. Knappen, *Revenue Bonds and the Investor* (New York: Prentice-Hall, 1939), 283.
34. City of Denton v. Denton Home Ice Company, 119 Tex. 193, 201, 193 (1930).
35. In addition to the Schenectady case, courts became involved in nine other conflicts over attempts by municipalities to produce and sell ice according to the LexisNexis database and Oscar Pond, *A Treatise on the Law of Public Utilities* (Indianapolis: Bobbs-Merrill, 1913), 65. Courts ruled against the local jurisdiction in the following four cases: *Mueller v. Thompson*, 149 Wis. 488 (1912); *Union Ice and Coal v. Ruston*, 135 La. 898 (1914); *Kansas City v. Orear*, 277 Mo. 303 (1919); and *Hill v. Port of Seattle*, 104 Wash. 634 (1919). In the last case, the Supreme Court of Washington prohibited the Port District of Seattle from selling ice to the public, incident to furnishing it to fishing boats and warehouses. Courts ruled for the local jurisdiction in five cases (only two of which were decided before 1926, both in Georgia): *Holton v. City of Camilla*, 134 Ga. 560 (1910); *Saunders v. Mayor of Arlington*, 147 Ga. 581 (1918); *Tombstone v. Macia*, 30 Ariz. 218 (1926); *Denton v. Denton Home Ice Co.*, 119 Tex. 193 (1930); and *Kellett v. Johnson*, 330 Mo. 452 (1932).
36. Charles C. Williamson, *The Finances of Cleveland* ([1907] New York: AMS Press, 1968), 209; McKisson quoted in Jon C. Teaford, *The Unheralded Triumph: City Government in America, 1870–1900* (Baltimore: Johns Hopkins University Press, 1984), 291; and Campbell, "Municipal Ownership," 715–17.
37. Lane W. Lancaster, "State Limitations on Local Indebtedness," in *The Municipal Year Book*, ed. Clarence E. Ridley and Orin F. Nolting (Washington, DC: International City Managers' Association, 1936), 319–24; and Williamson, *The Finances of Cleveland*, 210.
38. Ballard C. Campbell, "Tax Revolts and Political Change," *Journal of Policy History*, 10, no. 1 (1998): 156–61; and David C. Perry, "Building the City through the Back Door: The Politics of Debt, Law, and Public Infrastructure," in *Building the Public City: The Politics, Governance, and Finance of Public Infrastructure*, Urban Affairs Annual Review 43 (Thousand Oaks, CA: Sage, 1995), 202–36. The property tax is described as "the most central and massive flaw in state and local finance systems" in Clifton K. Yearley, *The Money Machines: The Breakdown and Reform of Governmental and Party Finance in the North, 1860–1920* (Albany: State University of New York Press, 1970), 37. Lancaster, "State Limitations on Local Indebtedness," 319–23. Quote from David T. Beito, *Taxpayers in Revolt: Tax Resistance during the Great Depression* (Chapel Hill: University of North Carolina Press, 1989), 2.
39. Williamson, *The Finances of Cleveland*, 209–10.
40. The assembly gave these specialized administrative units fiscal autonomy by grant-

ing them the power to tax. Lois Green Carr, "The Foundations of Social Order: Local Government in Colonial Maryland," in *Town and County: Essays on the Structure of Local Government in the American Colonies*, ed. Bruce C. Daniels (Middletown, CT: Wesleyan University Press, 1978), 95; Nancy Burns, *The Formation of American Local Governments: Private Values in Public Institutions* (New York: Oxford University Press, 1994), 46; Kathryn A. Foster, *The Political Economy of Special-Purpose Government* (Washington, DC: Georgetown University Press, 1997), 15–16; and Paul Studenski, *The Government of Metropolitan Areas in the United States* (New York: National Municipal League, 1930), 257–70.

41. Ellwood P. Cubberley, *Public Education in the United States: A Study and Interpretation of American Educational History* (Boston: Houghton Mifflin, 1934), 68–73, and chap. 6; and Edwin Grant Dexter, *A History of Education in the United States* (New York: Macmillan, 1922), 185–88.

42. Robin L. Einhorn, *Property Rules: Political Economy in Chicago, 1833–1872* (Chicago: University of Chicago Press, 1991), 15–19, 104–43. For a defense of the special assessment system as allowing modest-income families to become homeowners by giving them the option of voting against improvements that would price their properties beyond reach, see Roger D. Simon, *The City-Building Process: Housing and Services in New Milwaukee Neighborhoods, 1880–1910* ([1978] Philadelphia: American Philosophical Society, 1996), 24. On the use of special assessment financing to develop suburban residential enclaves, see Ann Durkin Keating, *Building Chicago: Suburban Developers and the Creation of a Divided Metropolis* (Columbus: Ohio State University Press, 1988), 79–97.

43. Joel A. Tarr, "The Evolution of the Urban Infrastructure," 28; Studenski, *The Government of Metropolitan Areas in the United States*, 256–87; and John C. Bollens, *Special District Government in the United States* (Berkeley: University of California Press, 1957), 46–92. Like special districts within cities, metropolitan special districts tended to be isolated from public input. See Sarah S. Elkind, "Building a Better Jungle: Anti-Urban Sentiment, Public Works, and Political Reform in American Cites, 1880–1930," *Journal of Urban History* 24 (November 1997): 55. On the "closed, self-contained nature of decision making," that characterizes some of the most influential contemporary special districts in the country, see Robert Gottlieb and Margaret FitzSimmons, *Thirst for Growth: Water Agencies as Hidden Government in California* (Tucson: University of Arizona Press, 1991), 109–46, esp. 110.

44. Frederic H. Guild, "Special Municipal Corporations," *American Political Science Review* 12 (November 1918): 680–81, quotes at 681.

45. C. Dickerman Williams and Peter R. Nehemkis, Jr., "Municipal Improvements as Affected by Constitutional Debt Limitations," *Columbia Law Review* 37 (February 1937): 187.

46. Foster, *The Political Economy of Special-Purpose Government*, 17; and Lawrence L. Durisch, "Publicly Owned Utilities and the Problem of Municipal Debt Limits," *Michigan Law Review* 31 (1932–1933): 504.

47. Morris A. Copeland, *Trends in Government Financing* (Princeton, NJ: Princeton University Press, 1961), 94. School districts are excluded for three reasons. The first is for comparability, since they are almost always excluded in the literature on special districts and authorities. This is because the metrics of school districts follow a different logic and would make statistics on special districts and authorities meaningless if included. For example, the number of school districts has diminished radically over the course of the twentieth century, as tiny districts, suitable for young

children walking to school, were consolidated. School district financing has also followed a distinct trajectory from other independent local government units. In 1902, school districts carried a debt load over nine times that of all other special districts combined. By the eve of the New Deal, total school district debt was less than twice that of all other special districts. In the immediate postwar period, the two totals were roughly the same. The second and more substantive reason for excluding school districts is that they are not part of the story told in this chapter and book. Primary and secondary education have been regarded as core functions of government from early in the life of the republic, rather than novel public activities to be instituted as industrialization and urbanization brought about a more complex, interconnected society and economy. James A. Maxwell, *Financing State and Local Governments* (Washington, DC: Brookings Institution, 1965), 73; and Bollens, *Special District Government*, chap. 6.

48. Winston v. Spokane, 12 Wash. 524 (1895).
49. U.S. Federal Emergency Administration of Public Works, *Revenue Bond Financing by Political Subdivisions: Its Origin, Scope, and Growth in the United States* (Washington, DC: GPO, 1936), 3–4; Durisch, "Publicly Owned Utilities," 506; John F. Fowler, Jr., *Revenue Bonds: The Nature, Uses and Distribution of Fully Self-Liquidating Public Loans* (New York: Harper, 1938), 21–22; and David Wilma, "Seattle Takes Over Ownership and Operation of the Streetcar System on April 1, 1919," HistoryLink.org (Online Encyclopedia of Washington State History).
50. Van Eaton v. Town of Sidney, 211 Iowa 986, 993 (1930). Even when an ad hoc authorization was granted, it often contained restrictions—far more rigid than those in the charters of private corporations—that made it hard for the new public enterprise to succeed. E. H. Foley, Jr., "Revenue Financing of Public Enterprises," *Michigan Law Review* 35 (November 1936): 22.

CHAPTER 4

1. George H. Nash, *The Life of Herbert Hoover*, vol. 3, *Master of Emergencies, 1917–1918* (New York: W. W. Norton, 1996), 10.
2. David Burner, *Herbert Hoover: A Public Life* (New York: Alfred A. Knopf, 1979), 94.
3. Wesley C. Mitchell, *History of Prices during the War, W.I.B. Price Bulletin No. 1* (Washington, DC: GPO, 1919), 52–53.
4. Frank M. Surface, *The Grain Trade during the World War* (New York: Macmillan, 1928), 18–31; and U.S. Department of Agriculture, *Yearbook, 1918* (Washington, DC: GPO, 1919), 469.
5. William Frieburger, "War Prosperity and Hunger: The New York Food Riots of 1917," *Labor History* 25 (Spring 1984): 217–39; Dana Frank, "Housewives, Socialists, and the Politics of Food: The 1917 New York Cost-of-Living Protests," *Feminist Studies* 11 (Summer 1985): 255–85, quote at 266; and Meg Jacobs, *Pocketbook Politics: Economic Citizenship in Twentieth-Century America* (Princeton, NJ: Princeton University Press, 2005), 53–55.
6. Tom G. Hall, "Wilson and the Food Crisis: Agricultural Price Control during World War I," *Agricultural History* 47 (January 1973): 33.
7. Meyer London, "The Government as Grocer," *Independent*, March 12, 1917.
8. Edward Mandell House to Wilson, May 4, 1917, in Arthur S. Link, ed., *The Papers of Woodrow Wilson* (Princeton, NJ: Princeton University Press, 1983), 42:220. For reactions to Hoover's personality, see Nash, *The Life of Herbert Hoover*, 3:23.
9. Quotation from closed-door, unpublished hearings before the House Committee

on Agriculture, May 7, 1917, quoted in Nash, *The Life of Herbert Hoover*, 3:13. Robert Cuff makes the point that the independent status of Hoover's agency should not be seen as inevitable, as witnessed by the fact that food control during the Second World War was handled by the Agriculture Department and during the First World War the Labor Department "managed to retain primacy in its traditional field." Robert Cuff, "Herbert Hoover, The Ideology of Voluntarism and War Organization during the Great War," *Journal of American History* 64 (September 1977): 362.

10. Wilson quoted in Francis William O'Brien, ed., *The Hoover-Wilson Wartime Correspondence* (Ames: Iowa State University Press, 1974), 49. Wilson's preferred plan was a commission that included representatives of agriculture, industry, and labor, with Hoover as chairman. Nash, *The Life of Herbert Hoover*, 3:16.
11. Nash, *The Life of Herbert Hoover*, 3:27–34.
12. Hoover to Wilson, June 29, 1917, in Link, *The Papers of Woodrow Wilson*, 43:49.
13. "Cut in Food Prices Is to Be Hoover's First Official Aim," *New York Times*, May 30, 1917. Hoover at one point suggested that explicit permission for forming government corporations be included in the food control bill but ultimately decided against this course. See Hoover to Wilson, June 30, 1917 in Link, *The Papers of Woodrow Wilson*, 43:56.
14. Monroe Lee Billington, *Thomas P. Gore, The Blind Senator from Oklahoma* (Lawrence: University of Kansas Press, 1967), 97.
15. Quoted in Nash, *The Life of Herbert Hoover*, 3:39.
16. "Attacks Hoover as Arch Gambler," *New York Times*, July 17, 1917.
17. 40 Stat. 276 (August 10, 1917), sections 1, 2, and 11. "Executive Order Establishing the United States Food Administration," August 10, 1917, reprinted in Surface, *The Grain Trade*, 517–18; and "Big Corporation to Control Wheat," *New York Times*, August 16, 1917.
18. "Authority to Organize Food Administration Grain Corporation," Executive Order 2681, reprinted in J. Reuben Clark, Jr., *Emergency Legislation Passed Prior to December, 1917 Dealing with the Control and Taking of Private Property for the Public Use, Benefit, or Welfare* (Washington, DC: GPO, 1918), 174–76, quote at 175.
19. Harold Archer Van Dorn, *Government Owned Corporations* (New York: Alfred A. Knopf, 1926), 86; and Harvey F. Pinney, "Federal Government Corporations as Instrumentalities of Government and Administration" (PhD diss., New York University, 1937), quote at 278.

    Hoover also established a second subsidiary organization to help carry out the program of the Food Administration. In 1918 he set up the Sugar Equalization Board, Inc., to purchase and distribute Cuban sugar in a manner that would not undermine American sugar beet growers. He incorporated this body under the laws of Delaware. In this instance, for reasons that are not clear, Wilson gave his permission in a letter, rather than by executive order. Van Dorn, *Government Owned Corporations*, 178–79.
20. "Modify Wheat Rule as Cereals Advance," *New York Times*, February 2, 1918.
21. Surface, *The Grain Trade*, 20. By 1917, the retail price of bread was up by 64 percent over 1913 levels, but advanced only 11 percent during 1918. Van Dorn, *Government Owned Corporations*, 101–2.
22. Burner, *Herbert Hoover*, 100. For Hoover's extensive public relations conservation campaign, see also Jacobs, *Pocketbook Politics*, 56–63; and Maxcy Robson Dickson, *The Food Front in World War I* (Washington, DC: American Council on Public Affairs, 1944). For Hoover's commitment to a noncoercive role for government, see

Joan Hoff Wilson, *Herbert Hoover: Forgotten Progressive* (Boston: Little, Brown, 1975), 54–63.

23. Hoover, "Introduction" to William Clinton Mullendore, *History of the United States Food Administration, 1917–1919* (Stanford, CA: Stanford University Press, 1941), 12; David M. Kennedy, *Over Here: The First World War and American Society* ([1980] New York: Oxford University Press, 2004), 119–120; and Nash, *The Life of Herbert Hoover*, 3:13, Hoover quote at 74.
24. Nash, *The Life of Herbert Hoover*, 3:81–92, 535–37n107; Surface, *The Grain Trade*, 70, 74, 83; U.S. Department of Agriculture, *Yearbook, 1918*, 469; Kendrick A. Clements, *The Presidency of Woodrow Wilson* (Lawrence: University Press of Kansas, 1992), 68–69; and Mullendore, *History of the United States Food Administration*, 23. Hoover quote from "Hoover Ready to Buy Whole Wheat Crop," *New York Times*, August 13, 1917.
25. Reed quoted in Nash, *The Life of Herbert Hoover*, 3:85: Surface, *The Grain Trade*, 150, 125.
26. Van Dorn, *Government Owned Corporations*, 99–100, 118–19; and Surface, *The Grain Trade*, 330, 459.
27. Arthur C. Townley, leader of the North Dakota Nonpartisan League, quoted in Hall, "Wilson and the Food Crisis," 46.
28. Quotes from "Farmer's Export Financing Corporation Act, 1921," Senate Report No. 192, 67th Cong., 1st sess., 2. Text of Norris's bill printed in Senate Committee on Agriculture and Forestry, *Farmers' Export Financing Corporation: Hearings on S. 1915*, 67th Cong., 1st sess., June 20–29, 1921, 3–6.
29. Murray R. Benedict, *Farm Politics of the United States, 1790–1950* (New York: Twentieth Century Fund, 1953), 183n 28; and Norman L. Zucker, *George W. Norris: Gentle Knight of American Democracy* (Urbana: University of Illinois Press, 1966), 88. Hoover quotes from "Hoover Opposes Government Aid to Farm Exporting," *New York Times*, June 26, 1921. James H. Shideler, *Farm Crisis, 1919–1923* (Berkeley: University of California Press, 1957), 159–62, Norris quote at 162.
30. Emergency Agricultural Credits Act, 42 Stat. 181 (August 24, 1921); John McDiarmid, *Government Corporations and Federal Funds* (Chicago: University of Chicago Press, 1938), 198–99; Van Dorn, *Government Owned Corporations*, 129–38, 198–205; and Agricultural Credits Act of 1923, 42 Stat. 1454 (March 4, 1923).
31. David Hamilton, *From New Day to New Deal: American Farm Policy from Hoover to Roosevelt*, 1928–1933 (Chapel Hill: University of North Carolina Press, 1991), 19–21; and Benedict, *Farm Politics*, 208–31.
32. H. Morton Bodfish, *History of Building and Loan in the United States* (Chicago: United States Building and Loan League, 1931), 207–9; and American Federation of Labor, *American Federation of Labor: History, Encyclopedia Reference Book*, vol. 2 (Washington, DC: American Federation of Labor, 1924), 298. Quote from Senate Committee on Banking and Currency, *Hearing on Federal Building Loans, S. 2492*, 66th Cong., 1st sess., October 8, 1919, 20.
33. Kennedy, *Over Here*, 252–58; Glenn E. Plumb, "Labor's Solution of the Railroad Problem," *Nation*, August 16, 1919, 200–201; Glenn E. Plumb and William G. Roylance, *Industrial Democracy: A Plan for Its Achievement* (New York: B. W. Heubsch 1923), 198; David Montgomery, *The Fall of the House of Labor: The Workplace, the State, and American Labor Activism* ([1987] Paris: Cambridge University Press, paperback reprint 1993), 401; and K. Austin Kerr, *American Railroad Politics, 1914–1920* (Pittsburgh, PA: University of Pittsburgh Press, 1968), chap. 7.

34. Preston J. Hubbard, *Origins of the TVA: The Muscle Shoals Controversy, 1920–1932* (Nashville, TN: Vanderbilt University Press, 1961), 1–7; Norman Wengert, "Antecedents of TVA: The Legislative History of Muscle Shoals," *Agricultural History* 25 (October 1952): 145–46; Paul K. Conkin, "Intellectual and Political Roots," in *TVA: Fifty Years of Grass-Roots Bureaucracy*, ed. Erwin C. Hargrove and Paul K. Conkin (Urbana: University of Illinois Press, 1983), 12–22; and Norman L. Zucker, *George W. Norris: Gentle Knight of American Democracy* (Urbana: University of Illinois Press, 1966), 118–19.
35. Van Dorn, *Government Owned Corporations*, chap. 9; McDiarmid, *Government Corporations and Federal Funds*, 31–32; and William J. Peterson, "The Federal Barge Line," *Palimpsest* 53 (September 1973): 390–401.
36. Herbert Hoover, "Third Annual Message" reprinted in William Starr Myers, ed., *The State Papers and Other Public Writings of Herbert Hoover* (Garden City, NY: Doubleday, Doran, 1934), quotes at 54, 47, 49; Albert U. Romasco, *The Poverty of Abundance: Hoover, the Nation, the Depression* (New York: Oxford University Press, 1965), 191; and Federal Home Loan Bank Act, 47 Stat. 725 (July 22, 1932).
37. Hoover, "Third Annual Message" 50; and Gerald D. Nash, "Herbert Hoover and the Origins of the Reconstruction Finance Corporation," *Mississippi Valley Historical Review* 46 (December 1959): 455–68. Hoover quote characterizing the banking sector from Jordan A. Schwarz, *The Interregnum of Despair: Hoover, Congress, and the Depression* (Urbana: University of Illinois Press, 1970), 88–89. Reconstruction Finance Corporation Act, 47 Stat. 5 (January 22, 1932).
38. James Stuart Olson, *Herbert Hoover and the Reconstruction Finance Corporation, 1931–1933* (Ames: Iowa State University Press, 1977), 24–39, McFadden quoted at 35 and Wagner at 36.

    With regard to the issue of expediency, it should be noted that Hoover had endorsed the popular concept of stabilization corporations to deal with agricultural surpluses while a candidate for the presidency in 1928, even though he had consistently opposed establishing such bodies during his tenure as Commerce Secretary. Historian David E. Hamilton describes this shift as "political opportunism." As it turned out, the stabilization corporations authorized by the Agricultural Marketing Act (June 15, 1929) did not turn out to be effective. During the war, Hoover's goal with the grain corporation was to stimulate production and hold down prices. The deteriorating economy of the late 1920s presented an opposite set of challenges—ones that were inherently harder to solve. In February 1930, with wheat prices falling since the previous summer, the Grain Stabilization Corporation attempted to create a price floor through buying operations, with the hope that it could dispose of its stores after world prices recovered. No upturn occurred, however, and the corporation exhausted its resources and ended its purchasing program in June 1931. The Cotton Stabilization Corporation, created in June 1930, suffered a similar fate. Benedict, *Farm Policies*, 262–63; and Hamilton, *From New Day to New Deal*, 66–108, quote at 42.
39. As always with these heterogeneous agencies, there is no single definitive count, because different researchers use different definitions. The figures used here are based primarily on the those in Joint Committee on Reduction of Nonessential Federal Expenditures, *Report of Joint Committee on Reduction of Nonessential Federal Expenditures Relative to Government Corporations*, Senate Doc. 227, 78th Cong., 2nd sess. (August 1, 1944), 2–3, which lists agencies in existence at the time the report was issued. Homogeneous instrumentalities, for example, the twelve land banks, are counted as single units. Information on corporate agencies established after March

1933 but no longer in existence by 1944 from McDiarmid, *Government Corporations and Federal Funds*, 34–47.

40. "New Deal Rules by Corporations," *New York Times*, October 22, 1933.
41. The ten that were established without explicit congressional authorization were the Commodity Credit Corporation, the Federal Surplus Commodities Corporation, the Public Works Emergency Housing Corporation, the Federal Subsistence Homesteads Corporation, the Electric Home and Farm Authority, the Public Works Emergency Leasing Corporation, the Tennessee Valley Associated Cooperatives, Inc., the Export-Import Bank of Washington, the Second Export Import Bank of Washington, and the Virgin Islands Company. For information on the circumstances of their creation, see the appendix.
42. The name would be changed in 1935 to the Federal Surplus Commodities Corporation. Roosevelt quoted in "Huge Corporation to Buy for Relief," *New York Times*, October 2, 1933. Certificate of incorporation of the Federal Surplus Relief Corporation printed in volume 79 of Congressional Record, 74th Cong., 1st sess. (February 6, 1935), 1556–57. Executive Order 6340, Creating the Commodity Credit Corporation, October 16, 1933. After listing several pieces of recent emergency legislation, in addition to the Federal Farm Loan Act of 1916, Roosevelt stated in this order that it was "expedient and necessary that a corporation be organized with such powers and functions as may be necessary to accomplish the purposes of said acts." As justification for his ability to establish an agency independent of the standard departmental structure of the federal government, the president cited the National Industrial Recovery Act, 48 Stat. 195 (June 16, 1933), sec. 2. (a): "To effectuate the policy of this title, the President is hereby authorized to establish such agencies . . . as he may find necessary."
43. "Work Relief Corporation to Spend 8 to 9 Billions, Hopkins Plan to End Dole," *New York Times*, November 29, 1934; "Flurry over Hopkins Finds His 'EPIA' at Work," *New York Times*, December 2, 1934; and June Hopkins, "The Road Not Taken: Harry Hopkins and New Deal Work Relief," *Presidential Studies Quarterly* 29 (June 1999): 306–16. For Sinclair's authorities, see his *I, Candidate for Governor and How I Got Licked* ([1934] Berkeley: University of California Press, 1994), 242–49. Hopkins lobbied hard, but ultimately unsuccessfully, for a work relief corporation to be added to the administration's social welfare proposal that ultimately became the Social Security Act.
44. National Industrial Recovery Act, 48 Stat. 195, Title II, sec. 208; Arthur M. Schlesinger, Jr., "The Coming of the New Deal (Boston: Houghton Mifflin, 1959), 361–68, quote at 364; and Paul K. Conkin, *Tomorrow a New World: The New Deal Community Program* ([1959] New York: Da Capo Press, 1976), chap. 5, Bankhead quote at 87. The sketch of the substinance homesteads program in this section relies heavily on Conkin and Schlesinger.
45. Executive Order No. 6209, July 21, 1933.
46. Philip M. Glick, "The Federal Subsistence Homesteads Program," *Yale Law Journal* 44 (June 1935): Cummings quoted at 1333n27, Glick quote at 1333. Glick was the program's general counsel.
47. Ibid., 1333–37, quote at 1335.
48. McDiarmid, *Government Corporations and Federal Funds*, 40–41, 200–201; and Conkin, *Tomorrow a New World*, 119.
49. Letter from McCarl to Ickes, dated January 11, 1934, entered in Congressional Record, 73rd Cong. 2nd sess. (January 22, 1934), 1053.

50. Dale L. Flesher, "Remembering J. Raymond McCarl," *Government Accountants Journal* 42 (Spring 1993): 22; "J. R. M'Carl Dead," *New York Times*, August 3,1940; and John Raymond McCarl, "Government-Run-Everything," *Saturday Evening Post*, October 3, 1936, 9. The agency largely abandoned pre-audits after McCall's tenure ended. It transitioned from focusing on specific expenditures to investigating and analyzing the efficacy of government programs more generally. Reflecting this more expansive conception, in 2004, Congress changed the formal name of the GAO to Government Accountability Office. *GAO: Working for Good Government Since 1921*, http://www.gao.gov/about/history (accessed June 22, 2011).
51. Congressional Record, 74th Cong. 1st sess. (February 6, 1935), vol. 79, pt. 2, 1546, 1547. Reputation as second most unpopular from "Death of Schall" *Time*, December 30, 1935. The least liked was assumed to be Huey Long.
52. Albert W. Atwood, "The New Deal Corporate Maze," *Saturday Evening Post*, October 26, 1935, 68.
53. National Industrial Recovery Act, 48 Stat. 195 (June 16, 1933), Title I, sec. 2.
54. Letter from McCarl to Ickes (January 11, 1934) printed in Congressional Record, 73rd Cong. 2nd sess. (January 22, 1934), vol. 78, pt. 1, 1052–53.
55. The President's Committee on Administrative Management, *Report of the Committee* (Washington, DC: GPO, 1937), 32–33, quote at 32. The key studies of the administrative reorganization battle are Richard Polenberg, *Reorganizing Roosevelt's Government: The Controversy over Executive Reorganization,1936–1939* (Cambridge, MA: Harvard University Press, 1966); and Barry Dean Karl, *Executive Reorganization and Reform in the New Deal: The Genesis of Administrative Management, 1900–1939* (Cambridge, MA: Harvard University Press, 1963).
56. Polenberg, *Reorganizing Roosevelt's Government*, 22; and President's Committee, *Report of the Committee*, 7–9, 121–30, quotes at 7, 64.
57. Senator Burton Wheeler quoted in "Wheeler for Curb on Reorganization," *New York Times*, March 9, 1938. Hoover quoted in Carl Brent Swisher, *American Constitutional Development* (Cambridge, MA: Houghton Mifflin, 1943), 763. Hoover's message to the Senate on reorganization of executive departments is in Congressional Record, 72nd Cong., 2nd sess. (February 17, 1932), vol. 75, pt. 4, 4109–10.
58. Byrd quoted in *Current Biography 1942* (New York: H. W. Wilson, 1942), 117. Paul Y. Anderson, "Reorganization and Bunk," *Nation* 146 (April 8, 1938): 406.
59. Byrd quoted in David L. Porter, *Congress and the Waning of the New Deal* (Port Washington, NY: Kennikat Press, 1980), 94.
60. Ronald L. Heinemann, *Harry Byrd of Virginia* (Charlottesville: University Press of Virginia, 1996), 179, 219; and *Current Biography, 1955* (New York: H. W. Wilson, 1955), quote at 90.
61. Heinemann, *Harry Byrd of Virginia*, 227, quote at 221.
62. "Byrd Committee Called Wasteful," *New York Times*, February 25, 1950; Carl Solberg, *Hubert Humphrey: A Biography* (New York: Norton, 1984), 160–61, 141–45; and Frederick C. Mosher, *The GAO: The Quest for Accountability in American Government* (Boulder, CO: Westview Press, 1979), 127n10.
63. U.S. Congress, Joint Committee on Reduction of Nonessential Federal Expenditures, *Report on Government Corporations*, Senate Doc. 227, 78th Cong., 2nd sess. (August 1, 1944), quote at 2, table 7 on 49.
64. Government Corporation Control Act, 59 Stat. 597 (December 6, 1945).
65. The reincorporated agencies were the Panama Railroad Company, the Commodity

Credit Corporation, the Institute of Inter-American Affairs, the Virgin Islands Company, and the Export-Import Bank. Allowed to lapse at this time were the Defense Plant Corporation, the Metals Reserve Company, the Rubber Reserve Company, the Defense Supplies Corporation, and the Disaster Loan Corporation. Senate Committee on Government Operations, *Audit Reports of Government Corporation and Agencies*, Senate Report 861, 83rd Cong., 2nd sess. (January 1954), 7.

66. The St. Lawrence Seaway Development Corporation (SLSDC) was chartered by Congress in 1954, 68 Stat. 92, to develop, operate, and maintain, in cooperation with the government of Canada, the seaway between Lake Erie and Montreal. The SLSDC operated as an independent agency until 1958, when it was transferred to the Department of Commerce. In 1967 it became part of the Department of Transportation. The FFC was chartered in 1954 by the secretary of the treasury pursuant to Executive Order 10539 and dissolved in 1961 by an act of Congress, 75 Stat. 418. Data from *Guide to Federal Records in the National Archives of the United States*, compiled by Robert B. Matchette et al. (Washington, DC: National Archives and Records Administration, 1995), web version.

67. Senate Committee on Government Operations, *Audit Reports*, 8.

68. The Resolution Trust Corporation (RTC) was established by the Financial Institutions Reform, Recovery, and Enforcement Act (FIRREA) of 1989, 103 Stat. 183. By 1986, the Federal Savings and Loan Insurance Corporation (FSLIC), the federal insurer of the thrift industry (banking institutions that specialize in residential mortgage loans), had been left insolvent due to the failure of hundreds of thrifts. FIRREA created a new thrift insurance fund to be administered by the Federal Deposit Insurance Corporation (FDIC) and established the RTC, initially capitalized at $50 billion (later raised to $105 billion), to handle the assets of failed or troubled thrift institutions. By 1999, the cost to U.S. taxpayers to back up the commitment extended to insured depositors of failed thrifts came to approximately $124 billion. Timothy Curry and Lynn Shibut, "The Cost of the Savings and Loan Crisis," *FDIC Banking Review* 13, no. 2 (2000): 26–35.

The United States Enrichment Corporation (USEC) was established by the Energy Policy Act of 1992, 106 Stat. 2776, as a wholly owned government corporation for the purpose of privatizing the two facilities. (The process was modeled on Conrail, a government corporation that Congress established in 1976 from seven private bankrupt railroads in the Northeast. After ten years and an investment of $10 billion, the operation was able to demonstrate commercial viability such that private investors came forward and bought the freight rail system for $2 billion.) The USEC was sold in 1998, but the transition was not successful. This was because the company was not able to compete successfully with other for-profit enrichment firms while carrying out the public purposes that Congress had envisioned being continued under private ownership, such as keeping the facilities in both states open and purchasing, at above-market rates, large quantities of weapons-grade uranium from the former Soviet Union as a way of keeping it out of the hands of unfriendly nations and terrorists. Ronald C. Moe and Kevin R. Kosar, *Federal Government Corporations: An Overview* (Congressional Research Service, March 23, 2006), 14–15; Peter Passell, "The Sticky Side of Privatization: Sale of U.S. Nuclear Fuel Plants Raises Host of Conflicts," *New York Times*, August 30, 1997; and Dan Guttman, "The United States Enrichment Corporation: A Failing Privatisation," *Asian Journal of Public Administration* 23 (December 2001): 247–72.

69. Atwood, "The New Deal Corporate Maze."
70. Arthur W. Macmahon, John D. Millett, Gladys Ogden, *The Administration of Federal Work Relief* (Chicago: Public Administration Service, 1941), 116.
71. Polenberg, *Reorganizing Roosevelt's Government*, 9, 10.
72. Schlesinger, Jr., *The Coming of the New Deal* , 533.
73. Ibid., Tugwell quoted at 534.
74. Jordan A. Schwarz, *Liberal: Adolf A. Berle and the Vision of an American Era* (New York: The Free Press, 1987), 138–39; William J. Barber, *Designs within Disorder: Franklin D. Roosevelt, the Economists, and the Shaping of American Economic Policy, 1933–1945* (New York: Cambridge University Press, 1966), 125–26; and Adolf A. Berle, Jr., "A Banking System for Capital and Capital Credit," chap. 5 in Berle, *New Directions in the New World* (New York: Harper and Brothers, 1940).
75. For example, Harold Archer Van Dorn, *Government Owned Corporations* (New York: Alfred A. Knopf, 1926); Robert H. Schnell and Robert H. Wettach, "Corporations as Agencies of the Recovery Program, *North Carolina Law Review* 12 (February 1934): 77–98; Maurice S. Culp, "Creation of Government Corporations by the National Government," *Michigan Law Review* 33 (February 1935): 473–511; John Thurston, "Government Proprietary Corporations I," *Virginia Law Review* 21 (February 1935): 351–96; John Thurston, "Government Proprietary Corporations II," *Virginia Law Review* 21 (March 1935): 465–503; Oliver Peter Field, "Government Corporations: A Proposal," *Harvard Law Review* 48 (March 1935): 775–96; John A. McIntire, "Government Corporations as Administrative Agencies: An Approach," *George Washington Law Review* 4 (January 1936): 161–210; and John McDiarmid, *Government Corporations and Federal Funds* (Chicago: University of Chicago Press, 1938).
76. Glick, "The Federal Subsistence Homesteads Program," 1333.
77. James S. Olson, *Saving Capitalism: The Reconstruction Finance Corporation and the New Deal, 1933–1940* (Princeton, NJ: Princeton University Press, 1988), 45.
78. Herbert Morrison, *Socialisation and Transport: The Organisation of Socialised Industries with Particular Reference to the London Passenger Transport Bill* (London: Constable, 1933), passim, quotes at 77, 156. The greater London region consisted of two thousand square miles, in which over nine million people then lived. Terence H. O'Brien, *British Experiments in Public Ownership and Control* (London: George Allen and Unwin, 1937), 203.
79. C. R. Attlee, "Post Office Reform," *New Statesman and Nation* (November 7, 1931): 565–66, quotes at 565.
80. Kenneth O. Morgan, *Labour in Power, 1945–1951* (Oxford: Clarendon Press, 1984), chap. 3.
81. E. Eldon Barry, *Nationalisation in British Politics: The Historical Background* (Stanford, CA: Stanford University Press, 1965), 116, 147–48, 162–64; and G. N. Ostergaard, "Labour and the Development of the Public Corporation," *Manchester School of Economic and Social Studies* 22 (1954): 192–226. The text of the bill appears in Frank Hodges, *Nationalization of the Mines* (London: Leonard Parsons, 1920), 151–70, quote at 154.
82. Charles Loch Mowat, *Britain between the Wars, 1918–1940* (London: Methuen, 1955), 342; and John Singleton, "Labour, the Conservatives and Nationalisation," in *The Political Economy of Nationalisation in Britain, 1920–1950*, ed. Robert Millward and John Singleton (Cambridge: Cambridge University Press, 1995), 13–33.
83. A. Snow, "The First National Grid," *Engineering Science and Education Journal* 2 (October 1993): 219.

84. Morrison, *Socialisation and Transport*, 123, 153.
85. C. Herman Pritchett, "The Government Corporation Control Act of 1945," *American Political Science Review* 40 (June 1946): 509.
86. William E. Leuchtenburg, "The New Deal and the Analogue of War" in Leuchtenburg, *The FDR Years: On Roosevelt and His Legacy* (New York: Columbia University Press, 1995), 75.

CHAPTER 5

1. Seligman quoted in Glenn W. Fisher, *The Worst Tax? A History of the Property Tax in America* (Lawrence: University Press of Kansas, 1996), 4.
2. Census study cited in Paul Studenski and Herman E. Krooss, *Financial History of the United States* (New York: McGraw-Hill, 1952), 432n11. For Detroit, see Eric H. Monkkonen, "The Politics of Municipal Indebtedness and Default, 1850–1936," in *The Politics of Urban Fiscal Policy*, ed. Terrence J. McDonald and Sally K. Ward (Beverly Hills, CA: Sage Publications, 1984), 148.
3. Lane W. Lancaster, "State Limitations on Local Indebtedness," *The Municipal Year Book, 1936* (Washington, DC: International City Managers' Association, 1936), 313; and David T. Beito, *Taxpayers in Revolt: Tax Resistance during the Great Depression* (Chapel Hill: University of North Carolina Press, 1989), quote from 2. Clifton K. Yearley describes the property tax as "the most central and massive flaw in state and local finance systems" in *The Money Machines: The Breakdown and Reform of Governmental and Party Finance in the North, 1860–1920* (Albany: State University of New York Press, 1970), 37.
4. Arthur D. Gayer, *Public Works in Prosperity and Depression* (New York: National Bureau of Economic Research, 1935), 315–32; Joel William Canaday Harper, "Scrip and Other Forms of Local Money" (PhD diss., University of Chicago, 1948), 113, 51–62; American Municipal Association, *Municipal Scrip: A Report of Experience* (Chicago: American Municipal Association, 1934), 5; and Loren Gatch, "Local Money in the United States during the Great Depression," *Essays in Economic and Business History* 26 (2008): 47–61. Thanks to Stephen Mihm for help finding sources on the scrip movement of the 1930s.

   The high point for defaults was November 1935, when 1,170 general-purpose local governments (towns, cities, and counties) were reported to be simultaneously in default. When all local government bodies, such as school and other kinds of special districts, are included the figure rises to 3,251. (This is out of a total of 175,369 total taxing districts then in existence.) It should be noted that most of these defaults represented only temporary delays of payments, not actual repudiations of debt. And while it is true that a few large cities and even some states went into default at some point during the 1930s, most of the defaulting government entities were, as economist Albert Gailord Hart noted, "trifling affairs." As a proportion of all municipal debt, past due payments probably never amounted to more than 2 percent. A. M. Hillhouse, *Municipal Bonds: A Century of Experience* (New York: Prentice-Hall, 1936), table 7, 19; and Albert Gailord Hart, *Debts and Recovery: A Study of Changes in the Internal Debt Structure from 1929 to 1937* (New York: Twentieth Century Fund, 1938), 224.
5. James T. Patterson, *The New Deal and the States: Federalism in Transition* (Princeton, NJ: Princeton University Press, 1969), 7–10; Studenski and Krooss, *Financial History of the United States*, 346; David Brian Robertson and Dennis R. Judd, *The Development of American Public Policy: The Structure of Policy Restraint* (Glenview, IL: Scott,

Foresman, 1989), 23; Ballard C. Campbell, *The Growth of American Government: Governance from the Cleveland Era to the Present* (Bloomington: Indiana University Press, 1995), 86–87; Paul V. Betters, J. Kerwin Williams, and Sherwood L. Reeder, *Recent Federal-City Relations* (Washington, DC: United States Conference of Mayors, 1936), 8; B. U. Ratchford, *American State Debts* (Durham, NC: Duke University Press, 1941), 433, table 38; Jerome J. Shestack, "The Public Authority," *University of Pennsylvania Law Review* 105 (February 1957): 558n28; and W. Brooke Graves, *American State Government* (Boston: D. C. Heath, 1936), 195.

6. Hoan quotes are from his "Letter to Mayors," July 29, 1931, file 135, box 35, Daniel W. Hoan Papers, Milwaukee County Historical Society. Edward S. Kerstein, *Milwaukee's All-American Mayor: Portrait of Daniel Webster Hoan* (Englewood Cliffs, NJ: Prentice-Hall, 1966), 77, 178.
7. Mark I. Gelfand, *A Nation of Cities: The Federal Government and Urban America: 1933–1965* (New York: Oxford University Press, 1975), 35–37, Murphy quote from 36; and Sidney Fine, *Frank Murphy: The Detroit Years* (Ann Arbor: University of Michigan Press, 1975), 349–51.
8. Gelfand, *A Nation of Cities*, 396n31; and Carlos A. Schwantes, "Industrial Armies," in *Encyclopedia of the American Left*, ed. Mari Jo Buhle, Paul Buhle, and Dan Georgakas (Urbana: University of Illinois Press, 1990), 351–52.
9. Lester V. Chandler, *America's Greatest Depression: 1929–1941* (New York: Harper and Row, 1970), 34–35. Quote from Jordan A. Schwarz, *The Interregnum of Despair: Hoover, Congress, and the Depression* (Urbana: University of Illinois Press, 1970), 155. Udo Sautter describes the spectrum of opinion in early 1932 on the issue of federal aid for relief in *Three Cheers for the Unemployed: Government and Unemployment before the New Deal* (Cambridge: Cambridge University Press, 1991), 300–305.
10. Press release, February 3, 1931, in William Starr Myers and Walter H. Newton, *The Hoover Administration: A Documented Narrative* (New York: Charles Scribner's Sons, 1936), 63.
11. Ibid.
12. See, for example, Walter I. Trattner, *From Poor Law to Welfare State: A History of Social Welfare in America*, 3rd ed. (New York: Free Press, 1984), 260–61. Hoover quote from Myers and Newton, *The Hoover Administration*, 182. This was one of twenty-one public warnings against deficit spending that Herbert Hoover issued between December 1931 and April 1932. Albert U. Romasco, *The Poverty of Abundance: Hoover, the Nation, the Depression* (New York: Oxford University Press, 1965), 222.
13. Udo Sautter, "Government and Unemployment: The Use of Public Works before the New Deal," *Journal of American History* 73 (June 1986): 82–83; T. H. Watkins, *The Hungry Years: A Narrative History of the Great Depression in America* (New York: Henry Holt, 1999), 123–34; Irving Bernstein, *The Lean Years: A History of the American Worker, 1920–1933* ([1960] Baltimore: Penguin, 1966), 433–34; "Letter to Mayors," July 29, 1931, file 135, box 35, Daniel W. Hoan Papers (Milwaukee County Historical Society, Milwaukee, Wisconsin.); Edward S. Kerstein, *Milwaukee's All-American Mayor: Portrait of Daniel Webster Hoan* (Englewood Cliffs, NJ: Prentice-Hall, 1966), 133–41; Gelfand, *A Nation of Cities*, 34–37; James Stuart Olson, *Herbert Hoover and the Reconstruction Finance Corporation* (Ames: Iowa State University Press, 1977), 62–73; and Schwarz, *The Interregnum of Despair*, 146–73.
14. Emergency Relief and Construction Act, 47 Stat. 709.
15. Myers and Newton, *The Hoover Administration*, 209.
16. Although only $30 million had been expended before the PWA took over, ERCA

officials actually had authorized $219 million. One problem with getting money out the door was that the bulk of the projects approved were large and complex, requiring sophisticated engineering and architectural work before construction could begin. James S. Olson, "Harvey C. Couch and the Reconstruction Finance Corporation, *Arkansas Historical Quarterly* 32 (Winter 1973): 222; J. Franklin Ebersole, "One Year of the Reconstruction Finance Corporation," *Quarterly Journal of Economics* 47 (May 1933): 482; Secretary of the Treasury, *Final Report of the Reconstruction Finance Corporation* (Washington, DC: GPO, 1959), 268–69, table PA-2; Olson, *Herbert Hoover and the Reconstruction Finance Corporation*, 78; and Paul Y. Anderson, "Buying California for Hoover," *Nation*, October 26, 1932, 392–93.

17. Senate Committee on Banking and Currency, "Further Unemployment Relief through the Reconstruction Finance Corporation: Hearing on S. 5336," 72nd Cong., 2nd sess. (February 2–3, 1933), 70–71.
18. Robert G. Smith, *Ad Hoc Governments: Special Purpose Transportation Authorities in Britain and the United States* (Beverly Hills, CA: Sage, 1974), 109; and Studenski and Krooss, *Financial History of the United States*, 433. Revenue-bond statistics are computed from Lawrence S. Knappen, *Revenue Bonds and the Investor* (New York: Prentice-Hall, 1939), 279–86.
19. The legislatures of just five states held yearly sessions in this period: Massachusetts, New Jersey, New York, Rhode Island, and South Carolina. All others met every two years, except for Alabama, which met every four years. Graves, *American State Government*, 203; Ballard C. Campbell, *The Growth of American Government: Governance from the Cleveland Era to the Present* (Bloomington: Indiana University Press, 1995), 86–87; and Betters et al., *Recent Federal-City Relations*, 8.
20. The RFC financed the Bay Bridge project by purchasing $71 million worth of bonds from the California Toll Bridge Authority. 1929 Cal. Stat., chaps. 762 and 763; and California Legislature, Joint Legislative Budget Committee, *Financial History of the San Francisco–Oakland Bay Bridge* (Sacramento: Senate of the State of California, 1953), 12–16, 71–84. The RFC purchased $148,500,000 worth of bonds from the Metropolitan Water District of Southern California in support of the Metropolitan Aqueduct. 1927 Cal. Stat., chap. 429; Norris Hundley, Jr., *The Great Thirst: Californians and Water, 1770s–1990s* (Berkeley: University of California Press, 1992), 215–32; Wylie Kilpatrick, "Federal Assistance to Municipal Recovery," *National Municipal Review* 26 (July 1937): 339; and John McDiarmid, "California Uses the Government Corporation," *American Political Science Review* 34 (April 1940): 300–306.
21. Knappen, *Revenue Bonds and the Investor*, appendix A, 279–86; and J. Kerwin Williams, *Grants-in-Aid under the Public Works Administration* (New York, 1939), 38–39. It might be argued that some of the 1933 laws were passed in response to the New Deal public works program that took over administration of the Emergency Relief and Construction Act (ERCA) in mid-June of that year. Harold Ickes, who administered the program, took a more activist approach to helping states pass laws that permitted revenue-based borrowing than Hoover's public works directors had. But considering the start-up time for a new federal agency under a new presidential administration and the fact that most state legislatures met early in the year, most of the new state laws passed in 1933 should probably be credited primarily to the impetus of ERCA.
22. *Detroit News*, May 9, 1933, 6; *Detroit Free Press*, May 27, 1933, 1; and 1933 Mich. Pub. Acts, chap. 94 (May 26, 1933), introduction and sec. 11.
23. 1933 S.C. Acts, chap. 299 (May 9, 1933), introduction and sec. 11.

24. National Industrial Recovery Act, 48 Stat. 195. For in-depth treatments of the PWA, see Jason Scott Smith, *Building New Deal Liberalism: The Political Economy of Public Works, 1933–1956* (New York: Cambridge University Press, 2006); and Robert D. Leighninger, Jr., *Long-Range Public Investment: The Forgotten Legacy of the New Deal* (Columbia: University of South Carolina Press, 2007).
25. Williams, *Grants-in-Aid*, 41n2; Jack F. Isakoff, *The Public Works Administration* (Urbana: University of Illinois Press, 1938), 81, 28; James S. Olson, *Saving Capitalism: The Reconstruction Finance Corporation and the New Deal, 1933–1940* (Princeton, NJ: Princeton University Press, 1988), 199; Laurence S. Knappen, *Revenue Bonds and the Investor* (Englewood Cliffs, NJ: Prentice-Hall, 1939), 173–79; and E. H. Foley, Jr., "Some Recent Developments in the Law Relating to Municipal Financing of Public Works," *Fordham Law Review* 4 (January 1935): 11.
26. When the Emergency Relief and Construction Act of 1935, which continued funding for the agency, failed to specify a ceiling for grants, the president raised the limit to 45 percent. In actuality, this new level doubled the impact of grants, because the initial grants of 30 percent were calculated on the cost for labor and materials only, which according to PWA statisticians worked out to be approximately 20–22 percent of the total cost of projects. The larger grants of 45 percent were based on the cost of the entire project. Williams, *Grants-In-Aid* , 133, 122; Jack F. Isakoff, *The Public Works Administration* (Urbana: University of Illinois Press, 1938), 88–93; and Olson, *Herbert Hoover and the Reconstruction Finance Corporation*, 79.
27. Winston P. Wilson, *Harvey Couch: The Master Builder* (Nashville: Broadman Press, 1947), 94; Linda J. Lear, *Harold L. Ickes: The Aggressive Progressive, 1874–1933* (New York: Garland, 1981); Harold L. Ickes, *Back to Work: The Story of the PWA* (New York: Macmillan, 1935), 59, 224; Jeanne Nienaber Clarke, *Roosevelt's Warrior: Harold L. Ickes and the New Deal* (Baltimore: Johns Hopkins University Press, 1996), 71; Franklyn Waltman, Jr., "New Dealists Are Drafting States' Bills," *Washington Post*, January 31, 1935, 1; and Harold Ickes, testimony May 18, 1936 to Senate Committee on Appropriations, *Hearings on First Deficiency Appropriation Bill for 1936*, 74th Cong., 2nd sess., 314 (hereafter: Ickes testimony on *First Deficiency Appropriations Bill*).
28. Frank LeRoy Spangler, *Special Report of the State Tax Commission, No. 5: Operation of Debt and Tax Rate Limits in the State of New York* (Albany: J. B. Lyon, 1932), 18.
29. State ex rel. Hamilton v. Martin, 23 Pac (2d) 1 (Wash. 1933); Williams, *Grants-In-Aid*, 231–32, 246; and James A. Maxwell, *The Fiscal Impact of Federalism in the United States* (Cambridge, MA: Harvard University Press, 1946), 170.
30. Williams, *Grants-In-Aid*, 233–34; and Jones v. City of Detroit, 277 Mich. 272, 269 N.W. 171 (October 5, 1936). Quote from Bacon v. City of Detroit, 282 Mich. 150, 275 N.W. 800 (November 10, 1937).
31. Ickes, *Back to Work*, 224; Williams, *Grants-in-Aid*, 249; and E. H. Foley, Jr., "PWA and Revenue Financing of Public Enterprises," *Proceedings of the First Annual Meeting: Section of Municipal Law* (Chicago: American Bar Association, 1935), 58–59.
32. Ickes testimony on *First Deficiency Appropriations Bill*, 323.
33. U.S. Federal Emergency Administration of Public Works, *Revenue Bond Financing by Political Subdivisions* (Washington, DC: GPO, 1936) 21.
34. C. C. Ludwig, "Cities and the National Government Under the New Deal," *American Political Science Review* 29 (August 1935): 640–48.
35. U.S. Federal Emergency Administration of Public Works, *Revenue Bond Financing*, 22.

36. Secretary of the Treasury, *Final Report of the Reconstruction Finance Corporation*, 149–50.
37. Franklin Roosevelt, "Letter to Governors" (1934), cited in Robert G. Smith, *Ad Hoc Governments*, 108.
38. As Jerome J. Shestack comments, "It is not entirely clear why certain courts should have found it easier to appreciate that the pledge of revenues of authority facilities is less a debt within the constitutional sense than the pledge of a municipality of the revenues from improvements. Nevertheless, whether through subtlety or sophistry, it was the authority that demonstrated the victory of indirection." Shestack, "The Public Authority," *University of Pennsylvania Law Review* 105 (February 1957): 559.
39. Jerry Mitchell, *The American Experiment with Government Corporations* (Armonk, NY: M. E. Sharp, 1999), 26–30; Jameson W. Doig, *Empire on the Hudson: Entrepreneurial Vision and Political Power at the Port of New York Authority* (New York: Columbia University Press, 2001), 171–73; Roosevelt quoted in "Two Governors Open Great Hudson Bridge As Throngs Look On," *New York Times*, October 25, 1931; Bernard Bellush, *Franklin D. Roosevelt as Governor of New York* (New York: Columbia University Press, 1955), chap. 10; and Laws of New York, chap. 772, 1931. The focus of the New York State Power Authority was initially on the St. Lawrence River, rather than the Niagara, since at this point private power companies were using Niagara waterpower on the U.S. side.
40. Emergency Relief and Construction Act, 47 Stat. 709, Title II, sec. 201 (1).
41. "Roosevelt Proposes Lake Sewage Action," *New York Times*, July 11, 1931; E. H. Foley, Jr., "Revenue Financing of Public Enterprises," *Michigan Law Review* 35 (November 1936): 20; quote from "Buffalo Seeks Aid on Disposal Plan," *New York Times*, December 16, 1934; and State of New York Temporary State Commission on Coordination of State Activities, *Staff Report on Public Authorities Under New York State* (Albany, NY: Williams Press, 1956), 294.
42. 1933 Laws of New York, chap. 391.
43. 1935 Laws of New York, chap. 349. Capitalization as in the statute.
44. Dan Cupper, *The Pennsylvania Turnpike: A History* (Lebanon, PA: Applied Arts Publishers, 1990), 6–9, 22–24; Phil Patton, "A Quick Way from Here to There Was Also a Frolic," *Smithsonian* 21 (October 1990): 96–108; and Smith, *Ad Hoc Governments*, 121.
45. James A. Maxwell, *Financing State and Local Governments* (Washington, DC: Brookings Institution, 1965), 188–194.

    The question of whether the federal government should tax the earnings from state and local bonds ("municipals") has long been a point of contention, with the tax treatment of revenue bonds a particular flash point. In 1895, the Supreme Court ruled that the 1894 federal income tax was unconstitutional because it constituted a "direct tax." In the same decision, the court concluded that the legislation's attempt to tax income from states and their subdivisions was "repugnant to the constitution." Pollock v. Farmers Loan and Trust Co., 157 U.S. 429, quote at 586. The Sixteenth Amendment (1913), which allows for a federal income tax, does not mention anything about immunity for state bond issues, and in fact, specifies that "Congress shall have the power to lay and collect taxes on incomes, from whatever source derived." Nevertheless, Congress has never assented to taxing interest income from state securities. The Revenue Act of 1913 (38 Stat. 114, sec. 2) stated "that in computing net income . . . there shall be excluded the interest upon the obligations of a State or any political subdivision thereof." Efforts over the years by Treasury officials under administrations of both parties to end this practice were unsuccessful.

Unable to get legislation through Congress ending the tax exemption for all municipals, the Roosevelt administration pursued a legal strategy focusing specifically on the revenue bonds of the New York Port Authority and the Triborough Bridge Authority, presumably on the assumption that authorities "were more vulnerable than traditional government agencies." The Second Circuit Court of Appeals ruled against the administration in 1944, and, in 1945, the Supreme Court refused to hear the U.S. Treasury's appeal. In 1988, the Supreme Court overturned its decision in *Pollock,* ruling that the exemption rested on statutory, not constitutional grounds (South Carolina v. Baker, 485 U.S. 505). The specific issue in question was the right of the federal government to deny tax exemption to bonds that were not formally registered (thereby making them attractive vehicles for tax evasion and money laundering). South Carolina contested the federal government's right to do this on the basis of the Tenth Amendment and the doctrine of intergovernmental tax immunity. Thus, it is now settled law that Congress has the power to withdraw all exemptions, although it has made no move to do so. Commissioner of Internal Revenue v. Estate of Shamberg, 144 F. 2d 998 (2d Cir. 1944); Commissioner of Internal Revenue v. Estate of White, 144 F. 2d 1019; certiorari denied in both cases 323. U.S. 792 (1945); Doig, *Empire on the Hudson,* chaps. 9–10, quote at 229; Ratchford, *American State Debts,* 509–10; B.U. Ratchford, "Intergovernmental Tax Immunities in the United States," *National Tax Journal* 6 (December 1953): 319–20; Lawrence E. Chermak, *The Law of Revenue Bonds* (Washington, DC: National Institute of Municipal Law Officers, 1954), 193–96; Dennis Zimmerman, *The Private Use of Tax Exempt Bonds: Controlling Public Subsidy of Private Activity* (Washington, DC: Urban Institute Press, 1991), chaps. 2–3; and Alberta M. Sbragia, *Debt Wish: Entrepreneurial Cities, U.S. Federalism, and Economic Development* (Pittsburgh, PA: University of Pittsburgh Press, 1996), chap. 9.

46. Julian E. Zelizer, "The Forgotten Legacy of the New Deal: Fiscal Conservatism and the Roosevelt Administration, 1933–1938," *Presidential Studies Quarterly* 30 (June 2000): 331–58.

CHAPTER 6

1. The total of forty-seven is based on the list produced by the General Accounting Office for the Byrd Committee. U.S. Congress, Joint Committee on Reduction of Nonessential Federal Expenditures, *Report on Government Corporations,* Senate Doc. 227, 78th Cong., 2nd sess. (1944). See also chart A. The total of thirty was derived by subtracting the nineteen agencies no longer in existence in 1960 and adding the two new ones that had been created. Those no longer in business by 1960 were the Disaster Loan Corporation (dissolved 1945), the Reconstruction Finance Corporation (dissolved 1954), and the Home Owners' Loan Corporation (dissolved 1954), plus the sixteen agencies set up to support the war effort (which Congress began liquidating even before VJ Day). The two new agencies, both created in 1954, were the St. Lawrence Seaway Development Corporation and the Federal Facilities Corporation (dissolved 1961).
2. Harvey C. Mansfield, Sr., "Special Government Corporations: A Middle Way," in *Nonprofit Organizations: A Government Management Tool,* ed. Harold Orlans (New York: Praeger, 1980), 71; Kevin R. Kosar, *The Quasi Government: Hybrid Organizations*

with Both Government and Private Sector Legal Characteristics (Washington, DC: Congressional Research Service, 2008), 14–16; Ronald C. Moe, "The Emerging Quasi Government: Issues of Management and Accountability," *Public Administration Review* 61 (May–June 2001): 295–96; and Paul C. Light, *The True Size of Government* (Washington, DC: Brookings Institute Press, 1999), 26. Historian of science Larry Owens has suggested that contracting with the semiprivate research institutes "resonated symbolically" with American economic ideology in an era when officials were anxious to differentiate the U.S. approach to scientific development from that of its totalitarian rival. Aaron L. Friedberg, "The United States and the Cold War Arms Race," in *Reviewing the Cold War*, ed. Odd Arne Westad (London: Frank Cass, 2000), 212.

3. As time went on, RAND began providing research services for other defense agencies, rather than working for the air force exclusively. In the 1960s it started doing social research for a diverse range of clients, including federal, state, and local governments, and even private foundations. Thus, the RAND organization evolved from an air force–sponsored FFRDC into a complex corporate entity that functioned as an independent research contractor, as well as operating FFRDCs. By the early twenty-first century it was serving as administrator of three FFRDCs: Project Air Force, the Arroyo Center, and the National Defense Research Institute. Daniel Guttman, "Public Purpose and Private Service: The Twentieth Century Culture of Contracting Out and the Evolving Law of Diffused Sovereignty," *Administrative Law Review* 52 (2000): 868–72; U.S. Congress, Office of Technology Assessment, *A History of the Department of Defense Federally Funded Research and Development Centers* (Washington, DC: GPO, June 1995), 16, 41–44; and Alex Abella, *Soldiers of Reason: The RAND Corporation and the Rise of the American Empire* (Orlando, FL: Harcourt, 2008), 184–87, 202–12.

4. National Science Foundation, *Master List of Federally Funded Research and Development Centers*, at http://www.nsf.gov/statistics/ffrdclist/ (accessed September 12, 2010). The Los Alamos HIV web system is at http://www.hiv.lanl.gov/content/index (accessed July 24, 2011). The role of the Lawrence Berkeley Laboratory was already shifting in the 1950s, but the clear break came in 1971, when the Lawrence Livermore Laboratory, as a newly independent entity, took over weapons research from the Berkeley lab; see http://www.lbl.gov/Publications/75th/files/04-lab-history-pt-4.html (accessed July 24, 2011).

5. With respect to the formal characteristics of these entities, the Office of Technology Assessment explains that "the defining trait of an FFRDC is a sponsoring agreement with the federal government, clearly identifying the entity as a FFRDC and placing limitations on competition with non-FFRDCs. The federal government's commitment to the existence of a FFRDC implies that there will be a long-term stable financial relationship." U.S. Congress, Office of Technology Assessment, *A History of the Department of Defense Federally Funded Research and Development Centers*, 11.

6. Harold Seidman, *Politics, Position, and Power: The Dynamics of Federal Organization*, 5th ed. (New York: Oxford, 1998), 208–9; Harold Seidman, "Nonprofit Intermediaries: Symptom or Cure?" in *Nonprofit Organizations: A Government Management Tool*, ed. Harold Orlans (New York: Praeger, 1980), 45; and Kosar, *The Quasi-Government*, 16.

7. Kevin R. Kosar, *Federal Government Corporations: An Overview* (Washington, DC: Congressional Research Service, 2009), 15. This total includes only corporate entities

wholly owned by the government, as distinct from government-sponsored mixed-ownership enterprises such as the Federal National Mortgage Association, known as Fannie Mae. National Science Foundation, *Master List.*

8. Ronald C. Moe and Kevin R. Kosar, *Federal Government Corporations: An Overview,* (Washington, DC: Congressional Research Service, March 23, 2006), 17; and Jonathan G. S. Koppell, *The Politics of Quasi Government: Hybrid Organizations and the Dynamics of Bureaucratic Control* (Cambridge: Cambridge University Press, 2003), 183–85.
9. Harold Seidman, "The Quasi World of the Federal Government," *Brookings Review* 6 (Summer 1988): 42; Seidman, *Politics, Position and Power,* 113–16; N. Eric Weiss, *Government Interventions in Financial Markets: Economic and Historic Analysis of Subprime Mortgage Options* (Washington, DC: Congressional Research Service, April 18, 2008), 8; Joseph Stiglitz and Bruce Greenwald, *Towards a New Paradigm in Monetary Economics* (Cambridge: Cambridge University Press, 2003), 239–44; and Seidman quote from Harold Seidman, "Government-Sponsored Enterprise in the United States," in *The New Political Economy: The Public Use of the Private Sector,* ed. Bruce L. R. Smith (New York: Macmillan Press, 1975), 85. A. Michael Froomkin has referred to REFCORP as "little more than an accounting trick," in Froomkin, "Reinventing the Government Corporation," *University of Illinois Law Review* 1995 (1995): 615.
10. David Osborne and Ted Gaebler, *Reinventing Government: How the Entrepreneurial Spirit is Transforming the Public Sector* (Reading, MA: Addison-Wesley, 1992); Ronald C. Moe, "The Emerging Federal Quasi Government: Issues of Management and Accountability," *Public Administration Review* 61 (May–June 2001): 290–93; and Nancy J. Knauer, "Reinventing Government: The Promise of Institutional Choice and Government Created Charitable Organizations," *New York School of Law Review* 42 (1997): 946, 954–58.
11. Ronald C. Moe, "The 'Reinventing Government' Exercise: Misinterpreting the Problem, Misjudging the Consequences," *Public Administration Review* 54 (March–April 1994): 111–22; and Albert Gore, *From Red Tape to Results, Creating a Government That Works Better & Costs Less: Report of the National Performance Review* (Washington, DC: GPO, 1993), 61. Other agencies identified by the NPR as appropriate for transformation into deregulated, self-funding operations include the U.S. Patent and Trademark Office, the U.S. Mint, the St. Lawrence Seaway Development Corporation, the Department of Defense Commissary Agency, and the Seafood Inspection Program. Alasdair Roberts, "Performance-Based Organizations: Assessing the Gore Plan," *Public Administration Review* 57 (November–December 1997): 465–78; and U.S. General Accounting Office, *Government Corporations: Profiles of Recent Proposals,* GAO/66D-95-57FS (Washington, DC: GPO, 1995).
12. Robert W. Poole, "The Urgent Need to Reform the FAA's Air Traffic Control System," *Backgrounder* #2007 (The Heritage Foundation, February 20, 2006), 6, http://www.heritage.org/Research/Reports/2007/02/The-Urgent-Need-to-Reform-the-FAAs-Air-Traffic-Control-System (accessed July 6, 2011).
13. As with any attempt to count public authorities, Preston's list reflects gaps in available information, as well as personal judgments with respect to definitions. For example, Preston did not include housing authorities and redevelopment authorities, based on their close institutional and fiscal relationship with the federal government. Nathan Stone Preston, "The Use and Control of Public Authorities in American State and Local Government" (PhD diss., Princeton University, 1960), 36. For postwar growth, see also Annmarie Hauck Walsh, *The Public's Business: The Politics and Practices of Government Corporations* ([1978] Cambridge: MIT Press, 1980), 118.
14. Dan Cupper, *The Pennsylvania Turnpike: A History* (Lebanon, PA: Applied Arts Pub-

lishers, 1990), 6–9, 22–24; Phil Patton, "A Quick Way from Here to There Was Also a Frolic," *Smithsonian* 21 (October 1990); and Robert G. Smith, *Ad Hoc Governments: Special Purpose Transportation Authorities in Britain and the United States* (Beverly Hills, CA: Sage Publications, 1974), 121.

15. Council of State Governments, *Public Authorities in the States: A Report to the Governors' Conference* (Chicago: Council of State Governments, 1953), 30–31; and Michael R. Fein, *Paving the Way: New York Road Building and the American State, 1880–1956* (Lawrence: University Press of Kansas, 2008), 205, chap. 5.

16. U.S. Department of Transportation, *America's Highways, 1976–1976: A History of the Federal-Aid Program* (Washington, DC: GPO, 1976), 472–74. States built 2,937 miles of tolled highways between 1947 and 1959, when this kind of construction tapered off. During the 1960s, states opened only a thousand new miles of toll roads. José A. Gómez-Ibañez and John R. Meyer, *Going Private: The International Experience with Transport Privatization* (Washington, DC: Brookings Institution, 1883), table 10–1, 169.

    In an interesting sidelight, the plan to use earmarked taxes to finance the federal interstate system was adopted only after Congress rejected the Eisenhower administration's proposal to establish a Federal Highway Corporation. As conceived by the administration, this public corporation would issue $21 billion in bonds to the general public. This debt would be considered outside the debt limit of federal government and not guaranteed by it. The bonds were to be paid off with taxes on vehicle fuels, although the corporation was also to be given authority to borrow up to $5 billion from the U.S. Treasury. Mark H. Rose, *Interstate: Express Highway Politics, 1939–1989*, rev. ed. (Knoxville: University of Tennessee Press, 1990), chap. 6; and John M. Martin, Jr., "Proposed Federal Highway Legislation in 1955: A Case Study in the Legislative Process," *George Washington Law Journal* 44 (1955–56): 236. A major obstacle to the administration bill was Virginia senator Harry F. Byrd, a fierce opponent of government borrowing in general and government corporations specifically, who by this time was the chairman of the Senate Finance Committee.

17. John A. Jackle and Keith A. Schulle, *Lots of Parking: Land Use in a Car Culture* (Charlottesville: University of Virginia Press, 2004), 82–83; Arthur Pound, "No Parking," *Atlantic Monthly* 161 (March 1938): 391; Orville C. Peterson and George A. Warp, "Tort Liability Aspects of Governmental Efforts to Relieve Urban Traffic Congestion," *Virginia Law Review* 36 (December 1950): 1050; International Parking Institute, "History," copyright 2010, http://www.parking.org/about-ipi/history.aspx (accessed January, 1, 2011); Constance A. Cunningham, "Homer S. Brown: First Black Political Leader in Pittsburgh," *Journal of Negro History* 66 (Winter 1981–82): 308–10; and William D. Heath et al., *Parking in the United States: A Survey of Local Government Action* (Washington, DC: National League of Cities, 1967), 114–37.

18. *Public Authorities in the States: A Report to the Governors' Conference* (Chicago: Council of State Governments, 1953), 2–3.

19. "Robertson Visions High Sewer Rental," *Buffalo Evening News*, April 8, 1935, 8.

20. For Smith quote, *Revised Record of the Constitutional Convention of the State of New York, 1938*, vol. 3 (Albany: J. B. Lyon, 1938), 2287; Norman Hapgood and Henry Moskowitz, *Up from the City Streets: The Life of Alfred E. Smith* (New York: Grosset and Dunlap, 1927), 256–77, esp. 269; and William J. Quirk and Leon E. Wein, "A Short Constitutional History of Entities Commonly Known as Authorities," *Cornell Law Review* 56 (April 1971): 561–79.

21. Walinske v. Detroit-Wayne Joint Bldg. Authority, 325 Mich. 562 (1949), quotes at

572, 580, 578. The earlier opinion was Bacon v. City of Detroit, 282 Mich. 150 (1937).

22. Quotes from Joseph F. Gricar, "Municipal Corporations—Circumventing Municipal Debt Limitations," *Michigan Law Review* 48 (May 1950): 1019–20. See also Eugene C. Lee, "Use of Lease-Purchase Agreements to Finance Capital Improvements," *Municipal Finance* 24 (November 1952): 78–81; and Jon Magnusson, "Lease Financing by Municipal Corporations As a Way around Debt Limitation," *George Washington Law Review* 25 (March 1957): 377–96.
23. Walinske v. Detroit-Wayne Joint Bldg. Authority, 566–68, quote at 566.
24. B. U. Ratchford, "New Forms of State Debts," *Southern Economic Journal* 8 (April 1942), 470; and Michael J. O'Malley III, "Built by the New Deal," *Pennsylvania Heritage Magazine* 34 (Fall 2008): 16–27.
25. Walsh, *The Public's Business*, 122; Preston, "The Use and Control of Public Authorities," 61; and Pennsylvania General Assembly Joint State Government Commission, *Public School Building Subsidies* (Harrisburg, PA: Joint State Government Commission, 1955), 5.
26. "Message from the President of the United States Proposing a Plan of Federal Cooperation with the States in Regard to Building Additional Classrooms for School Children," H.R., Doc. 84, 84th Cong., 1st sess., 3.
27. W. H. Lawrence, "Eisenhower Asks 7 Billion Program to Build Schools," *New York Times*, February 9, 1955, includes Hill quotes, as well as additional information about proposal's financing design beyond the president's published message.
28. Ibid.
29. Joseph A. Loftus, "Eisenhower Asks Fund of 2 Billion to Build Schools," *New York Times*, January 29, 1957.
30. Preston, "The Use and Control of Public Authorities," 46, 418; and C. Robert Morris, "Evading Debt Limitations with Public Building Authorities: The Costly Subversion of State Constitutions," *Yale Law Journal* 68 (December 1958): 240n13.
31. Janice C. Griffith, "'Moral Obligation' Bonds: Illusion or Security?" *Urban Lawyer* 8 (1976): 54–93 ; and Walsh, *The Public's Business*, 132, 166.
32. "John N. Mitchell Dies at 75; Major Figure in Watergate," *New York Times*, November 10, 1988. Section titles such as "Nelson Rockefeller: The Stunting of Fiscal Viability and the Rise of Moral Obligation Bonds" make clear the viewpoint of Peter D. McClelland and Alan L. Magdovitz in *Crisis in the Making: The Political Economy of New York State Since 1945* (New York: Cambridge University Press, 1981), 225.
33. Laws of New York 1932, chap. 548, sec. 4; and Moreland Act Commission on the Urban Development Corporation and Other State Financing Agencies, *Restoring Credit and Confidence* (Albany, NY: Moreland Act Commission, 1976), 86. See also B.U. Ratchford, *American State Debts* (Durham, NC: Duke University Press, 1941), 517–21.
34. The New York State Limited Profit Housing Companies Act (1955) is commonly known by the names of its sponsors, Senator MacNeil Mitchell and Assemblyman Alfred J. Lama. By 1972 HFA debt was $ 3.8 billion compared to the state's full-faith and credit debt of $3.4 billion. Figures from James E. Underwood and William J. Daniels, *Governor Rockefeller in New York: The Apex of Pragmatic Liberalism in the United States* (Westport, CT: Greenwood Press, 1982), table 6.9, p. 174, and table 6.6, p. 168.
35. McClelland and Magdovitz, *Crisis in the Making, 156–61, 199–202, 233–34*; and William K. Reilly and S. J. Schulman, "The State Urban Development Corporation:

New York's Innovation," *Urban Lawyer* 1 (1969): 135. For the section of the statute that makes this quasi guarantee: Laws of New York, 1960, chap. 671, sec. 346 (d). Walsh, *The Public's Business*, 72–77.

36. Annmarie Hauck Walsh, "Public Authorities and the Shape of Decision Making," in *Urban Politics: New York Style*, ed. Jewel Bellush and Dick Netzer (Armonk, NY: M. E. Sharpe, 1990), 204.
37. Comereski v. City of Elmira, 308 NY 248 (1955), 254; and William J. Quirk and Leon E. Wein, "A Short Constitutional History of Entities Commonly Known as Authorities," *Cornell Law Review* 56 (April 1971): 583–85.
38. Walsh, *The Public's Business*, 133.
39. In 1973 the combined debt of all New York State public authorities was $13.8 billion compared to the state's full-faith and credit debt of $3.5 billion. Figures from Underwood and Daniels, *Governor Rockefeller in New York*, table 6.5, p. 166, and table 6.6, p. 168.
40. Alan G. Hevesi, *Public Authority Reform: Reining in New York's Secret Government* (New York State: Office of the State Comptroller, February 2004), 14.
41. For "nonguaranteed" debt specific revenue streams serve as collateral. "Full-faith and credit" debt is backed by the tax-based resources of state and local governments themselves. Data in figures 6.1 and 6.2 from Council of State Governments, *The Book of the States*, vol. 38 (Lexington, KY: Council of State Governments, 2006), 400.
42. Comereski v. City of Elmira, 254.

EPILOGUE

1. Koch quoted in Annmarie Hauck Walsh, "Public Authorities and the Shape of Decision Making," in *Urban Politics: New York Style*, ed. Jewel Bellush and Dick Netzer (Armonk, NY: M. E. Sharpe, 1990), 214.
2. Alberta M. Sbragia, "Politics, Local Government, and the Municipal Bond Market," in *The Municipal Money Chase: The Politics of Local Government Finance*, ed. Alberta M. Sbragia (Boulder, CO: Westview Press, 1983), 99.
3. Joseph E. McLean, "Use and Abuse of Authorities," *National Municipal Review* 42 (October 1953): 444.
4. Daniel W. Hoan, *The Failure of Regulation* (Chicago: Socialist Party of the United States, 1914), 88.
5. Frederic C. Howe, *The Confessions of a Reformer* (New York: C. Scribner's Sons, 1925), 5.
6. Franklin Roosevelt, "Letter to Governors" (1934), cited in Robert G. Smith, *Ad Hoc Governments: Special Purpose Transportation Authorities in Britain and the United States* (Beverly Hills, CA: Sage, 1974), 108.
7. David C. Perry, "Building the City through the Back Door: The Politics of Debt, Law, and Public Infrastructure," in *Building the Public City: The Politics, Governance, and Finance of Public Infrastructure*, Urban Affairs Annual Review 43 (Thousand Oaks, CA: Sage, 1995), 202–36; and Donald Axelrod, *Shadow Government* (New York: John Wiley and Sons, 1992), 313.
8. Jon Magnusson, "Lease-Financing by Municipal Corporations as a Way around Debt Limitations," *George Washington Law Review* 25 (March 1957): 395.
9. Harold Seidman, "Government-Sponsored Enterprise in the United States," in *The New Political Economy: The Public Use of the Private Sector*, ed. Bruce L. R. Smith (New York: Macmillan Press, 1975), 84.
10. Florida State Department of Transportation, "Organizational Structure," http://

www.dot.state.fl.us/personnel/OfficeOrg.shtm (accessed January 12, 2011). Cleveland's electrical company was officially renamed Cleveland Public Power in 1983. "CPP History" from the organization's website, http://www.cpp.org/history.html (accessed January 7, 2011). Information about the Norfolk Parking Division found on pages related to parking on the city's website, http://www.norfolk.gov/Parking/ (accessed January 7, 2011).

11. Calls for greater bureaucratic flexibility within a structure of accountability to elected officials should not be confused with advocacy of radical deregulation and privatization of bureaucratic units as envisioned within the "entrepreneurial" paradigm of public administration popularized by Osborne and Gaebler in *Reinventing Government* and embodied to a significant extent in the National Performance Review chaired by Vice President Al Gore discussed in chapter 6.
12. San Francisco City and County have the same borders and are served by a single government combining municipal and county functions.
13. What the program provides, rules, fees, the network of clinics providing medical homes, participating hospitals, and so on are described on the program website, http://www.healthysanfrancisco.org/visitors/ (accessed November 6, 2010). For an early evaluation by the Kaiser Foundation, see http://www.kaisernetwork.org/daily_reports/print_report.cfm?DR_ID=51941&dr_cat=3 (accessed November 6, 2010). Participants survey results were found at http://articles.sfgate.com/2009-08-26/bayarea/17176230_1_health-care-universal-health-poor-health (accessed November 6, 2010).
14. Information on the SFCCC and the member clinics is provided on the consortium website, http://www.sfccc.org (accessed November 6, 2010).
15. Technically, the law requires that for-profit employers with more than twenty employees working in San Francisco, or nonprofits with more than fifty, spend a certain amount per employee hour (including the hours of part-time staff) on providing health care for employees, either through private health insurance, HSF, or reimbursement (by the company) of employee health care expenses. (Managerial employees above a certain income level—$81,450 for 2011—are not counted.) At the outset, in 2008, the required amount to be spent was $1.17/hour/employee for companies with fewer than one hundred employees, and $1.76 for larger ones. In effect, if a company does not provide health insurance, or provides only bare-bones coverage, it ends up having to pay into HSF. Information on these provisions are found in an American Medical Association newsletter article at http://www.ama-assn.org/amednews/2007/08/20/gvsa0820.htm (accessed November 6, 2010). The plan is defined legally by the city/county Health Care Security Ordinance (HCSO), found at http://www.municode.com/content/4201/14131/HTML/ch014.html (accessed November 6, 2010). Many administrative details are found on the city/county website, at http://sfgsa.org/index.aspx?page=418 (accessed November 6, 2010); the regulations are set out in a document at http://sfgsa.org/Modules/ShowDocument.aspx?documentid=1246 (accessed November 6, 2010). A general summary is provided at http://sfgsa.org/Modules/ShowDocument.aspx?documentid=6776 (accessed November 6, 2010).
16. A timeline of the legal struggle is found at http://www.sfcityattorney.org/index.aspx?page=22 (accessed November 6, 2010).

INDEX

Page numbers followed by "f" refer to figures.